TEN LESSONS THAT WILL GET YOU FIRED

(But You Must Teach Immediately)

ALEX CAMPBELL

Jan-Carol
Publishing, Inc

Ten Lessons That Will Get You Fired
(But You Must Teach Immediately)
Alex Campbell

Published May 2016
Little Creek Books
Imprint of Jan-Carol Publishing, Inc.
Cover Design: Tara Sizemore

ISBN: 978-1-939289-92-6
Library of Congress Control Number: 2016941703

You may contact the publisher:
Jan-Carol Publishing, Inc.
PO Box 701
Johnson City, TN 37605
publisher@jancarolpublishing.com
jancarolpublishing.com

Looking back upon my life, there are very few instances that I can point to that changed the direction of my life. One of these moments, however, I remember fondly. It was when I first read John Taylor Gatto's masterpiece, Weapons of Mass Instruction. They say that a great author does not tell you things you do not know, only crystallizes thoughts that you already had, just could never put into words. I felt exactly that way when I first wrestled with Gatto. Since then, I have been inspired to read, study, and learn all I can about education. I was challenged to think about my preconceived notions about schooling. Today, this book is a culmination of those struggles to create an educational environment like Gatto advocates. Gatto is now getting older and has worn himself out from his struggle against the schooling behemoth. I sometimes wonder, "Who will take his place when he is gone?"

PREFACE

As I began my career as a teacher, I kept noticing more and more things seemed designed to keep students from actually learning. As my career continued, I decided that so many strategically placed hindrances could not be accidental. Something or someone was trying to keep my students from getting the education they desperately needed to be successful people. I frantically searched for solutions to the problem through the public school bureaucracy, but found no antidote for this educational sickness plaguing the system. I decided to take it upon myself to create an atmosphere in my classroom where we could short circuit the school machinery that threatened to strangle us all. After years of pushing the boundaries of education with my own classroom, I have discovered that although I have come close to being fired many times, I have actually created a place where a real education can be fostered. This journey is not for the faint of heart, but with perseverance and a little luck, any teacher can learn how to confront the darkness that permeates public schooling and create a beacon of hope for generations to come.

ACKNOWLEDGEMENTS

This book could never have been written without God's blessings. He has allowed me to be on this inspiring journey to help young people, and I hope this book inspires many more people to reach out and take chances to change the lives of those around them. This book would not have been possible without my loving wife, Brittney. She is my sounding board, my inspiration, and my encouragement. When no one else believes in me, she does. My two sons, Braylon and Brogen, were also a tremendous source of inspiration. Looking at young boys growing into whatever example their father sets is an overwhelming experience. I hope they are inspired to live a good life, enjoy the journey, and help others along the way. My parents have also been a great blessing to me. Without the patience, guidance, and love of my parents to help shepherd a type A, easily obsessed, over the top, mischievous, know it all, there is no way I would have survived this long, much less written my first book. Finally, I would like to thank my students. Without the wonderful young people with whom I have the pleasure to work, none of these stories and lessons would ever have been experienced. I appreciate their patience with me and their willingness to follow me wherever it leads in the pursuit of education.

LETTER TO THE READER

In college, the professor that had the greatest impact on me once said that if a new teacher were to just keep a little journal of the happy, exciting, funny, and interesting things that happened during their career, that any teacher would have enough material for a great book by the time he or she retired. She was absolutely correct. I do not know if I have had any more of an interesting teaching career than the average educator, and I definitely do not feel that I am superior to all of the other teachers in my ability to relate my experiences to others. For whatever reason though, I took those wise words from my professor to heart. I do not think I ever intended to write a book about them, but somehow that is exactly what happened.

I love being a teacher because no two days, even no two classes, are alike. Teenagers are unpredictable, and I love that about them. Normally when people ask what my occupation is, and I tell them I am a high school teacher they reply with, "Oh, I am sorry" or "I don't know you put up with them." or "Now, there's a job I couldn't do." I do not know if the job is as difficult as they make it out to be, but it is definitely not as miserable. I do feel that you have to be born to be a great teacher. Sure you can do some things that will make you better at it, but people just need that little something down inside that makes them want to be locked in a room with thirty hormonal, sweaty, energetic teenagers for seven hours a day. I know I was born with that little whatever it is down inside. I do not dread going to school; I love it. That is not to say that there are not aspects of school that grate on me, wear me down, and sometimes even infuriate me. But they usually have to do with the adults and the decisions they make; not the kids.

Sometimes I think back to the teacher I was when I started (or even 5 years ago) and cringe. I have learned so much as a teacher so quickly, that sometimes I even find myself feeling sorry for the kids because of the teacher that my former students had to endure. Being surrounded by hundreds of young people every day for 15 years will teach someone how to adapt, improvise, be flexible, and grow. I am amazed at how much and my teaching changes every single year. I think I am a better teacher now because of all of the experiences I have had, the young people I have the pleasure of meeting, and the successes and failures that come with struggling to become better at my craft.

Over the years I found myself retelling certain stories over and over again to fellow teachers, students, and even many people throughout the community. I must admit that many times I have been surprised by how many people sat around a dinner table enthralled at my stories about what happened at school. I decided that it was time to stop repeating those stories to a small audience, and put them down into words for anyone who wanted to hear them. I hope new teachers find encouragement to be creative, keep adapting, and hang on through the difficult times. I pray that old teachers are reminded why they became teachers in the first place. Former students can even look back on their time and school and think about the people that worked hard to make a difference in their lives.

There are even plenty of lessons in this book for people who never have or never will call teaching their profession. If you love the human spirit, there are plenty of stories in there that I hope will brighten your day. When you question whether this modern form of schooling that America is slogging through can ever obtain positive results, there are a few life lines in here to remind you that indeed it can. If you only receive your information about the youth of America from the news media about the gangs, school shootings, apathy, and desire to play video games all the time, there is just enough in this book to remind you that there is still an infinite amount of good in the young people of America.

I am grateful for the students that have taken this ride with me, the parents that have entrusted me with their most precious possessions, the administrators that were crazy enough to take a chance on a young and unorthodox teacher, and my family that supports me in all that I do. It has been a great journey through my first 15 years of teaching. I hope that through this book, many more people can experience the journey with me.

Best regards,
Alex Campbell

TABLE OF CONTENTS

Chapter I: Admit You Don't Know Anything About Teaching   1

Chapter II: Brag About an Awesome Event in Public When   17
                There Isn't One

Chapter III: Never Give out Textbooks   45

Chapter IV: Let Your Students Do Work That Is Well Below   65
                Their Grade Level

Chapter V: Make Enough Noise to Bother Everyone Else   90

Chapter VI: Let Your Students Play   106

Chapter VII: Brainwash Your Students   135

Chapter VIII: Make Your Students Die   160

Chapter IX: Make Your Students Cry   180

Chapter X: Let Your Students Refuse to Do Assignments   199

CHAPTER I

ADMIT YOU DON'T KNOW ANYTHING ABOUT TEACHING

The education industry in this country is a cathedral. Its colleges are not just buildings where professors impart knowledge; they have been built into so much more. They are massive, outdated, gothic cathedral shrines built to the gods of industrialized schooling; holdovers from some bygone era, still meant to impress the lower classes with the majesty of their massiveness. To become a teacher, one must not only pass through thirteen years of institutionalized learning to receive a high school diploma, but also complete four to five years of college. Of course, that does not include the masters, educational specialist, and doctoral degrees that abound in the field of education. Additionally, there are the tests that are required to obtain licensure: the test to be admitted to the college of education, the test to get out of the college of education, and the multiple tests to prove you are competent in your content area. Add to all of that the one or two student teaching semesters (the growing trend is two) that can only be served after observing, planning, and teaching for dozens to hundreds of hours before that final placement. Include the ongoing in-services and local, state, and national training, licensure and relicensure requirements, and the constant push to return to school to complete advanced degrees, and a massive cathedral—replete with flying buttresses, steeples, and bell towers—has been erected. This is the sprawling cathedral of formal education that trains the high priests of education: the modern American educator.

There is so much that goes into being an educator or teacher these days that the process has polluted our idea of what a teacher is or should be. Is it just someone who has read the books, heard the lectures, and passed the tests, but has no wisdom associated with living life, facing death, and conquering the moral dilemmas of adult living? Yes, teachers learn much about planning, classroom management, teaching strategies, reading strategies, phonics, exceptional learners, and a myriad of other things in the long and tedious process of becoming a teacher. However, we sometimes forget that education is really not as mysterious and difficult as it has been built up to be.

There have always been teachers in our world. Maybe it was the wise and wrinkled oldest man of the tribe who sat cross-legged by a dying flame, listening patiently while the hot-blooded young warriors passionately made their pleas to the group. When everyone was quiet, the old sage spoke up with just a few simple words, and left the others feeling silly for their previous rash remarks. Everyone knew they were in the presence of a wise teacher. He had no degree, license, or sheepskin on his wall: just a lifetime of experiences, which when shared let everyone know they were in the presence of a master facilitator of knowledge. No one rose from the fading light in the back, stood, and pointed their bony, incriminating finger at the wise elder and cried, "But where's your teacher's license?" Everyone just knew, and that was enough.

When my grandfather was in the intensive care unit of the hospital, the doctors told all of my family "Grandpaw" would soon die. We gathered around his bed, held his hand, and waited. Finally, a thought burst forth into my mind. "Your grandfather will soon be gone," it screamed. "Ask him something important before he dies and takes a lifetime of wisdom with him," it thundered. So I knelt beside his bed and whispered into his ear, "What is the most important thing you have ever learned?" As we all held our breath waiting for his tired words to come to us, I bent down and placed my ear beside the mask that supplied his oxygen and muffled his words. What he told us in that room that day I will never forget, and it didn't matter if he only had a fourth-grade education. We all knew that in that bed lay a wise man, whether he had the academic credentials or not.

Once, a custodian in my building came to my room early one morning. I do not recall how we began talking about our younger lives, but we did, and I am glad it happened. She was nearly a generation older than me, and as she stood in my doorway propped against the door jamb, she told story after story about her life. I was transfixed by her narrative. When she was finished, I knew I was in the presence of a master teacher. So what if she was a janitor? She had just as much right to be in front of a classroom as I did, if not more. She had lived many of the things I had only read about. How could my words, stolen from the pages of a book, ever convey the history that her broken heart and quivering lips could?

I allowed my students to produce a veterans program once. It was amazing how much work they put into it, and how it brought so much healing to our community. A friend of a veteran who died in Vietnam asked to speak to my class personally the next day, a request which I gladly obliged. When he came into the room with his oxygen unit in hand and the hose running into his nostrils, it got very quiet in my room. I pulled my most comfortable chair to the front of the room for him to sit in, and he began to share his heart with us. He told us of his best friend who died in Vietnam, and the last time he saw his friend. He recounted every detail of the moment his parents told him that his best friend had died in Vietnam. He made us relive with him the time his eyes locked with his friend's the first time he heard of the Vietnam War, while in a high school class. I could almost feel the eerie stare of his close friend as he peered so deeply in my eyes, and it felt as if he would pierce my very soul. The man only stopped to remove the oxygen tube and wipe his eyes and nose with a handkerchief. My students did not make a sound, and neither did I. When the man finished talking, I was in awe. I had just met a teacher in every sense of the word, yet he had no credentials. What could a cheap piece of paper in a gilded frame on the wall, with some gold leaf and calligraphy, from a cathedral of education, do for this man to make him any more effective as a teacher? He had just told a story that my students and I will never forget.

I learned this lesson with my own children at a nursing home. I took my two boys, ages four and six, to visit an elderly lady from our church who had fallen and broken her hip. The kind man at the front desk told us where her room was, but she was not there. As we walked back to the front door, we passed a rather passionate game of bingo taking place in the cafeteria; sure enough, she was there. The activities director invited us to stay and play with the residents. My children love playing games. Before I could even answer, they ran to the director, grabbed their game pieces, and took seats on each side of our elderly friend.

The bingo cards went all the way to the number 99, and my four-year-old was still learning to count to 100. I thought it would be a great opportunity for him to receive a bit of schooling while also playing a game with a friend. My youngest son was doing pretty well filling in his card, until a really large number was called. The number called was indeed on his card, but he overlooked it. I had determined I was not going to help him play. If he overlooked a number or two, that was fine. I was content to just let him look and learn his numbers for himself while having a bit of fun. Then the most amazing thing happened.

This old lady, who had not made a sound the entire time we were there, was sitting beside my four-year-old. I had resigned myself to the fact that she was most likely a mute, without thinking. As she placed her chip on her card, she looked over at my son's card as well. Seeing that he had made a mistake and realizing I was not coming to the rescue, she was determined to help him. She picked up a chip, gave it to my son, pointed at the number and said softly, "You missed one." My son did not speak, but he looked up at the lady sheepishly and smiled. She smiled too and turned her attention back to her own card. In that moment, I realized that this lady had become the most unlikely of teachers.

Maybe she never talked, because she never felt it was necessary. Possibly she was silent, because she never felt anyone needed her. Perhaps she was still because she felt she had nothing to offer the world. However, for one day, this little tow-headed boy needed her. This little innocent boy was right beside her; no one else saw the mistake, and no one (not even his father) was coming to his rescue. In that moment, this lady was needed to be a teacher. To my son, she was wise; to her, my son was in need; to the world, a teacher was born. How dare the world have the audacity to say, "You cannot teach! You are not licensed to give out bingo chips to children!" What right do we have? After all, there was a certified and licensed professional in the room who was an expert on activities like bingo. The truth is that when we only let the professionals and specialists do all of the work, we not only rob from the learner, but from the potential teacher as well. There is no room for high priests in education, only a community of believers.

About a dozen years into my teaching career, I went crazy with this concept when I was teaching an elective class in history. I started to realize that history is nothing more than what people did between the time they were born and the time they died. But how many teenagers even have a concept of what life or death is? To overcome this hurdle, I decided to do an intensive study of "What Is Life?" and "What Is Death?" Each of these units would be one week long, and would take up the first two weeks of my class. I racked my brain all summer to come up with the perfect combination of speakers. I wanted a variety of perspectives, so my students could see life and death from all angles. That first year, I decided on seven speakers.

For the life unit, I invited four speakers. The first was a doctor who had delivered hundreds, possibly thousands, of babies. He also had an adopted son who had nearly died of cancer as a small child. This man got to witness children being born, the pain and effort that it takes to bring that life into the world, and the joy on parents' faces on a daily basis. I knew that he would have a very unique perspective, and he was also a new school board member. He was also the man who told me that my second son would be a boy. I still remember the handshake he gave me when he told me, and how caring he was as he went through all of the ultrasounds to assure us all was progressing normally. A soft-spoken man, with a caring heart and tons of experience, he was a perfect choice.

The second speaker was a friend of mine who had just had a new child. This friend of mine, with his bundle of joy only a couple of months old, his first girl, would make a perfect fit by showing the parent's perspective of how precious life is to those who are entrusted with it. This knowledge is something which many teens are unfortunately familiar with, in our society. I wanted them to see how beautiful, important, and powerful the responsibility of being given someone else's life is. He was also a local businessman, and had spoken to schools before. I have known him since we were both small children. He was a youth leader at my church, and he came from a great family.

The third speaker was someone I met by accident. I was at the local state park with my youngest son, and on the way in I saw the back of a huge motorized wheel chair with "MARINE" embroidered on it. I quickly caught up to him, and we realized we were both natural talkers. We had a nice fifteen-minute conversation about how he got in that wheelchair. The story he told had me mesmerized the entire time, and left me wanting more when he finished. He left a violent home as a young teen, lived in a basement, got help from a teacher/coach, worked nights to pay his rent, joined the Marines, went to Afghanistan in the 1980s, and saw dozens of countries throughout the next twenty years. After the September 11th attacks of 2001, he went to Afghanistan and Iraq several times, and was hit by an improvised explosive device (IED) inside a building with his squad of five Marines. He told me how the IED blew him through a plate-glass window on the fourth floor, how he hit the ground in a seated position and pushed his pelvis so far up into his spine that it crushed every vertebra from the chest down. His elbows hit the ground, forcing his arms out of the shoulder sockets and through the skin. When he looked to his sides while seated in that road, he saw the bones of his arms sticking up so far through the skin of his shoulders that they were even with his eyebrows. He then looked deep in my eyes and said, "If you had a magic time machine and you could go back in time and show my teenage self how I would end up thirty years later, I would still have joined the Marines in a heartbeat!" Then he asked me a question. "You want to know why?" I nodded my head, dumbfounded, to the affirmative. "Because you remember that squad of five Marines I was with, in that building when the IED went off?" he asked, reminding me. "I was the only one that survived. I'm glad I'm alive," he whispered. Then he mentioned that he spoke to small groups, and gave me his business card. How could I, a high school teacher in my thirties who had only left the country twice for vacations, stand in front of my class and pretend I was an expert on the military, life, pain, tragedy, nearly anything? Especially when I had this man locally who knew more about life than I probably ever would? I called him back, and couple of months later he was my third speaker. However, all of these were just the opening shots of my educational salvo. I was ready to bring out the big gun, my final speaker.

There is a guy I have known all of my life. We were not really close, but we kept running into each other throughout life. We played in the same small little league in town. We only played each other's team about three times per year, but it was more than that. Kids would hang out all day at the ball park, come hours early, or stay late to watch all of the other games. I might not have played on the team with everyone, but I knew just about everybody in that league. He was one of them. Later in middle school basketball, we found ourselves on two of the top local teams. I went to a county school, and he went to the city school. Both of those schools fed into the same high school by a quirk of district lines. This game was more than about who was good that year; it would become bragging rights for years to come, as many of the players from both teams would become members of the same high school team the next year. I will never forget our eighth-grade showdown, when we played a home game at their place. The crowd was massive and energetic; everyone knew what was riding on the game. It was a close game all the way, and our teams were never separated by more than seven points, but we lost. I shook hands with my friend and slunk back to our locker room. It was what happened in that locker room, though, that would really impact me.

They had a coach who was one of the finest men you could ever meet. He came into the locker room and told us that although we were down about the loss, what he saw was a great team. He continued by stating that our team would send players to the same high school as his team the next year. He told us that he was excited that both teams' players would get to play together the next year, and he felt they would make an amazing high school basketball force in years to come. With those few words, he gave me back some of the pride that I lost on the court. He healed wounds between young boys that would allow them to become friends in years to come, instead of festering into bitter rivals. My old acquaintance did continue to be my friend, but as fate would have it (and as their coach had laid the groundwork for it), we became ever closer in the years to come.

We saw each other occasionally throughout our teen and young adult years, but when I got my first high school teaching job in the county system where I grew up, I found myself helping the feeder middle school football team. The first day I walked into the locker room to meet the rest of the staff, and there he was. We quickly recounted our glory days, caught up on the missed time, and were old friends again. I only coached one year with the middle school, but I was really struck by the man he had become. He had such a great way of speaking to those kids. He always gave our pregame speech. I remember us sitting in the coach's office and talking about what we needed to win, the importance of the game, and what the boys needed to do to win it. We would go out to talk to the players one final time; the head coach would say a few words and then bring on my friend. I would have all of these great things that needed to be said, but by the time he was done, he would have said everything I was thinking. When his part of the speech was finished, the head coach would look at me and say, "Anything you want to add, coach?" I would just have to sheepishly shake my head to the negative; nothing else needed to be said.

My friend went on to move to the city school district in our county. A couple of years later I would make that same jump, and when I did, he was the principal of one of the elementary schools. It did not surprise me. He always was a likable, hard-working guy who related so well to younger kids. About four years passed, with me seeing him at in-services and random times throughout the school year. However, my feelings about him really changed the summer before I decided to make my most radical experiment with outside experts speaking in my class. At church, a lady who knew we were friends told me she heard he was sick. It was bad, but he was going for a second opinion before he announced anything. A few weeks later, the cold reality of what he found would shake me (and our whole community) to the core.

He had Lou Gehrig's disease (ALS). It progresses at a different rate for each person; his was moving quickly. In a few months he had gone from a recreational runner able to handle 3k, 5k, and even half marathon races easily to a man who became weak and tired from running. He even began tripping during his training runs when he could not lift his toes properly anymore. He finally gave up running and tried various other forms of exercise, but just a few months later, he had to stop exercising his legs at all. There was just no strength left. By the time we got back to school at the end of that summer, I would be in for one of biggest shocks of my life.

It was not that I was ignorant of the ravages of the disease. I remembered when I was a very young boy, there was a lady at our church who had the disease. She and her husband ran one of the larger furniture stores in town. She was also a very kind and elegant lady. She and her husband had always been close with our pastor and his family, as was my father. I remember many dinners and social gatherings at our pastor's house when she would be there. I saw her transform from that elegant lady I had always known into a wheelchair-bound invalid. My last memory of her was at my pastor's house having dinner one night. Her husband rolled her in and parked her wheelchair beside the couch. My pastor's wife got down in the floor beside her feet. I thought this was weird, but the muscles of her neck, shoulders, and even eyes would not allow her to lift her chin from her chest; the only place she could focus was in a small area near her feet. If you wanted this lady to see your face when you talked, you had to get down in the floor at her feet, just as my pastor's wife was doing.

Another local man I knew had also been struck with the disease. There was a little convenience store very close to my house. My dad and several other local men would stop there every morning for coffee (and a bit of small talk) on their way to work. My brother and I would sit in the vehicle and wait. This local guy had kids about our age, and we often played softball and other sports in the field behind the store in the summer. He would always wave through the window, yell cordialities if the window was down in the warmer months, and even sometimes come over to the door to open it and spend a few minutes talking with us. I remember one day my dad getting back into the truck with a frown on his face. We drove for a few minutes up the road toward our school. About halfway there, he asked, "Do you know the man who stops and speaks to you every morning at the store?" Of course we did, and we told him so. "He's dying," my father uttered in a small voice. "He has Lou Gehrig's disease," he continued quietly. I remember not really paying attention to the second part. The shock that he was dying was too much for my young mind. I remember thinking that he looked so healthy. *But I just talked to him this morning, and he was fine,* my naive brain said. Finally, I was awakened from my thoughts when my brother asked, "What's Lou Gehrig's disease?" My father told us as best he could that it was a nerve condition, like the one the lady from our church had suffered through. It makes the nerves that control the muscles weak. It is always fatal, and usually within the first five years. My dad said that our friend told him while in the store, standing beside him, both holding their morning coffee. Then the man put the small, frail Styrofoam cup in his right hand and told my dad he was squeezing with all of his might—but the cup did not budge. It was a very visual example of a disease that destroys.

As I walked into our general in-service meeting, there he was, standing at the door greeting all of the teachers back for another year. He looked good, but when we spoke his speech sounded off. I couldn't really place it; he sounded tired, maybe. After a couple of hours in the meeting, we all went outside to have our pictures made. I was able to talk to him a bit more, and that is when it hit me. His speech was slurred from the disease. He could not talk with that same charismatic tone and command of the language that had made him such an effective communicator. He had always spoken with a slow southern accent, but now it was much slower, more methodical, even strained. He was working hard to form every word. Gone was the ease with which he had held middle school boys captivated before a game, made friends everywhere he went, and became one of the most beloved principals in the area. That realization, however, would not prepare me for what I witnessed when we finished our conversation and he walked away.

There he was, the multi-sport athlete and lifelong fitness freak, was limping. I stood and stared. I elbowed a friend and pointed. I did everything my mother taught me not to do in public when you notice someone with a physical handicap, but I could not control myself. A friend and I went to lunch and talked about it; I spoke with other teachers after lunch at my school about it, my wife and I discussed it that night, and the next day I detailed the events to mutual friends of ours. I just could not stop thinking about him, his disease, and the rapidity with which it was consuming him. As I drove to school the next day, I had already been planning my speakers for that first unit's study of life, when it hit me. I was missing one more expert I had to have. This man would be my final speaker. Many of the kids knew him from school, the community, and even family ties. Many of them had read in the paper about him finally receiving his doctorate degree in educational administration (although I never heard him refer to himself as doctor), seen his picture in the local section of the paper when he had gotten married less than a year ago, and read a recent feature article about his struggle with Lou Gehrig's disease and how he would continue to work with kids until he was physically unable to do so. He loved kids, was a great speaker, and now had a story that would grab hearts like never before.

I called him immediately on his office phone. It was way before school started; I just figured I would leave a message, and wait to hear back from him. I should not have been surprised to find he was already there in his office working. I told him about my unit, about the other speakers, and about my desire to have him be the final expert on our study of life. He accepted with a graciousness that took me aback a little. He said, "If anyone gets help from what I am going through, all of this is worth it." I booked him as my final speaker of that week, and he finished with, "I think I have a whole new perspective on what life is that I can share with the kids this year, compared to last year." Indeed, because he was now becoming an expert.

I began to get more and more excited as that week approached. I knew it was going to be a very emotional yet educational week, not just for the kids, but also for me. Maybe I was even more excited than the kids, because I knew a bit more about these people and what their stories would tell me. I even began to tell my friends, both inside and outside of the teaching profession, and they were excited as well. Several even insisted that I record the talks with the students that week. I agreed, but when I started to really think about it, it was amazing what they were saying. When was the last time someone said to me, "What is getting ready to take place in your class is so awesome that you must record it so others can see it who are not able to be there?" My assistant principal even said she was going to try to come down. When was the last time a principal said to me what was happening in my class was so awesome she was going to try to make time in her busy schedule to come down? My assistant principal even said I needed a box of tissues it was going to be so emotional. When was the last time someone told me to be ready with tissues because the class would be so awesome? Once I really thought about what these statements were really saying about my class, I was awed. Those things were never said when I was teaching, and that was fine with me. I do not have to be the expert in my class all the time. If we are on a topic where I am obviously not the expert, then I am more than happy to step to the side and let the real master take over. When my ego gets out of the way, real education can take place, no matter who the educator is.

The next week's study of death, although at first sounding somewhat morbid, was possibly more important than the first week's study of life. You see, every student had experienced life to some degree, but they had little experience with death. I feel that nothing is truly real until it is experienced. Yes, my students had lived life—not to its fullest, but they had lived. None of my students had personally experienced death (or they would not have been my students). Some had learned much about death through the death of a grandparent. A tiny few had experienced the loss of a parent or maybe a close friend, but that was rare. However, none had really come close to the precipice of death itself and stared into its cold, dead eyes. Sure, I could not take them all the way to that bitter edge (that WILL get you fired... fast), but I hoped to showcase people who had stories so real and personal that they took themselves there in their minds.

The first thing I thought of when planning the unit about death was the funeral home. We have several excellent family-run funeral homes in our area, and I called the first one that came to my mind. They were more than happy to come down. We even arranged for them to bring the hearse, coffin, and some flowers. I wanted the shock value of seeing that hearse outside, wiggling by the coffin on their way to their seat as it filled the entire aisle way of the class, and the flowers up front to remind them of the many they had seen before when death was in the air. The man from the funeral home even agreed to bring some of the tools and materials used to prepare the body for cremation, preservation, and display at the receiving of friends. Hopefully, these items would really get the kids to think about what death meant to them.

I live in a small town, and so thankfully we have little major crime like murder, kidnapping, and sexual assault. Unfortunately, the summer before I decided to try the study of life and death, we had several children die in our county. I know the county sheriff, as his family attended our church when I was younger. In a freak occurrence, when my family and I went on vacation that summer, the sheriff was at the same hotel for a conference and we were able to talk a bit. We discussed the terrible deaths of those young people in our county in the preceding few weeks. He told us how hard it was to see those crime scenes and talk to those parents. He said it made him go home and hug his small son, and appreciate the time they had together more. When I started planning my unit, his name came to mind. He was an excellent speaker, and has a passion for young people. He would make a perfect speaker for the unit. When he returned my call, he was more than happy to be a guest speaker that week. We talked a bit about what I wanted him to address, and he had some great ideas. He volunteered to bring some chilling crime scene photographs so students could see what the actual room looked like when someone died. Second, he agreed to talk about what happens to the body when it dies, such as decomposition, and what it is like when they find bodies that have been dead for a while out in the elements. It may be gruesome, but it is a great way to get them to think about the tragic impact of death. He agreed to mention some local deaths of the past summer (one, a girl hit by a car; another, a boy shot in the head with a pellet gun; and another, a person sucked down a drain pipe during a local cloud burst), as they had valuable lessons for young people. The students in my class knew these stories from the paper. Some possibly even knew the families, or were friends with the victims. Our county sheriff would be a very personal and powerful speaker.

The final speaker actually came to me with the idea of speaking. He is one of my best teaching friends. He has always taught near my room, and for some reason my two small boys were just drawn to him and his wife. They are an older couple, old enough to be my parents, and I respect them just as much. You will never meet a finer couple than my dear teacher friend and his wife. I often run ideas by him when they run through my scattered mind. He is always kind enough to listen to my ramblings, and often has some great insight. The school year before I tried this grand experiment with the study of life and death, I told him about it to see what he thought. After I discussed bringing in some speakers on the meaning of death, he calmly looked at me and said, "I will come and speak." I was a bit shocked because I did not know why he would be an expert on such a subject, but after he told me about his past, I knew I would conclude with this quiet man who taught next door.

I would never have guessed the amount of pain that this solemn man and his family had gone through to acquaint him with death. He told me how he had three wonderful children, the oldest about my age. How they grew up all doing great with school, music, church, activities, etc. They were just a great family, but no one knew the tragedy that would befall them. When their oldest son was fourteen, he was playing with his dad's gun; it went off, killing the boy. As he told me the story, I was crushed. I could still feel the incredible grief and emptiness that was in his soul. Then I began to feel very stupid for even bringing up my crazy idea of the study of death to him. Why did I have to come to him, of all people? I was sorry I'd made him relive this obviously very painful event by talking to him about my unit of death. When he finished his story, I apologized and told him it was not my intention to cajole him into speaking, as I did not even know about his family's tragedy. I was even embarrassed that he might think I did know, and had set the whole thing up just to get him to speak. I would never ask any parent to relive something so tragic. I told him that I appreciated his willingness to speak, and reiterated that he did not have to speak about such an emotional event. "I want to!" he said. "These kids need to hear it. I may cry," he said, "but that is just part of the grieving process." In my original discussion with him about my idea, I told him that if teenagers understood how precious life is and how final death was, they could understand their decisions much better. It was their feeling that life was long and they had all the time in the world to mess up, fix it, and correct their mistakes; that would change during the units on life and death. He brought up my own sentence as justification for why he must speak. "That's what killed my son; he thought he was invincible," he reminded me. "These kids need to hear what I have to say," and he persuaded me. I agreed to let him be the last speaker, although deep inside I still felt bad for even insinuating I was coming to him to underhandedly persuade him to speak; but what a powerful message the quiet man down the hall with a painful secret would deliver to my students.

My seven speakers were set for my first study of life and death. Maybe it was because I realized how important what these people would say was, but I felt that after the students heard these stories from the people of their community, they, too would feel the gravity of life and death and the decisions they make. I was feeling pretty good about myself when I emailed the main office secretary about all of the speakers I had coming in the next two weeks. I just wanted her to be aware that there would be a steady trickle of unusual guests through the office at about the same time every day, asking for me. It was when I received her return email that I realized how extensive the feeling of the teacher as the absolute authority on education really could be.

She only replied one word, but that one word really hit home: "Slacker." Now, the secretary and I have a great relationship. She is probably one of the most professional secretaries with whom I have ever worked. She was even a friend of mine, so that word hurt me a little. My dad was always giving out these wise sayings, and one of them instantly sprang into my consciousness: "Whatever is in the well will come up in the bucket." In other words, I know she was not trying to be hurtful, she was joking that I was just being lazy and not teaching my own class. It was all a joke; I got that part. However, if she hadn't felt, down deep that I was taking the easy way out, then she would not have said it even in jest. She may not have even realized what she was insinuating, but it really helped me to realize the culture that has been built up around the teacher as the expert. If a teacher is willing to admit that they don't know very much and people throughout the community with no degree, no specialized training, and no license can teach anything better than themselves, many people think there is something wrong with the teacher.

There have been countless examples, both big and small, of people or groups that have admitted that they were not the expert. During and after WWII, there was a huge push by our country (and the Soviet Union) to get the German rocket and propulsion scientists to immigrate to our country. We brought them in and put them in charge of our rocket and missile programs, basically admitting that even the most powerful country in the world was not the expert when it came to that specific technology. Think about it: our technological production might have proved superior to all other countries in the world, yet here we were fighting for the scientists from the country we just defeated for their "loser" scientists. How did that work out for America? As a result, we did become the first and only country to put a man on the moon, using the technology developed by those same scientists.

I have a friend who is one of the top Olympic weightlifters in America. One summer, the United States Olympic Committee (USOC) flew him to Los Angeles and put him and a few other top lifters up with all expenses paid, to allow him to train for a month with a Bulgarian coach brought in from Europe. It really floored me when I thought about what America was really saying. Here we were, the country that has dominated the Olympic Games for decades. We always win more gold than anyone else at the Olympics, and we have become a society obsessed with sports. Yet here we were, admitting that basically there was not one weightlifting coach in America as good as the ones in Bulgaria. That is pretty amazing when you consider all of the strength coaches we have in America, the money that is pumped into the U.S. Olympic Training Center, and all of the high tech scientific training tools we have to help those athletes. We were admitting that the coaches in a second-world country still trying to break free from the doldrums of the Eastern Block have coaches that are better than ours. We were basically saying that the only way for our athletic coaches to get our weightlifters any better was paying to bring in their old retired coaches, and paying big money for our athletes to train with them. At first, it is kind of shocking what the USOC is admitting; then again, it is amazing to consider that the American experts on weightlifting would admit there are others who know more than they do. They were humble enough to admit there were people in other countries who knew more.

One of my best friends is a teacher, but that is his second profession. For over a decade, he was a security guard in prisons. After he grew tired and slightly depressed from the routine of working with people who had already broken their lives, he decided he would try his hand at helping keep younger lives from being broken. He went back to school and became a math teacher. He taught next door to the criminal justice instructor. When the criminal justice teacher, who had some law enforcement experience, realized there was an expert on prisons next door, he immediately scheduled him to speak to his classes when they came to the unit on the prison system. He wore his old guard's uniform, and he described the state and federal prison system. These were things that could easily be found with a bit of online research by any high school student. But then, he launched into an hour of personal stories from his decade in the system. Stories that could not be told by anyone else, each with a unique lesson on what it was to be a prison guard. The students were mesmerized by his stories of shankings, homemade alcoholic beverage experiments by the inmates, and the times he was stabbed. The kids loved it. They wanted to see the scar where the shank went all the way through his massive twenty-inch bicep, the knuckle he broke punching a prisoner in a life and death struggle, and hear about the time he had to subdue a greased-up, naked inmate who had set his cell on fire. It was one of the students' favorite lessons all year. What was the criminal justice teacher, who was supposed to be an expert on law enforcement, doing bringing in the math teacher to teach his class about prison? He was finding an expert on the subject at hand, admitting he didn't know everything, and letting the kids reap the rewards of his wise decision.

The sooner teachers realize that they do not have a monopoly on education, the better our educational system will be. Sure, I have learned many amazing things from some wonderful teachers in college, but I have learned more from my personal mistakes and victories in my own classroom over the last twelve years. Possibly I have learned the most just by living life as a child, student, parent, pall bearer, Sunday school teacher, visitor to a hospital room, volunteer at the nursing home, husband, son, neighbor, and citizen. We teachers must realize that there are people all around us with so much to offer that we could never dream of teaching ourselves. All we have to do is give up the idea that we are some type of high priests of education, blessed with Gnostic knowledge in a sacred book meant to be dispersed to the ignorant masses at our whim. Admit you are not the expert, let others help you educate your students, and see them flourish like you never could have imagined.

How did those units on life and death go in my classroom? It was one of the most effective and meaningful times I have ever had in my class. Unbelievably, the students took notes while each speaker presented. I did not have to tell, remind, or force them; they just did it, because they wanted to remember what these people had to say. You could have heard a pin drop in my room when the Marine told them about how on Christmas he calls the families of the Marines that he says he killed and checks on them, because he feels responsible for taking their dads and husbands away. There were students sharing tissues when my friend pulled up his pant leg and showed them his leg, wasting away day by day before his very eyes.

When the quiet teacher down the hall shared his painful secret with the students, as promised, he began to cry. I looked into the students' faces, and you could see the empathy they shared with him. When the doctor told of how his first son died just a few minutes after he was born, gasping for breath and fighting to live just one more second, the students were focused on his every word. The students felt the fear of a new father and mother, as they rushed their child to a special hospital two hours away, praying their baby would not die. The youths felt the unfamiliarity of climbing into a casket and looking up to see their life, for the first time, from the other side. And the students felt a cold chill run down their spine as they looked at the sheriff's pictures of bloated bodies, murder victims, teen suicides, and drug overdoses. These were real life lessons and experiences that I could not provide. Only by using the experts from throughout the community could the students ever be exposed to these eye-opening experiences.

I hope that by now you are convinced of the benefits that can come from using other possible teachers throughout the community. All it takes is the courage to admit that you are not the expert on everything, and you have as much to learn about certain subjects as your students. I know that I learned so much from the unit on life and death that it gave me a new perspective, and helped me to be a better teacher and person. However, be prepared; there will be those who do not like your audacity. If you admit that as a teacher, you do not know everything and are not always the expert in the classroom, that implies that the educators around you are also not experts and do not know everything. That is a bitter pill for many in any profession to swallow, and you may be surprised how much people can get offended by such insinuations. Disrobing the priest, removing the miter, and questioning his authority are never popular things to do in the cathedral of education. What will happen when the parishioners learn that the omniscient and omnipotent priest is little more than an average flawed and fallible human? This type of rebellion will not garner you many friends in the educational world, and may leave anyone who dares suggest it experiencing their very own Inquisition. However, if you care about the true education of young people, you must be willing to take this often unpopular step to ensure the ascension of your students to a paradise of real education.

CHAPTER II

BRAG ABOUT AN AWESOME EVENT IN PUBLIC WHEN THERE ISN'T ONE

A s soon as I hung up the phone, I remember thinking What have I done? I had just finished talking to a reporter from our local newspaper. I had raved for twenty minutes about our upcoming veterans' program. My history classes were going to give the Vietnam veterans of our city a welcome home that was fifty years overdue. Hundreds of people would be there. A huge reception was scheduled afterwards. Students would perform live music, special presentations would follow, eulogies for the fallen from our school would be read, audiovisuals created by students would be displayed, and so much more. The whole thing sounded fantastic, and the reporter could hardly wait to come to the school and interview the two students in charge of the entire program. She arranged to meet with them the next day. She said she would get it printed in the newspaper the day following the interviews, so the whole town would know that in less than a month this tremendous special occasion to honor the community's Vietnam veterans would take place. There was only one problem: there was no ceremony.

It all started when my classes were going through the Vietnam unit. I try to make it really personal, and not just an overview of military movements or political posturing. The students loved reading several first person accounts of American POWs, such as James Stockdale, Robert Stirm, and others. They watched dumbfounded as the newsreel videos from the Tet Offensive showed the execution of

Viet Cong soldiers in the street. They were held in rapt attention when we watched the end of the video *Four Hours in My Lai*, as an American veteran discusses his suicide attempts because of what he did at the small village years before. The students seemed to get into the unit a bit more than the classes from previous years, but there was no way of knowing what was about to happen next.

I make a conscious effort to help my students understand the thankless sacrifice that many of our veterans make. I came to this decision after my uncle visited the then recently debuted World War II memorial in Washington D.C. As my uncle walked around the memorial on a weekday, when the crowd was not too large, he saw a man and his wife also taking in the sights. My uncle said it was obvious the man was a WWII veteran. He was the right age, and had one of those black baseball caps with the yellow writing that told the name of a certain military group with which the man served. Those caps are always dead giveaways about a person's military service. My uncle was moved by the power of the moment, being at this new WWII memorial alongside a man in whose honor it was built. As the couple neared, my uncle felt he needed to tell this man how much he appreciated what he did for our country. Using this as his opening, my uncle said, "I would just like to say thank you for your service to our country." Those seem like very safe words to say to a veteran; however, my uncle was not prepared for what happened in return.

The veteran bit his lip and tried to fight back the tears, but it was no use. He began to cry and then to sob. His wife put her arm around him for support while my uncle looked on, heartbroken. "I did not mean to hurt you," he blurted toward the man, as his wife helped him to a bench close by. She sat beside him, clutching him while his body heaved with huge sobs that had been held back for nearly seventy years. My uncle just stood there, kind of dumbfounded and feeling very badly for what he had caused. Then he saw the lady get up from the park bench and come his way. "I didn't mean to bring back any bad memories or bother you guys on this obviously special day," he said. The lady just smiled back at my uncle and told him it was okay. My uncle's words had not hurt her husband at all. Actually, he had been waiting to hear from someone like my uncle for a very long time. The lady told my uncle that her husband had just whispered to her some words that were almost impossible to believe. "My husband said that it was nearly seventy years ago when he returned from WWII, and you are the first person to ever thank him for his service," said the lady, fighting back her own tears. She went on to say that he was sorry he was overtaken by his emotions, but it was fine. He was glad to finally hear those words from someone, anyone, no matter if they were from a stranger and it was long overdue.

When it comes to wars in American history, most people agree that comparatively speaking, WWII was a very popular war. It had the most men involved, we were attacked to be brought into it, and the home front really got behind the effort. It was nothing like Vietnam; when the country was so divided and many felt the country was in a war of aggression, not survival, no matter the threat of Communism. Still more were upset that the government refused to declare Vietnam a war while men were being drafted and dying. Vietnam was also the first true media war; reports came directly from the field, and were not sanitized by the government before hitting the airwaves and newsstands of America. If ever there was a war that the American people supported, it would have to be WWII. How could it happen that a man could serve, come home to the tickertape parades of a grateful nation, and never hear anyone utter the words "Thank you?" My uncle was astounded. As my uncle recounted the story to me several years later, I was also amazed—and a bit heartbroken. I realized that even in the most popular of wars in American history, there were many people just like the man my uncle happened upon who never had been thanked by anyone. I was just a small-town history teacher, but I was determined to change that in any way I could, no matter how small my influence. I was going to help our veterans, and the only way to do that was to make the sacrifices personal for my students.

To make it personal, I took the students down to the Vietnam Veterans Memorial Wall in our own school to investigate the personal connection. There were ten pictures on that wall, of men who graduated from our high school and later died in Vietnam. The memorial wall is located in our cafeteria; however, many of the students admitted they had walked by that wall for three years and never even bothered to stop and look at it. Each student chose a person from the wall and wrote down all of the information available. This included their full name, rank, branch, birth date, date of death, and where in Vietnam they died. My original plan was for each student to write a letter to the family of their veteran. They would then research how to find their family, and if they could find them, mail them a letter so they would know their loved one was not forgotten. They would also make a book mark for them to keep the entire unit, to remind them that each death was a person who impacted a family, and shook a community. I wanted to make the war very personal to each student in my class, and this activity was to be the linchpin of the unit. Little did I know my paltry ideas would soon be overshadowed.

My plan was a solid one, and the students seemed to enjoy the start of the project, but the thing that really set the trap for me was the Vietnam veterans' welcome home video I found on YouTube, from Fort Campbell, Kentucky. The short video clip showed the amazing event the people of the Fort Campbell community put on for the veterans who had never received a proper welcome home from Vietnam. It showed some of the interviews with the veterans, telling their stories of how they were treated horribly when they returned to our country. It showed some of the speeches that were given by the current soldiers of Fort Campbell. The most powerful point of the short four-minute video was the part where the Vietnam veterans were walking into the hanger pushing their comrades in wheelchairs, holding their hands, and putting their arms around each other's shoulders while the crowd wiped tears from their eyes. It was a very powerful video, but it was the words spoken by one student in the room that really got me into trouble.

Normally, it is the talkative social butterflies who always speak up first, but I was a bit shocked when one of the quietest girls in the class immediately piped up. "That was awesome! It wasn't right how those men were treated when they came back," she said. I am not really sure why I said what came out of my mouth next. Maybe I had been reading too much John Taylor Gatto, and thinking too much about how he says you have to let students do more and not just sit and listen to the teacher. Out it came without me really thinking about it: "So what are you going to do about it?" It may have sounded a bit condescending to my students, but I really did not mean it that way at all. I was only trying to empower the student to think about how she could make a difference. I was also a little bit shocked when she replied so quickly and emphatically. "We could put on our own Vietnam veterans' welcome home." My answer was an almost instantaneous, "Yes, we can, and you are in charge!" Her mouth gaped wide open and she was stunned for a moment; she quickly snapped her mouth shut, and I could tell by the way she set her eyes that she was going to take this challenge very personally.

I showed the video to my next class and almost as soon as the video was over, a student's hand shot up. He was the talkative type. He was never shy about speaking in public; actually, he relished it. Anytime we had activities where he presented in class, he wanted to be the first one to go and the other students loathed him for it. No one wanted to follow a natural public showman like him. It turned out he felt the same way as the student in my previous class, and for him it was personal. His grandfather was a Vietnam veteran, and one of his personal heroes. I asked him the same question, "What are you going to do about it?" He replied without a moment's hesitation, "We will have our own ceremony." To which I quickly replied, "Good! You're in charge!" After class, I asked him if he knew the girl from my previous class, and he said he did not. I introduced them the next day and told them they were in charge; by the next day of class, they had a list of a dozen things they wanted to do in their ceremony. After they presented their list to both classes, there were many suggestions from the other students. After a few more minutes of haggling, they had a whole new list of things they wanted to do. After reviewing their wish list, I suddenly felt like maybe this whole thing was a bad idea.

I had possibly let them bite off more than they could chew. Could I have given a bunch of sixteen-year-old kids too much freedom? Sure, a Vietnam veterans' welcome home sounds like a great idea, but did they truly understand how much work *inviting the entire community* would be? Did they know how much setup it would take for 300 chairs and a reception for 150 people? I needed to step in and explain to them the real gravity of all the things they wanted to do. I told them we would have to secure the school facilities, and before I could shut my mouth, a hand was already up volunteering to go down and talk to the administration. I asked them how we were going to get enough chairs for everyone, and again as soon as my question ended, another hand was up like a flash volunteering to go talk to the custodian about it. Eventually, no matter what potential pitfall I brought up, there was a student who was ready to tackle it. We still did not have a real event yet, but I had some students who were willing to work on it. There was only one glaring problem I saw: *we had no veterans to welcome.*

I realized we had a major problem in getting the word to all of the Vietnam veterans in the community, both those from our town who had moved away over the last half century, and the members of the families of those Vietnam veterans who had already died or were killed in Vietnam. This problem is what led me to call the local newspaper. I figured there was probably no better way than to have them do a story describing what we were planning, and ask people who wanted more information or were coming to call the school and let us know. It was still a gamble. How many of those took the newspaper? Would this type of announcement reach the veterans that had moved away? Only time would tell if the gamble would pay off, but there was still this nagging voice in the back of my head saying, "Did you really just announce to the world that you were going to have a great program and all you have is some kids agreeing to talk with people about borrowing chairs?"

We continued discussing the event for the first few minutes of class the next day. I just stood up at my desk and asked the kids what they had discovered, listened to what they wanted to change, fielded new elements to the event they wanted to add, and tried to give them a bit of guidance. I guess what I was really trying to do was make them see a bit of reality about the difficulty of some of the things they wanted to add. They had never planned an event for hundreds of people before, and I had. I was the Sunday School Superintendent at my church and one event I was over was Bible School. We had hundreds of kids and dozens of workers; it was quite an undertaking, requiring months of planning. I was also the state chairman for the largest powerlifting federation in the world. I had organized one of the largest deadlifting competitions in America; nearly fifty of the top strength athletes came from all over the world, and nearly 400 spectators attended, with national television coverage. These events took me months to a year to coordinate. How were a bunch of teens, with me at the helm, going to pull this off in less than a month?

An even bigger aspect of the ceremony was brought to me by the students. They wanted to take their research into the veterans on the wall and turn the information into full-blown eulogies, which they would read to the families and friends of the fallen Vietnam soldiers from our school during the ceremony. I was not sure if they fully understood what that really meant. Writing a biography of a person from the wall to be read in class was one thing; writing a personal eulogy to the family of a fallen soldier to be read in front of the whole community was on a whole other level. This was going to really push the envelope of their skills. I asked the students if they understood they would have to contact the families, including those difficult to find after fifty years. They would have to speak with them about things that may be difficult for loved ones to discuss with anyone, much less strangers. The students would then have to craft the perfect eulogy that would make the family proud; after all, they had been waiting a half century to hear those words. They would also have to present them in front of hundreds of people, television cameras, and news reporters in an eloquent way that would do their lives proud. My students agreed they understood, and were prepared to do whatever it took to make those eulogies everything the family could have dreamed of over these last tortuous decades.

The gravity of the situation never really seemed to bother the students. I once heard that research tells us the part of a person's brain that assesses risk does not fully develop until we're about 25. I believe it, because where I saw potential problems, all the kids saw were opportunities. At first it was annoying, but eventually it became infectious. I found myself feeling that we could do anything we wanted with this program, no matter how monumental the task. There was one thing that we needed to have a very heartfelt discussion about the next day, though—our expectations. I pulled up a chair right in the middle of the room and sat down. I leaned forward, looked them right in the eye, and spoke directly to them. I was no longer the teacher standing over them, but a friend and mentor speaking with them. I told them I was proud of all of the hard thinking and planning they were doing and would continue to do, but I wanted to make them aware of a few very important things they probably had not considered.

The students had never been involved in anything like this, and I wanted to make sure a few things were clear to them up front. I did not want to discourage them; I just wanted to be sure they would not be hurt if certain unexpected things happened. First, I told them that anytime you do anything, there will be detractors who try to tear it down. Some people might say, "That's nice, but how come they didn't include the WWII veterans?" Others may question why we did not do it on Veterans Day or Memorial Day. I told them they just needed to be aware that there are always people like that; no matter what you do, someone won't like it. It just meant we were actually doing something worth talking about. They all nodded their heads with understanding. Second, I told them that they were bringing up some painful memories. They were going to talk to people whose loved ones had been dead for fifty years. Many of them had grieved and moved on in their own ways. They might not want to come back to our ceremony and be part of it. Maybe it was just too painful, and maybe the family member would even hang up on them when they called. They all nodded their heads with insight yet again, undeterred. Then I delivered the final blow: What if they went through all the trouble of preparation and planning, and no one showed up? I told them candidly that when it was revealed in the newspaper that a bunch of kids were putting this on, maybe people wouldn't be as impressed as we were. Remember, the last time many of these veterans had any dealings with school children was when they returned home to the protestors throwing cups of urine in their faces, yelling "Baby killer!" All of the students were very quiet, and a few dropped their heads for a moment. Finally, after a few seconds of silence, I was surprised by the boy who spoke up. He was not your typical class leader. He was not even what most teachers would consider a good student. He was the stereotypical football player who did just enough to get by, and spent more time figuring out how to have fun at school than how to make good grades. He was even suspended for a few days, just a couple of weeks before (for what I am not sure, as I never asked). So, to say that I was a bit surprised when he was the one that spoke up is an understatement. "Mr. Campbell," he said, "if we have just one veteran come, then it is all worth it." The rest of the class immediately raised their faces, nodded their heads, and exploded in smiles and small talk echoing their sentiments; our fate was sealed. We would have a Vietnam Veterans' Welcome Home for our town, and, if it came to that, the students were prepared for the worst.

The day the story came out in the paper, to my surprise, it was on the cover above the fold. That is big news, and I was a bit shocked. There were the two student organizers of the event, and I was amused by seeing one of the quietest girls in the school on the front page of the paper, looking confident. *She must have been scared to death*, I thought. It was a great article and the students did a wonderful job with the questions. That day, I began to receive correspondence both by personal email through the school website and phone messages left in the office. Normally, I get about five messages a year from the office; I was getting nearly a dozen a day, after the article. People I had never met came to the school or my classroom randomly and told me personal stories. Our gamble to use the paper as our main source of advertising had paid off in a big way. The feedback I was receiving was more amazing than I ever could have dreamed.

Each day at the beginning of class, I would show the students the emails, tell them about my phone conversations, and inform them of the people I was meeting. I had to let them know how much what they were doing meant to the people of our community. One illustration I gave them was about a lady who worked just down the hall from me. Her husband was a Vietnam vet. They subscribed to the paper, but she told me he usually just glanced at the front page and then left it on the table for her to read when she came home. When she got home the day the event made the headlines, she was in for a surprise. She said her husband was in his chair reading the paper when she rounded the corner into the living room. He looked up at her with tears in his eyes and said, "Look what the kids down at the school are going to do for us." He never received a welcome home when he returned from Vietnam, and evidently he had been waiting, hopelessly, for nearly fifty years. She told me he reread the story over and over again until he went to bed. She came to me the next day so that my class would understand what just hearing of this event was doing for veterans in our community. When I retold this story to my classes, they were resolute; they would not let the veterans down. It would be everything they ever dreamed it would be, and that is when things started to get really intense.

The students had brainstormed all the previous day at lunch, by text, and on social media. They were ready to take this event to the next level. "We need a Facebook page!" they shouted. "Every veteran and family of a veteran deserves a real boutonnière," they demanded. "We want to sing a choral piece that we design ourselves," a group of girls insisted. "I'm calling the governor's office," another said, because he wanted to get some type of special governmental recognition. Unbeknownst to me, an ad hoc decorating committee had even organized itself. Some even decided to organize a welcoming committee so that this time, when the men that served in Vietnam confronted students, the first faces they saw would be happy, smiling faces welcoming them home. They wanted to greet them and thank them earnestly, then walk them to their seats personally. They had determined to make this the greatest event in the history of our community.

I felt we needed to discuss how to speak with people, so first I tackled the issue of the veterans. So many people do not talk to veterans, because they honestly just do not know what to say. I told my students that there are two phrases that should always be okay. First, "Thank you for your service" was always appropriate. Second, "Welcome home" was something that many Vietnam soldiers never got to hear. We practiced saying it as a class. I had a few students come up to me in front of the class; I played the part of a veteran, and they spoke to me one on one. It may seem silly, but none of my students had ever really done this before. I wanted them to be at ease and confident when speaking to veterans. No matter how silly it seemed, this was a skill that would benefit them throughout life.

Next, we discussed how to talk to family members of deceased veterans. We talked about how painful losing your spouse, brother, sister, father, or possibly child was for someone. If we add to that the hurt caused by the political turmoil surrounding the war, with the protests, lack of respect for the returning military, and so on, we could be digging at old wounds with some of these family members. As a class, we even developed a generic statement to use when they first called the family members. I remembered learning these phone skills at one of my early jobs, when I had to answer the phone. I recounted my boss saying, "When you answer the phone, you tell them who you are, where you are, and what you would like to do for them." Those words echoed back to me, and we put them to use when talking to the families. "Hello. My name is _____, and I am a student at the high school. We are planning a Vietnam veterans' welcome home, and I would like to talk to you about it." We practiced many times before I could tell they felt comfortable.

The one aspect of this event that I felt would really make it something exceptional was a special eulogy ceremony for the ten Vietnam soldiers from our school who died in the war. Each soldier had two or three students researching and writing a eulogy for their lives. The class decided that one person would be selected for each of the ten deceased to read a eulogy at the ceremony. I challenged them to not just read the information that was under their picture on our memorial wall. If we were going to read this in front of their families and a community that had been waiting fifty years to finally get this recognition, it had to be special. The students agreed, and that is when the real research began.

The students began to comb online resources trying to find next of kin so they could be contacted to find out more about the deceased, on a very personal level. We asked the paper to run a small article asking the families to contact us. The students contacted our town's chairperson for the veterans' memorial wall program, which allowed people to buy bricks for any veteran from our town to be placed along the memorial walk. Seven of the ten of the Vietnam veterans killed in action from our school had a brick on the town's wall, and the chairperson brought us the info about the person who purchased the brick so we could contact them. He came to our class to personally deliver the information. I had already spoken with him on the phone, and he told me that he was also a Vietnam veteran. I shared with my class that he would be coming down, he was a veteran, and he was excited about what we were doing. I heard a knock at my classroom door while the kids were divided into their groups working on the event, and I went to the door. The chairman of the town's veterans' memorial wall was there and he introduced himself. I brought him into the class, got all of my students' attention, and then introduced him to the class. Without prompting, they used what we had practiced. "Thank you for serving," the students said. They followed with "Welcome home." At that moment, we turned yet another powerful corner in this journey.

You can never really understand the power of that moment unless you were there. To the kids, it was just words; a social nicety that you say to people in the military. It was the thing I taught them to say when they were unsure of exactly what to say. To this veteran who had waited fifty years to hear those words, it was so much more. He turned and looked at me; behind his horn-rimmed glasses, I could see tears welling up in his eyes. He stared for a moment, blinked a few times, then composed himself before uttering a choked "Thank you." He gave us the information and told the class he appreciated what they were doing, then said he needed to get back to work. I did not bring up the fact that he had been emotionally taken aback when those few simple words were uttered by my class. I think they all noticed and understood the power of what they were doing. The project had a face, and they had seen what this project meant to at least one veteran of our community. They were more determined than ever to give their all for this project.

The chairman called me that afternoon. I picked up the phone and was a bit surprised at his words. "I just wanted to call and apologize," he said. "Apologize for what?" I asked. "I did not mean to get all choked up on you," he said. He went on to tell me that for half a century he had never heard those words. He'd wanted to hear them, he'd dreamed of hearing them, but no one ever said them to him. He had almost forgotten his desire to hear them spoken, when from the most unlikely of places, he heard those long overdue words. It was a bunch of kids born thirty years after he left Vietnam who had finally broken the silence. He then apologized for leaving so quickly. "I should have stayed," he said, "but I was afraid I would lose it. I went to my car and cried like I had not cried in a long time." I told him I was sorry if the emotions were too much, but before I could even finish my sentence, he cut me off. "Don't be. I have been waiting most of my life to hear those words."

When I told the students about the phone conversation the next day, they were blown away and more determined than ever to find those families, thank those veterans, and honor the ones who did not live long enough to ever receive their proper welcome home. The students called our school's former principal, who was over the creation of the Vietnam Memorial Wall in our school (luckily for us, he is now our director of schools). They looked at websites like the Virtual Wall, where people posted articles about their friends and loved ones who died in Vietnam, and often left email addresses for others to contact them. Some decided to call the nearest Veterans Administration facility (luckily, for us it was the largest one in the country and only fifteen minutes away). Others found national groups, like the Vietnam Veterans Association of America, that sponsored local chapters. By the time they were done, we had tons of contacts for veterans around the area, ways to help spread the word of our upcoming event, and (the best part) my students were actually getting to speak with real Vietnam veterans.

Possibly the most daunting part of the entire event was that we only had two weeks to organize this event. My room turned from a classroom into what felt like the nerve center of a political campaign. The first few days I taught the planned lesson for the first half, then would break and discuss our event. As the event grew nearer, we spent the entire class period on it. I felt more like an administrator or a facilitator than teacher. I would just get up and read a few emails, tell a story about someone I had met, then receive updates about what the students were supposed to get done the day before, then move on to what needed to be accomplished that day. That is when I realized that I really was no longer a teacher. Instead, each student in the class was their own teacher. I had been a teacher for over a decade, yet this was the time that I felt most like a teacher...when I was not doing much of anything at all.

One day I looked around the classroom and was amazed at what was happening. I had a group who had their cell phones out, but not to text their friends about what was going on after school; they were instead looking up telephone numbers of contacts we needed, finding emails of organizations and people who had to be reached, and then calling these important people. I had another group working on food for the receptions. I heard them talking about how many of each item, what kind of food was best, and even concerns about diabetes, since many of these veterans were getting older and many others had been exposed to Agent Orange (which increases the likelihood of diabetes). The very quiet girl who was one of the student organizers was giving an interview with a local radio station. I listened for a few minutes, so impressed with the changes that had taken place since the beginning of the year, especially since the beginning of the planning for this event.

Students did not even have to be in my class to be teaching themselves and learning independently. I had one group of students in the neighboring classroom, making boutonnières with the help of the horticulture teacher. There was another group of young ladies in the choral group who had decided they wanted to arrange and sing a patriotic song. They often went down to the choral room and practiced their song. When students needed peace and quiet to speak with people on the phone, they just dug out their cell phones, called people, and excused themselves to the room next to mine (which happened to be unoccupied during the times we were working on the event). Many teachers may find it hard to believe that students would pour themselves into school work with so much enthusiasm that you could just let them roam around the school unsupervised, and they would still stay on task and do what they were supposed to do. But that is not entirely the case; they were supervised, but it was a supervision of self. They knew they had two weeks to pull off an event they, and I, had been bragging about to the community. They knew that veterans had waited fifty years for this, and my students were not going to disappoint them. The students had totally seen the importance of this event, and when that happened, they became their own teachers.

I was reading Sir Ken Robinson's excellent book *Out of Our Minds*, and he talked about meeting a big time producer of live theater. Robinson asked him what the essence of theater was. I will never forget the answer: "The connections between the actor and the audience." The producer went on to say that you can add a stage, lights, music, fog, electronic amplification, and a huge theater to watch it in, but if there is no real connection between a performer and a spectator, there is no genuine theater. That made me start to think about what real education was. If some expert came up to me and said, "Hey! You have been teaching for over ten years. What is the essence of education?" what would I say? I thought back on what the theater producer said, and after some thought, I began to form my answer: Education is the connections between student and teacher, with the ultimate form coming when the student and teacher are in the same body.

I know that when there is a real connection between the classroom teacher and the students, amazing things happen. Humans long for that connection with others. We can have teachers, overhead projectors, buildings, tests, worksheets, study guides, curriculum, ball games, clubs, teams, and a lunchroom, but if there is no real connection between teachers and students, then we do not have real education. As I think about it more, I sometimes feel that the more of those peripheral things we have, the more it distracts from the essence of education. Teachers become so concerned with the worksheets, tests, lectures, and PowerPoints that it actually tears down the relationship between them and their students. This project allowed my students to have a relationship with the Vietnam veterans. At first tacitly, through learning about the ones who died from our school, and then through watching videos and completing readings in my class. Later, they got to meet a Vietnam veteran and have a very powerful effect on him, hear stories of others who were touched, and even talk to some on the phone. It had not been much interaction, but there was the prospect of some amazing interactions to come in the next few weeks, if the students just persisted and actually pulled off this colossal endeavor. The existing small connections with the promise of more were all it really took to transform my students from kids sitting in a room into real students...and even teachers.

As the event drew closer, all of the logistics seemed to be falling into place. It was time to make sure that the most important aspect of the event was perfect. The students and I discussed it, and agreed that the eulogies would most likely be the most powerful point of the ceremony. All of the students had written a eulogy, and now it was time to select the person from the group of two or three assigned to each fallen soldier to present the eulogy. The students huddled together and read each other's eulogies, discussed who could speak in public better, and who was already working on the presentation of some other aspect of the ceremony; they decided who would present on their own. Some of the students chosen to read the eulogies were not the most obvious choices; to me, it did not matter. I did not worry for one minute, because the students had started to see the importance of what they were doing. They were totally focused on doing everything in their power to honor these veterans and their families.

When students are allowed to see the relevance of their work, it becomes important to them. Something I learned in my first few days as teacher was that kids can spot fakery very well. When something is not important, but teachers only say it is important, they know the truth. When adults tell kids they may need it someday, knowing full well they probably will not, the kids know. Why are teachers surprised when kids are uninterested in our fake worksheets, study guides, and bold words? Give them something real, and watch them seize it. The class clown in my room stopped trying to be funny and started working. He actually became one of the most sensitive students in the class to the needs of the veterans and their families. Shy people became outspoken in their groups, and would even become project leaders and public speakers to the point that other teachers were shocked when they witnessed the ceremony. Poor writers worked on their grammar like never before, and wrote beautiful eulogies that would make any family proud. I used to wonder how people hundreds of years ago never went to school, instead spending their time playing and working with their families, yet did the most amazing things that stump the most "educated" in our society. The amazing accomplishments of Nikola Tesla, Isaac Newton, and Ben Franklin astound us, even though they were mostly home- or self-educated. It is all because those people were forced to tackle real problems in real settings, not just given fake problems in cathedrals of education by people who some government institution said were experts. If teachers will allow students to work on real problems with real consequences, then most of the perceived discipline problems and educational setbacks will evaporate.

I had a big talk with the students about how important real educational tasks were. I explained it like this: If a student messes up on a worksheet, the consequences are minimal. There would most likely be just a few points taken off of the final score. If a student answered a question wrong in class, it is no big deal; most teachers just say, "Nice try," and move on to the next student. "What happens when you are presenting a eulogy in front of hundreds of people, but most importantly a loving and hurting family that has been waiting half a century to hear the words you have prepared, and you let them down?" I asked. Now, that is real education. I told them that this assignment was real, the dead soldiers on the wall were real, the families were real, the hurt they felt was real, and the consequences of their performance were real. I also told them that the healing their words could provide was also very real. These eulogies, if done in spectacular fashion, may go into family Bibles to be passed down for generations; be placed in caskets at funerals; be delivered to the Vietnam Memorial wall in Washington DC by family members; or possibly be taken out and read on the anniversary of their dearly departed's birthday. This was the students' chance to make a real impact on a family, and it was 100 percent up to them. When they stood up behind that podium in front of the community and delivered their speeches, there would be no place to hide. They all nodded their heads in understanding, and went to work feverishly to make their eulogies something of which their parents would be proud.

The students kept tweaking their speeches until they were absolutely satisfied that they were perfect. They had other students read them and give input. When they felt they were getting close or maybe had a problem with some part of it, they brought them to me to read and give input. The students learned about how to say things in the right tone, how to present painful information in a way that inspired pride, and how to avoid opening decades-old wounds. I had one student named Rachel who worked so hard on her eulogy, but just could not get one part perfect. She kept looking at it, thinking about it, having other students read it, and rewriting it; no matter what she did, it was still not quite right. It was said in words that were not untrue or harsh, but when she spoke of how he died, it was just a bit uncomfortable. I was afraid my constant insistence that she keep changing it might give her the impression that she had not done a good job, could never get it right, or was not up to the task (which was far from the truth). I had a great idea. There was a veteran who taught just down the hall. I told her to take it to him and get his input. She returned in a few minutes, said he was very helpful, and started rewriting. The next day she came in with her eulogy, and it was perfect. There is nothing like the input of a real expert who has been there, lost friends, and understood the pain himself to help out in a situation like this one.

It wasn't until a teacher in-service day shortly before the event that I really understood what kind of effort the students were putting into this. One of my students came to the school on a day when he was supposed to be out going to the lake, sleeping late, hanging out with friends, or a million other things besides coming to school. However, there he was, in a shirt and tie in the doorway. He proceeded to tell me what he had been doing on his day off from school. He called the local archivist at our city library, and scheduled a meeting for his vacation day.

He went down and found the newspaper that had the death announcement of his soldier in the microfilm room with the help of the archivist. He read the article, and found it had the address and names of the immediate family at the end. He was intrigued, and decided to go to the home to see if they still lived there. That was a bold move for a high school kid, knowing that fifty years had passed.

When he arrived at the house, a lady met him and told him the family no longer lived there; but she knew where they had moved to and pointed out the house, which wasn't too far away. When he arrived at the next house, he introduced himself and they immediately welcomed him. They treated him just like an old friend, and began to call all of their relatives to come over and meet him. Before long, the kitchen was full of relatives, each telling stories that would help him craft a eulogy so personal no one in attendance would ever forget it. "I just left the house," he said with a smile. "I was there two hours, and they told me to come back any time. The sister even hugged me when I left," he said, shaking his head almost in disbelief. I think he was finally understanding the true gravity of what he was doing, and (maybe for the first time) so did I.

Other students went on their own to meet families too, and they had similar stories. They were always welcomed by the family, and the family always called others to come over or directed them to other homes to get a more complete story. Some families had moved too far away or remarried, but my students still tracked them down and emailed them or telephoned, gathering special insights. I encouraged them to make sure they wove the special stories they had heard into their eulogies to make it personal for each family. In all, the students were able to personally contact the families of seven of the ten veterans on our school's memorial wall. Possibly the harder job belonged to the students who could find no one to talk to about their soldier. I encouraged them to use their imagination to craft their eulogies as personally as possible. They had to do extra study to find out about their person, since there was no one to tell the history quickly and directly.

Not only were the eulogizers working hard on their presentations, I gave the two student organizers special tasks as well. The shy girl would give the welcome address, and the outspoken boy would give the closing. I emphasized that no matter which part they were working on, their words would either set the tone for the rest of the ceremony, or would be the last words ringing in the ears of the crowd. The quiet project leader worked very hard and did several rewrites, bringing each to me to get my input until she felt satisfied it would be the right way to begin the event. She did a great job, and while I was never worried about her writing it, one question lingered in my mind: *Can she deliver it?* The other project leader, the outspoken one, went to work on his with gusto. He brought rewrites to me before school, which he had stayed up working on until late in the night. He brought them to me during school, when he had neglected his other classes to change some details. We talked several times at length about how to make this the perfect capstone to the entire event. He spoke to his grandfather (who was a Vietnam veteran) several times to glean his wisdom about what should be said, and finally, he had the closing that would be perfect.

The event they had envisioned and worked so hard to bring to fruition was now only two days away. I took all of my students down to the school's courtyard where the event would be held. We brought the podium and set it up, then I had the students read their openings, eulogies, closings, or invocations, and sing their songs. I wanted each one to be honed to perfection when the time came. I gave them a ten-minute tutorial on public speaking, how to handle nervousness, and even how to handle it if they became emotional or cried. One student said, "Why would we cry?" I explained to them that they had become more connected to these soldiers, their families, and the war than they realized, and it might happen. Later on, I was very glad I had taken those few moments to discuss the emotional power they might experience. The students not speaking played the part of the crowd, and we even had a cell phone ring and a "baby" start crying. We left no stone unturned in our preparation.

The day arrived, and there was a flurry of activity throughout the school beginning at 7 a.m. There were students bringing food, decorations, boutonnières, copies of speeches, flags, ribbons, projectors, laptops, and so much more to my room. I was so busy that I didn't even eat anything after breakfast that day (that is a big deal for me). The crazy part is that I did not do even a small fraction of the work that went on that day. The event was so big there was no way I could do it all, and honestly, I had never intended it to be that way in the first place. This was the students' event; they knew their roles and did them, usually without even being told. I just walked around and put out fires when the blazes erupted, made a couple of decisions, offered some advice, and sat back and watched them amaze me with their maturity and attention to detail. There had been so much work done behind the scenes in the preceding two weeks, but now it was time to let the community in to reap the reward of their hard work.

When the first veteran arrived, I knew it was going to be a special event. As soon as the man's daughter dropped him off in the pull through in front of the school, and he saw the smiling faces of the student welcoming committee with boutonnières and ribbons in hand, he began to weep. Later, my students told me he cried the whole time they were attaching his flower, and the entire time they walked him to his seat. At this point, I felt the reality of what the students had cobbled together on short notice started to come into focus. I was inside, and I remember seeing a lady walking around like she was lost. My welcoming committee decided to give white flowers to veterans and red flowers to those who were families of veterans. I noticed the lady was wearing a red flower and just kind of standing there, looking around with a blank expression plastered across her face. I went over and introduced myself, and asked her if she was there with someone (I noticed her red flower). She dropped her head, let a few tears flow, and stammered, "No, but my late husband was a Vietnam veteran." The expression on her face was so powerful that I felt an emotional connection to a man whom I'd never met, as his widow stood before me. I felt the hot tears drop down my cheeks, too, when she gathered herself and raised her head to look me in the eye. "He would have loved this," she said with renewed strength, letting a tiny smile escape the corners of her mouth. I put my arm around her, and we both cried for a moment before I led her to the special seating for the families of veterans. Maybe this is when the reality of what they had done began to hit me, as well.

An entire book could be written about this event alone, but there were a few highlights that stood out to me about what kind of real education was taking place that day among my students. I looked around once to see some students setting up audio-visual equipment, while another greeted veterans with a smile; one group was being interviewed by the local television station news crew, and still another was being interviewed by the newspaper. No matter where I looked, students were interacting with people of all ages, but especially the veterans. We had nearly 150 experts (some call them veterans and their family members) on the Vietnam War attend that day, and my students learned from every one of them. I saw my students shaking hands with the veterans, getting hugs from veterans, and even choking back tears with the veterans. It was time for the program to begin, and that quiet young lady that had unintentionally become one of the project leaders kicked off the event flawlessly. I was in awe of the transformation that took place in that young lady in such a short amount of time. What was once a timid, quiet girl was now a confident young lady. She was followed by our director of schools, who was our keynote speaker and also a Vietnam veteran. The air felt like the ionized atmosphere right before a lightning storm that rolls through the country on a muggy summer afternoon. A storm of emotion was brewing, and there was going to be an outburst—maybe even some lightning. I was not sure when it was coming or where it would strike, but soon a spark was ignited and the entire morning was engulfed. All it took was one spark.

The program moved to the section where the eulogies were read, which I considered to be the main attraction of the day. The students had decided to have the friends and family of each fallen soldier stand in their honor, and then present that family with a copy of the eulogy. If there was no one present to receive the eulogy, we had several empty chairs in the front row where we would lay the eulogy with a white flower, as a symbol that even though there was not one friend or family member there, there was still a place for them. It came time for the boy who had visited the family on his vacation day from school to begin the most emotional part of the morning. He did an amazing job, and when he asked the family and friends to stand the crowd erupted in applause. When the young man walked to the sister to present the eulogy, the lady grabbed him in a hearty embrace so powerful that it nearly squished the tiny young man. I saw her whisper something in his ear as tears streamed down her face. He later told me she said, "I only wish our momma was here to see this." As I tilted my face toward the heavens, I felt the first few drops of the emotional storm spatter against my cheeks. Little did I know, there was a downpour awaiting us all.

Next, it was Rachel's turn. Remember she was the girl who struggled with the perfect wording for her eulogy? When she began, all was going well for a few lines; then I heard her voice change. *Nerves*, I thought. *She will be just fine.* Nerves would be natural for any of us in such a setting, much less for a quiet young lady only sixteen years old. In a moment, I heard her voice crack again, and I knew it was not just nerves; she was fighting back tears. The next second, she stopped talking and started to cry. I was not concerned. After all, I had prepared them for this just a few days before. I'd instructed her to just pause, let the emotions pass, and then resume where she left off. She tried to do what I told her, but she just could not stop crying. As I saw her tiny shoulders begin to heave up and down, I knew she was being consumed with powerful emotions that she would not be able to control. My eyes furtively darted toward the crowd. Many of them began to look down at their laps, either trying to avoid their own tears or trying to not embarrass the girl by looking on her in such an exposed emotional state (maybe some were doing a bit of both). I began to hurt for her, standing all alone, just a young bundle of raw nerves being exposed to the powerful emotions of the day in front of hundreds of strangers. I felt I needed to do something, so I jumped from my chair and put my arm around her. My original plan was just to stand with her and make her feel like she was not alone; as I stood beside her with my arm around her shoulder, I could feel the emotion radiating off of her. It permeated my skin, swam through my veins, and lodged itself in my soul. Soon, even though I had moved to her side to be strong for her, I felt myself begin to cry. So there we stood, teacher and pupil in front of hundreds, standing for a man neither of us had ever met, crying our eyes out. I offered her my handkerchief and she put both hands over her face. I let it pass a bit, then whispered into her ear, "Do you want to try and continue, or do you want to do yours at the end when you've had time to get composed?" She took a second, gathered herself, sucked in a huge breath and shuddered, whispering that she wanted to go on with her eulogy. I stood there for another second, letting her gather herself so she could begin anew, then made my way back to my seat and looked out over the crowd. There was not a dry eye anywhere. The storm had arrived, and everyone in attendance that day was soaked in the deluge of emotion that Rachel started.

I realized in that moment the power of what the students had done. Here was a girl crying for a man she had never met. In fact, he had died 35 years before she was even born. Through this event, which the students themselves designed, she formed a connection with a person whom she had not and would never know. It had moved her to a point where her emotions could not be held back, and neither could anyone else's. Everyone in attendance that day perceived the importance of real education at that moment. It's not about the textbooks, study guides, bold words, homework, worksheets, or standardized tests. Real education is about self-knowledge, and Rachel learned more about herself that day than any other day in school. She learned she could write a perfect eulogy, and she could create decorations; she was even the brilliant artist who designed the cover for our program (in about five minutes of scribbling in her ever-present art pad). The most important lesson she learned is that she can become emotionally connected to anyone, even someone she had never met, never would meet, and never could meet. She could learn to care about that person not because she read about Vietnam in a textbook, did a worksheet, or passed a standardized test; Rachel learned to care for a dead man because she studied and learned about what he went through, what the family experienced, what other veterans had recorded, and what all of the faces in the audience were radiating. For the first time in her life, history was real, learning was real, and a name on a wall was real; and it was because of nothing I had taught. Rachel had reached the ultimate level of education, when the teacher and the student are in the same body.

When Rachel completed her eulogy, she walked over to the family. The sister grabbed her face with trembling hands, looked her right in the eye, and said, "Thank you so much! That was beautiful." Rachel returned to her seat and others followed, but the outburst had begun. People were crying everywhere. I looked over my shoulder and all of my students were crying, the crowd's shoulders where heaving with tears, the veterans were sobbing, and the families were looking for handkerchiefs. I even looked over and caught sight of the newspaper cameraman. Here was a person who gets paid to remove himself from the events he covers in order to focus on his job; yet there he was, literally sobbing like a baby. I mean there was snot running out of his nose, his shirt sleeves were being used as handkerchiefs, and audible sobs were coming from this fellow. The cloudburst had begun, and it looked like it had set in for the day.

When it came time for the closing, it was already a special day. Everyone had regained their composure and they were smiling, yet many still had the tears in their eyes. The closing was amazing. With arms outstretched in an imaginary embrace, the student simply ended with "Welcome home," and then ran from the platform into the outstretched arms of his grandfather, the Vietnam veteran. He buried his face in that man's large chest and wet his shirt with his tears while his grandfather looked blankly into the air, fighting back his own emotions, pent up for the better part of half a century. That young man told me a few days later that his grandfather said that was the proudest he could ever be of his grandson. In a time when our culture is crazy about youth sports, focused on getting young people into the best colleges, and desires for their offspring to be wealthy, this grandfather understood what was important. That day, that grandfather received a large dose of what real education is supposed to be. He had a young grandson who received self-knowledge about his own family heritage, made a connection to a war he was way too young to understand, and used what he learned to make his own connections between the past and the future—all while giving back to the community. Do not think that the lessons were over just because the closing was given. There were still many history lessons yet to be taught on that day.

After the main event was over, the students were already scurrying like ants to move chairs, set up tables, and prepare food for the reception. The reception was all their idea. They wanted the veterans and their families to come into the school, sit down with their old friends, and talk or reminisce for as long as they desired. I thought it was a wonderful idea, because it would also give the students a chance to sit and talk with the veterans and families. I told them it would take a lot of work to have a reception, but they did not even blink. Students signed up eagerly to bake two dozen cookies each, and bring cakes, potato chips, napkins, drinks, or plates. They went all out, and thought of everything to make this a special day. Each table in the reception area was set with a centerpiece, and the whole serving line had a beautiful backdrop of latticework and red, white, and blue flowers. I was caught in the school's courtyard for a few minutes speaking with various friends, the media, and several veterans. When I made my way to the reception area, it was the first time I had seen what the students crafted. It was beautiful, and I am not just speaking of the decorations.

There were nearly 150 people there, and they were all having a great time. Old friends were backslapping each other. The veterans were moving chairs so they could sit beside their old friends, and families were together for the first time in decades. Many had not been inside the school in nearly half a century; they just enjoyed looking at the different classrooms and hallways, reminiscing about the glory days. The entire event was turning out just as the students had planned. All of their effort and thoughtfulness had paid off. It was a resounding success, but little did we know that a crisis was about to strike.

I have always heard that with success comes new challenges. That was never truer than when the young lady who was in charge of the reception came up to me in a panic. "Mr. Campbell!" she said. "We are almost out of food." We had planned for about 120 people; we were at nearly 150. Indeed, several dozen people were still in line and the food was getting very low. I was not shaken, because we'd planned for this. So I calmly told her to put out the reserve trays of food. "I already did!" she exclaimed. Before I could even think about what to do to remedy the problem, one of my students jumped up from her seat behind me, and said she would run to her car and drive across the street to get a couple of party trays. "Are you sure?" I asked, thinking that maybe she did not realize what it would cost. She insisted, and was out the door in a flash. She soon returned with enough food to satisfy even the hardiest of Vietnam veterans. The day was saved. After the reception, she told me that it cost nearly $60 for the trays. I offered to help pay her for the food. I knew that to a teenager who works a part time job, $60 was a tremendous amount of money. She flatly refused. "Absolutely not! It is the least I can do for these veterans and their families," she retorted, with an air of pride. She was another young person receiving a real education.

The reception was a smashing success; many of the attendees stayed for nearly two hours. They had so much fun talking with one another. As I made sure everyone had been served, I saw something that upset me very much. Some of my students were working so hard refilling the food, moving chairs, and clearing tables that they forgot the most important part of the day. They were too busy to talk to the veterans. That, to me, was the most important aspect of the entire ceremony. We had assembled the local experts with first-hand knowledge about something we studied in class, and they were missing the golden opportunity to interact with and learn from these amazing people. I quickly called for them all to gather around me, and I ordered them to stop whatever they were doing and go talk to veterans immediately. The students trickled into the audience, flowing into empty chairs here and there, introducing themselves to the veterans and their guests. They were greeted with hugs, hand shakes, and thank yous. I stood at the door to the reception area, admiring my favorite part of the day. Young people who were inspired to do something for others by watching a short video clip had actually done it. They had put on one of the most amazing events in the history of our community, and given these veterans and their families what every politician, veterans' group, and citizens' group had overlooked for several decades: a long overdue welcome home.

You may be wondering who would ever get fired for putting on a veterans' ceremony. To answer, my mind floats back to that day when I hung up the phone with the newspaper reporter and wondered what I had gotten myself into. I was worried the huge event I just bragged about couldn't actually be carried out by a few teenagers having no connection to Vietnam personally. What if we'd spent all of that class time (right before the standardized test, by the way) and the event bombed? What if the students spent their personal money and time making and buying food, but no one showed? What if we caused the administration and janitors all of these problems (like setting up, moving chairs and furniture, borrowing sound systems, etc.) and no one outside of our little group even cared? These are not ways to endear one's self to the school administration. What is worse, what if people did show up and it was a train wreck? What if the kids dressed sloppily, or fumbled through eulogies that were obviously rushed and careless? What if the students did not appear to care, and the school did not look beautiful? It would be a huge black eye, not just for our school (and those in charge of it), but also for the entire community. It would be a slap in the face to those veterans and their families, to invite them with the hope of the proper welcome home only to have a half-hearted effort that left them more hurt than they were before the event. What if the veterans learned that after fifty years and the promise of righting a wrong, the truth was still that no one really cared about those who sacrificed in Vietnam?

I learned some very big lessons while leaning up against that wall, smiling as my students spoke with and made personal connections with the veterans. If you gamble and let kids try something big, sometimes they may fail—but what if they do not? What are the stakes for the students and the community if they actually succeed? I hear teachers talking all the time about the negatives of letting the students try real projects with real consequences. "What if they don't do a good job and it looks ridiculous? What if they won't do the work, and the teacher has to work themselves to death to do it all, just to save the day? What if they don't take it seriously? My students are not mature enough to do something like that. I don't have time to do things like that, because I have to get through my curriculum." I have heard all of these excuses from teachers about why they don't believe in their kids, and don't trust them to do amazing projects that have real consequences. It is almost as if they are saying, "I don't have time to do what really works, because I am too busy doing what doesn't work." Another way of saying it would be, "I don't have time to trust my students to do something amazing, because I am too busy trusting myself to do something boring." We should not be focusing on the chance of failure, but on the possibility of success and the rewards that come with that accomplishment.

What happens if students actually live up to the expectations we have for them (or conversely, live down to them)? Inside each one of these young people is an amazing potential to change the world. Yet we almost never tap it, because we put them in boring schools with sanitized textbooks, mind-numbing worksheets, and straitjacket curricula that hold hostage their imaginations and spirits. Then we wonder why they never want to do anything, try anything new, take risks, put any effort in, get creative, or solve problems. The students do not want to do those things because they know they are not real life. Give a student the chance to do something real in life with real consequences, and watch them accept the challenge like never before. If all a teacher ever does is give worksheets, the students can't be expected to get excited and want to change the world. Teachers must find places where the students show interest, then challenge them to do something, guide and direct them with wisdom, and allow them to make decisions that affect the outcome.

There is an old adage and many quotes that say in some way without great risk there is no reward, and sometimes the greater the risk the greater the reward. That is how fortunes have been built in business, simple and shy men have found the beautiful loves of their lives, and sports legends have been made. So why do we not let our students take risks in schools? We cannot be paralyzed by the fear of what could happen. That is why the teacher is there. It is the teacher's job to gauge the interest of the students, making sure the students are really interested, that the students have been properly motivated through an effective study of the subject, and are constantly monitored to make sure the students lack of real-world wisdom does not allow them to go in the wrong direction. Yes, the teacher has an important place in education. But that place is not standing at the front of the class insisting they have the monopoly on knowledge, and the kids should just sit back and passively enjoy their ride through abstract subjects because they are imbeciles worthy of nothing better. It is time that schools and teachers started trusting their students with real-world problems, setting their passion and energy loose on a world the likes of which have not been seen in this county since the beginning of the Industrial Revolution.

"But how do you give the pupils a grade?" someone will cry. "Where is the empirical quantitative data that proves the students learned something?" they'll sneer. In this instance, I actually had a capstone project prepared from the very beginning, because I asked myself those very same questions. The day after the event, my students wrote an essay called "What I Learned Yesterday." They were going to tell me what they learned in their own words, and rationalize to me that they had learned enough on this project to deserve an exemplary grade for the past two weeks of class time. The next day, I gave them their assignment and told them they had complete freedom to write about whatever they wanted, but it better show me what they learned and explain to me how they learned it from the project. Nothing could have prepared me for what I read in those papers.

I read such fascinating titles as "Yesterday I Learned I Could Help a Man Exorcize His Demons." It was a jaw-dropping paper by a student who had listened to a veteran who was a medic in Vietnam. His job in Vietnam was to take dead bodies off of the choppers that were returning from the field, properly identify those corpses, and then place them in body bags. The student said that when the veteran started talking, he could feel how uncomfortable the veteran was in his voice and see the pain still present in his tortured eyes. Why the man began to talk of these very uncomfortable memories he had from so long ago, the student could not say; he only sat in nonjudgmental serenity and allowed the man to say whatever long overdue words he needed to put his haunting memories to rest. As the man talked for nearly thirty minutes, he told the student how for ten hours a day that is all he did. Some days there were hundreds of shiny, black, body bags lined up as far as the eye could see, by the end of his shift. Many times when he went to remove the body from the helicopter, there was no body; there was only a piece of a limb, a lump of flesh, or some bloody tattered clothing. Yet he still pulled it from the chopper and did his job, just stuffing those bodies (or parts of bodies) into bags for their return to the states and a proper burial. When the veteran medic finished his tale, the student noticed a difference in the man. His countenance had changed into one of peaceful calm. His eyes were not pained anymore, and his voice was no longer wavering, but even. The boy felt that somehow just listening to the man and allowing him to get his painful memories out was a huge help. Why the man had chosen such an innocent young boy, who really could not understand the ramifications of such heady topics, my young student was not sure. He ended by writing that he learned that even a young boy can be quiet and listen to an old veteran's painful stories, and help him remove his demons.

As I dove deeper into the pile of papers on my desk, it was one incredible story after another. One young lady said that no matter how old she was, she learned that she can make a difference in the world. At first she doubted whether a bunch of kids could really pull of such a huge event. When they did, it showed her that people of any age could do anything if they really wanted to. Wow, what a concept for a person of any age to understand—much less a teenager. If everyone in the world felt that way, there would be less injustice, more political activity, more grassroots efforts, more civic clubs and organizations, and a lot more people who needed it getting help. Even though this was not a civics class, this student learned a very powerful lesson about citizenship in a free society, and is a better member of our community because of it.

Another student said they learned that anyone can right a wrong, no matter how old. What an amazingly perceptive lesson! There are so many people who wait for others to do something, even though it is obvious to everyone that it needs to be done. It is called the bystander effect, or sometimes even Genovese Syndrome (named after the young lady who was sexually assaulted and murdered over a thirty-minute period on a New York street while dozens of people witnessed it, yet did nothing). People in groups always wait for someone else to do something. After all, they are in a huge group; someone had to see it, someone will do something, and that someone is better equipped to do it than they are. What happens is no one does anything, even though everyone sees the problem. This student learned that the politicians, veterans groups, and civic organizations knew of the problem, yet no one ever did anything about it. They were just a bunch of high school kids who watched a video and decided they would do something, whether they were the best equipped or not. I once heard a preacher say that "God does not always call the equipped, sometimes he equips the called." How many more wrongs are out there in the world that these students will notice throughout their lives? After this experience, when they see them they will have the confidence and skills to make them right.

One student even told me that before that day he had never spoken to a person over sixty who was not one of his relatives. I was shocked. I was stunned that he had never spoken to an old person at church, at his job, in a grocery store, or in the community. It really brought out a sad fact in our society; everything is designed to keep the young and old apart. It echoed a sentiment I received by email from a Vietnam veteran who said he was so proud we were having the event, but also a bit surprised that it was the students' idea to put on the ceremony. He said that when he was out in town and witnessed teenagers at the mall, grocery store, or shopping centers, they always acted like the older people did not exist. How sad that our society teaches the young that old people are dim-witted, old fashioned, boring, close minded, and (sadly) worthless The message is pervasive in our society. Many churches now have contemporary services separate from the adult services, complete with their own style of music and teaching, because it is obvious that young and old cannot enjoy the same music, or the same religious teachings, even though they worship the same God. When older people slow down instead of asserting that they have intrinsic value to our families, we take the easy way out and just put them in a nursing home—patting ourselves on the back when we visit twice a year. It does not take long for the young to internalize the very powerful messages our society sends them about the older generation. The student concluded by saying that after speaking with the veterans, he learned that the older generation was full of individuals, people just like the younger generation. Some were full of life, and others had the life drained out of them by terrible events such as Vietnam, and were still struggling fifty years later to recover. Some were great listeners, while others were just looking for anyone who would listen to them. Sure, some were short-tempered and mean, but others were funny and loving. What a powerful lesson to learn, that people (no matter their age) are still people, worthy of getting to know and evaluating on their own merits.

As I pored through the stack of papers reading what each student learned, I realized that this event was so much more than even I ever imagined. The students had thrown down an incredible gauntlet, buffeted themselves to rise to every lofty challenge, learned what they needed to jump each hurdle along the way, were proud of what they had accomplished when it was over, and were able to ascertain how they were different people after the challenge was completed. Isn't that what schools and teachers should really be teaching? We can put on the dog and pony show of standardized testing, we can teach kids to memorize steps and say they are educated, and we can pat ourselves on the back when students end up with mounds of college loan debt for meaningless degrees (for fields in which they can never find a job). Until we teach students how to seek out challenges, learn what they need accomplish the task, and reflect on what they have done to further prepare themselves for the next obstacle, we will not have true educational reform.

The time has come for the educational establishment, teachers included, to start letting kids take risks learning about things they truly care about. There should be no more charades, no more acting, and no more faking it. It is time to trust the students with their own real education. Have them create a huge event, tell the whole world about it, and watch as the real education unfolds. Sure, as a teacher, you may be scared at times. When educators realize that they are giving up control to a bunch of kids, it may be a bit frightening. As one looks around and sees what is happening in the classroom, it will be easy to realize you cannot plan ahead and keep everything to your schedule or lesson plan. When it becomes painfully obvious that there is no way to quantitatively evaluate the learning process, some may get scared. Persevere, for the shores of institutionalized, industrial-model schooling are being left behind in the distance, and the open waters of real-life education are dead ahead. Some may have to sacrifice that self-intoxicating sense of control on which some teachers thrive. Look to the students for encouragement. There is something about that youthful spirit, which knows no boundaries and never even considers failure as an option; it will encourage teachers to allow them to dream big. Sure, the whole project may become a monumental failure, and make the ones in charge look like fools—not only to your school, but also to the entire community. But what if the projects (and the students) do not fail? The possible rewards are just too great to be too afraid to take the risks.

CHAPTER III

Don't Give out Textbooks

When I was in college, I became an expert on textbooks. I had to review textbooks as part of my education courses. I compared the same event discussed over three texts, evaluated the teacher editions versus the student editions, and determined how different companies produced different supplemental materials for their texts. I learned the most about textbooks, however, when I bought them in the college bookstore. I always felt like I was being robbed at the beginning of each semester when I went to the bookstore to get my texts for classes. I remember seeing the numbers ring up on the register screen and thinking, *At least they could have the decency to use a gun or knife when they shake me down.* I felt as if there was nothing more I could learn about textbooks; after I became a teacher, something dawned on me. No one reads textbooks (at least, not if they can avoid it).

As my years as a teacher progressed, getting kids to read became more important. My first classes were biology and psychology, and the drive to read seemed less important because kids had fun labs in biology and fun activities in psychology to stimulate their thinking. Later, I started teaching advanced placement biology, where reading is stressed, and I began looking for readings to stimulate their minds and spark their reasoning abilities—yet the text always left me disappointed (even though we were using the most popular college-level biology text in the nation). I took to reading books like John Gribben's *The Scientists*, looking for stories and anecdotes to bring the science alive.

When I moved to my second school placement, I taught history. I really wanted the students to get the fascinating stories about the people we were studying, but again, the text had little to offer. I would often ask other history teachers around the school, and at in-service and training sessions, what their kids were reading. I often got the same answer. "You can't get kids to read!" they would say. They would bemoan the fact that they assigned textbook readings, yet the students never did their homework. If they assigned questions or bold words from the reading to force them to do it, they would only skim the sections until they found enough to answer the questions, but still would not actually read. Basically, the teachers were admitting that their subject was boring. They had no effective strategies to trick the kids into reading about their boring subject, even if it meant holding their grade hostage. Then a brilliant thought dawned on me.

I love to read. I read all the time. No one has to make me; I just do it. I love summer and Christmas breaks from school, because it gives me a chance to read more. I usually get books for my birthday and Christmas. I even put what I like in my Amazon cart online so my friends and family will purchase something on the list. I thought about legally changing my birth date to the end of May, because my birthday in late July only leaves me a couple of weeks to read the books I get before school starts back. However, no matter how much I love to read, I never found myself reading one type of book: a textbook.

I love history, but even history texts bore me. I love science, yet I have never read a biology text. Why should I expect a fourteen-year-old to do something that I cannot bring myself to do, as the teacher? It is the heart of folly. Instead, I decided that I should let the kids read what I, and they, actually like to read: biographical or autobiographical books about history's most interesting people and events. This is what I liked and, I reasoned, so would the students. Books about the risqué, absurd, scandalous, and mysterious are what got me reading, and I figured they would spark the students' interest as well. I began to really think about the books that got me excited about history. When I reflected upon books that drew me into reading and made me want to be a history teacher in the first place, none were textbooks. This little thought was the secret to getting the students in my class to read.

There was this nagging thought that kept creeping into my head, however: *Won't I get into trouble if I don't hand out the textbooks?* There were a couple of instances in my teaching career that made me think that way. Once, a struggling student and his parents came to see me on parent-teacher night. We talked about the student's struggles and what could be done to help. After I was finished, the parents said, "Our kid never has any homework; he never even brings his book home." They huffed, "Do you *give* homework?" They peered at me like a predator looking to pounce on wounded prey, if I gave the wrong answer. I told them that I did not give homework. (I felt like dropping some Alfie Kohn research on them about the uselessness of homework, but restrained myself). I told them the students had to work continuously in my class, from bell to bell, instead. "Our son never comes home and reads from his textbook either," they chided. "I do not really assign readings from the text to do at home either," I said. "We use the book some in class, but not at home," I finished. "Well, wouldn't bringing the book home and reading it *help*, even if it *wasn't* assigned?" the parents asked. "It is not going to hurt anything. There will be a general outline of the topics and time periods we are talking about, which should provide them a broad understanding, emphasizing the context I share in my teaching," I concluded. With that, they smiled and seemed pleased that they had found the solution to all of their son's academic problems: all he had to do was bring the textbook home, read it, and his grade would immediately improve. However, I was not smiling.

I was a bit perturbed that all of the solutions I offered the parents—like their son being more organized, turning in assignments on time, looking over notes, showing up for class, completing all of the items on each test, and interacting in group work—were ignored, while the parents thought that just reading the text would solve all of their son's problems. *Why do people think that?* I began to wonder. Why would they think that forcing textbook readings on a sixteen-year-old boy, from a book that the parents themselves would not even read, would solve all of their problems—and not even address the bigger issues? Why should textbook reading make up for the lack of effort, engagement, review, attendance, and all of the other things he was not doing on a daily basis? Someone had told these parents that reading boring textbooks was the Holy Grail to becoming a successful student. Most likely, they learned it through example from their teachers when they were in school, but there was one more part of that conversation that kept coming back to me.

I began to get mad at myself for saying, "It wouldn't hurt," when they asked me if reading the textbook at home would help their student. There are situations where a struggling student taking a textbook home *may* help. If they love and enjoy the subject *and* are putting forth effort, then reading the text would help. If they hate school, hate reading, hate the subject, and will not even try in the classroom, the chances of them putting in any effort at home are minimal. Expecting this would not be a very effective strategy. I think, however, there is an even more harmful repercussion potentially involved in forcing a student in that situation read a textbook—even if the parents can stand over him and make him (because that is what it would take). Maybe the kid agrees to read the text in the hopes it will make him enjoy the subject, learn more about it, pique his interest in history, and transform his educational world. Imagine his chagrin when he opens the text and starts reading, only to find a white-washed, boring, safe, monotone, book written well below his level—with bright pictures and graphs to distract him from the fact that the words are mind-numbing. There are no interesting stories, no biographies, no mountain man tales, no beheadings, not one atrocity, nothing risqué, and zero subjects that are controversial. Basically, the student would have his previous beliefs confirmed that history is boring and uninteresting, and he would vow never to read any more about it. So, I firmly believe that in many cases, reading a textbook is not only not benign, it is actively malignant. It will destroy students' interest in subjects and doom them to a life of avoiding reading.

Since textbooks are often students' first academic exposure to subjects, it often teaches them that school is boring, the adult world is boring, and these subjects are to be avoided at all costs. Possibly that is why 70 percent of people never read a complete book after high school, and 80 percent do not read one after college. We know kids love to read Facebook updates, tweets, blog posts, letters passed in class, comic books, video game guides, graphic novels, etc. They do love reading, but forcing them to read the worst books convinces them that the grownup world of books is terribly boring and not worth the effort. Maybe that is why so many adults are now reading books designed for children and adolescents. A few years back, I was amazed at how many adults I saw reading Harry Potter books. I am not saying they are bad books, but they are designed for children. However, adults were reading them instead of books designed for mature audiences. I am not here to debate why people read those books; I just find it interesting that you cannot get most adults to read books designed for mature minds at gunpoint, but instead, they will read books designed for children that have nothing to do with the subjects they were forced to learn in school. Possibly those adults are making up for lost time. Coincidence? I think not.

I was afraid that parents, who paid for these textbooks with their tax dollars, would be angry if their kid did not receive one. These texts are not cheap; they can cost up to $100 for each one. If a student has six classes, that's about $600 worth of books that the tax-paying parent has paid for—and believes their kid deserves (and rightfully so). I wondered how many parents were going to come rushing down to the school, when I did not hand out the text the first day, and demand to know why I was wasting their tax-paying efforts by not giving their kid the textbook for which they paid. I decided to give the books out, but not use them; that way I could at least say that the students had them, and could read them if they wanted. I was still bringing in tons of outside interesting readings to use in class, which I knew were more effective. I was soon to find out, however, that even this strategy would have its detractors.

I was out of the classroom for a history teachers' in-service on a Monday. I told the students on Friday to bring their books to class the following Monday, because they would need them to do some class map work (finally: maybe one reason to use the textbook). When I returned the next day and read the substitute's notes, he left me quite an exasperated message that read: "Several of the students did not have their books. What's wrong with these kids?" The blame was partly my fault, as humans are creatures of habit and they were not used to bringing their books with them to class. However, they shared books and had no problem completing the assignment. What was really bothered me was the *insinuation* of the substitute's letter.

First, there was the implication concerning the students. When I read the note, I thought that the substitute was disappointed in the students, as if to say, "Everyone knows that good students bring their books every day to learn." By that same line of reasoning, if they did not bring the book, then I guess that meant they were bad students who *could not learn*. Again, who is perpetuating that myth? Is the class that teaches the most the one that uses the textbook the most? Are great military leaders trained by the books, or on the battlefield? Are the best evangelists those who have read the most books and understand the most theory, or those who can deliver on the platform? Are the greatest coaches those who have read the books on coaching, or those who can coach well in games? Why do people keep missing this point? I am not saying that book knowledge cannot help in all walks of life, but I feel the most important knowledge is gained from *outside* of boring textbooks. The students in my class loved reading, learned so much, and were great students; for some reason, not bringing their text had already cemented in the mind of at least one adult that they were poor students.

The second element of the substitute's note that bothered me was the implication that reflected on myself. When I read the note I also heard, "What kind of teacher does not make the kids bring their books to class every day?" As if to imply that if I did not make them bring their books, I was not teaching them anything. The thought never crossed his mind that we were too busy engaging in *real* learning to bother with the textbooks. My students were too busy researching mountain man stories, writing letters to prison camp commandants, producing veterans' programs, researching their family histories, cooking Native American foods, working on assembly lines, doing manual labor with wheelbarrows, and growing gardens to bother with the book. I guess the substitute never bothered to look around the room and consider all of the evidence of real learning taking place in the classroom. This included the effects of talking on plant growth experiment taking place on the table up front, the cowboy eulogies my students had created that were posted on the walls, and the picture of Gustavus Swift on the door, wearing his crown for winning the title of Greatest Captain of Industry in our classroom tournament. All the substitute could see was the textbook, and when my students did not have theirs, he concluded that the teacher was not teaching.

This fear, that had been confirmed by this one small experience, held me back from not handing out textbooks for a couple more years. Finally, I decided to take the plunge into textbookless waters after one event gave me the courage. I proposed my idea to a class at the end of a semester. We had not used the textbooks at all, and the students noticed. As the semester was drawing to a close and I was taking up the textbooks, one student asked me in front of the class, "How come you even give out the books, if we never used them?" It was a valid question, and one I had been asking myself for a couple of years. I replied with a question: "What would your parents think if they paid taxes to support this school, which includes textbooks, if I did not give them to you?" One student spoke up to offer the logical and clear answer that had evaded me for so long: "What student in their right mind is going to tell their parents they don't have to read the stupid book?"

Wow—that was it. Students hated reading the text, because it was so boring. They were longing for a teacher to allow them to read the interesting stuff about their subjects. They were so excited when a teacher was daring enough to allow these interesting readings that the kids were pining for; the students were not going to sell out that teacher. How had I missed this point? It is similar to when a child visits her grandparents' or aunt's house growing up and they let you eat candy before bed, stay up too late, or watch too much TV. Did the child ever go home and complain to her mom about doing fun stuff? Of course not! She enjoyed the fun stuff when she could, yet understood that it was not going to happen most of the time. This short conversation with an honest student showed me that the students were not going to go home to their parents and complain about someone letting them do something fun and exciting in class. I finally had all of the confirmation I needed to pull off my grand scheme, and it was time for me to go to work.

After surveying all of my favorite books, articles, biographies, journal entries, and segments from history; I realized something. They all had two things in common. Including these two things in my selected readings for my students would make all of the difference. My favorite subjects in history were World War I, World War II, Vietnam, the 1920s' social revolution, and the emergence of rock and roll in the 1950s. Before I did this inventory of these topics, I did not really try to figure out why I loved these topics. For the first time, I critiqued why I loved them, and found something very interesting that I had not considered. All of the subjects I loved always had two things in common: scandal and violence.

World War I killed more people than every war in the history of the world *combined*, up to that time. It was a war of unbelievable destruction. The first fully mechanized war changed the way people would view international conflict. The amount of killing inflicted by machine guns, poison gas, artillery, airplanes, zeppelins, tanks, motorcycles, etc. would destroy the innocence of the world. The devastation of the soul can be felt through the poetry those young men created. A whole generation of poets, known as the Lost Poets, wrote the most brutal, graphic, depressing, and bitter verses ever conceived, but for some reason I love it. I call it poetry for guys who hate poetry. Whenever I tell my classes we are going to read poetry, all the boys roll their eyes in disgust; by the end of the unit they love that poetry, because it is violent. People have loved violence for thousands of years; it will work on the newest generation as well. When I hear English teachers complaining because their students, especially males, hate the poetry section, I always smile and say to myself, "Not mine." Everyone likes poetry. A teacher just has to use the kind that covers the two things from which people cannot separate themselves.

World War II, amazingly, was able to surpass the carnage of WWI. I always have several students who list their favorite history topic as WWII or the Holocaust. It is not because those subjects are fun, they love genocide, or they worship Hitler. They love the subject because it seems to encompass all of the human emotions into one huge stage, on a monumental scale. Everyone loves the emotions and passions that make us human; it just seems that the pressures of war amplify these. Students love the Holocaust and want to study why that happened, so I make it a lesson they will never forget. By the end of it, they all want the Nazis to be punished, "Payback!" they cry. "Payback!" The next day I show them what payback looks like, with a ninety-minute assault on the senses known as the Rape of Berlin. By the time it's done, the kids are begging for it to be over. They won't even look at the pictures anymore; "Enough!" they cry. "But I thought you wanted payback?" I ask. "Well, this is what payback looks like!" I say, as I continue to roll the brutal pictures, present the horrifying quotes, and flash the grisly statistics. My most powerful picture is saved for last. There is a young German mother lying in a bombed-out street littered with debris. Her skirt is torn up to her waist with her thighs laid bare. There is blood covering her inner thighs as she lies in the street. At her head is her young son. He has his fingers stuck in the slash made in his mother's throat by the offending soldier. After no doubt witnessing the violent sexual assault, he is trying to stop the bleeding so his mother may live. His mother is gritting her teeth in pain; he cries as he watches the life seep from his mother. Girls begin to cry while big, tough boys shift in their seats as they become uncomfortable. Violence and sex, much less the amalgamation of the two, should make people uncomfortable; however, it also makes them want to read.

Possibly the one article the students like the most all year is the four-page excerpt from Laura Hillenbrand's Unbroken. If you have not read it, it is the most amazing book I have ever read. Everyone I give it to agrees. The author is a magnificent story teller, and she found the most amazing story to tell. By the time the students get done reading all of the torture that Louis Zamperini is put through at the hands of his sadistic Japanese camp commander, Watanabe, the kids are begging to read more. I usually break it up and read it over two or three days. It is not that I intentionally want to delay the reading, it is just that I like to let it percolate down into their minds, allowing them to absorb little sips at a time instead of trying to swallow the bitterness all at once. One time, I realized that strategy can backfire.

As we worked through the four-page packet, I told the students we were going to stop and move on to another activity, and would pick up with the reading the next day. I talked for a few minutes, then asked a student a question. This girl was not your average student. She was an excellent young lady to have in class. She was quiet, intelligent, and hardworking. So, when I called on her then looked at her face, I was totally caught off guard. "Sorry," was her reply. "I wasn't listening." There was a short pause, as I am sure I (and the rest of the students) had to clear the shocked expressions off of our faces. Then she sheepishly answered, "I just couldn't stop reading the article. I had to finish it." She almost looked ashamed, and put her head down after squeaking out the words in a small voice. I felt like a horrible teacher.

First, I had for years made students read material that was so boring no one wanted to read it after I stopped making them. Now, I had this girl reading something very interesting, and she did not want to stop. The thing that really got me, however, was that she felt like a bad student (or even a bad person) for wanting to keep reading. What was the educational system (including my class) doing to her and millions of others just like her? When was the last time a student said they could not focus on the teacher because they were too busy reading something interesting about the subject? In educational jargon, it is often referred to as "time on task." My student was on task, just not on the task I was on at that time. Who was wrong, the student for caring so much she could not stop learning about it, or me for getting a student totally engrossed in a learning activity and then telling her it was not important and we needed to move on to something else? When was the last time I faced that dilemma when using a textbook? After we are through with the story of Zamperini (now often done in one or two days), the students are literally begging me to show them the letter Zamperini wrote to his torturer, Watanabe, years after the war. When was the last time kids begged to read the text book? Yes, the book is violent, has torture, and people die, but it gets at the human emotions that fascinate us all.

Vietnam was a brutal war with different tactics that, combined with increased media coverage, shocked America. My students love to read about the My Lai Massacre, not because it is fun to read of the killing, torturing, and raping of civilians, but because they cannot understand how it happened, how Americans could do it, and how it was suppressed. I also let them read personal profiles of several American prisoners of war. The students find their survival stories riveting, and their remaining lives inspiring. I tell them how one soldier, who had survived years in a POW camp by thinking about getting back home to his family, was given a letter from his wife when they found him. The students demand to know what was in that letter. Many of them look like they have been punched in the gut and betrayed when they find out his wife divorced him while he was in the POW camp. They call the wife bad names and demand an explanation for how she could do that to her husband; some even accuse me of playing some kind of sick prank on them. They care about those stories because they incorporate the critical two elements.

The 1920s are an amazing decade full of the most unbelievable happenings in American history. The more I learn about the decade, the more astounded I am. Just think about all of the sexual and violent things that went on in the Roaring '20s. A revolution in premarital relationships occurred that changed the way our entire country works. America went from courting, where a male suitor would call on the parents' home of a young lady, offer his calling card, and they would sit together and speak, to dating, where the male suitor would pick up the young lady in his car and whisk her off in the seclusion of his "struggle buggy" to a different location, while paying for everything. This one change rocked America to its foundations. The simple fact that the word dating had been used as the term for an appointment with a prostitute up until this time should tell us a little something about that era. When a person hired a prostitute to spend time with him, the person paid for it with cash; no one expected this relationship to have any long-standing meaning.

Think of all the inventions of the 1920s. First, there was the hair dryer; this just goes to show how important preparing for a date was becoming. Forget the fact that advertisements depicted it as something like a medieval torture machine; girls needed to get ready for a date quickly. Women also were going on multiple dates in one night. The hairdryer would facilitate that, but it does not lend as much insight as the next invention. Kiss-proof lipstick is the next creation of the era that fascinates me. Not only do ladies need to look good for all of their dates, they also need to be able to make out with multiple guys in one night while not fouling their makeup, so none of the guys are the wiser. Penicillin, used to treat gonorrhea, is the final invention that culminates the understanding of the Roaring '20s. If people are not quite sure how the changes in dating and the inventions surrounding it were really impacting the relationships between men and women, one only needs to see the advertisements for the treatment of this one sexually-transmitted disease on city mailboxes, store windows, and billboards. These inventions were provocative in nature, yet they give an important insight to just what kind of sexual revolution was taking place in the 1920s. I find these inventions mesmerizing, and so do the students.

The slang of the 1920s is another one of my favorite things to study. The language that developed is sometimes still in use today, so the students are able to familiarize themselves with a few of them. However, some have gone the way of courtship, and those are the ones that really spark students' thinking about that tumultuous time period. The struggle buggy is one of their favorites. It gives new insight into the importance of the car to dating. The handcuff is another favorite term of the students. That word refers to an engagement ring, and this gives further insight to how people felt about their freedom to be with whomever they wanted without the restrictions of pervious societal norms. This final slang word often receives the most discussion (and the most interesting answers from students) about its origin; the "drug store cowboy" is always a class favorite. After some interesting and sometimes hilarious guesses, I reveal to the students that it is a young man who hangs around in or near drugstores in an effort to pick up ladies. Every year I hear this phrase working its way into the common lexicon of the students, as they begin to refer to boys throughout the school with the word. I eventually decided to give the students a list of slang, have a competition to see who can get the most meanings of those words right, go over the answers with them while discussing the time period, and then challenge them to either write a story about a date or a fight (or sometimes both) using at least twenty of those words. The students really enjoy reading those aloud to the class, and they often end up on the classroom walls. Any type of reading that can get the kids excited about writing and even sharing that writing with others must be used as a tool of an effective teacher. Imagine a student getting excited about reading their textbook aloud to the class.

The violence of the 1920s is also amazing to the students. We cover the emergence of the mob during Prohibition. We even study a few of the famous ones: Bugs Moran, Al Capone, Baby Face Nelson, and Bonnie and Clyde. The kids find the portraits of these people fascinating, and devour the readings about them. The Ku Klux Klan also had a resurgence in that decade. Once, I was not going to present an entire lesson on the KKK, only mention it and move on, as I was a bit behind schedule for the semester. The kids begged to hear the lesson. They even made a deal that they would work as hard and as fast as possible to make time for the lesson. They kept their end of the bargain, so I kept mine; they were fascinated while reading the story of Mary Phagan and her role in the reemergence of the group. Combined with all of the race riots, which needed the use of the military to sometimes put it down, and the unemployment demonstrations that demanded the governor of Massachusetts (then Calvin Coolidge) fire most of the Boston police force and use the National Guard to keep the peace, a very violent cocktail is created that intrigues students about this amazing decade.

The emergence of rock and roll in the 1950s is also a favorite of both mine and the students. The '50s is one of those decades, like the Roaring '20s, when a great deal of social change happened after a major war. It is easy to draw similarities between the two, and the students get just as excited about the one as the other. Again, there are civil rights issues to discuss as well as the baby boom, which is very interesting to students, but the big hit of that unit is always rock and roll. We look at several of the influential artists of the decade by analyzing the lyrics to their popular songs. Kids just never really appreciate how much sensuality and inappropriateness are in the words of those songs that even their grandfather whistles. Some of our favorites are "Whole Lotta Shakin' Goin' On" by Jerry Lee Lewis, with its sexual implications; "Jailhouse Rock" by Elvis Presley, and its homosexual and gang-related overtones; and "Long Tall Sally" by Little Richard, which always opens a lot of students' eyes about the provocative nature of songs that they will never be able to hear the same way again. We don't just listen to those songs, or watch the videos or live performances: we really break those song lyrics down analytically enough to make even the finest music history or theory teacher proud. Once, about halfway through a lesson when I mentioned the next song we were going to analyze, a student cried, "Are you going to ruin that song for me too?"

It seems that scandal and violence is what history is mostly about. Maybe it is that way because that is what mankind is all about: and possibly, yet sadly, has been all about, for the entirety of history. If that is true—and the more I thought about it the more convinced I became—then that is what teenagers would be about, too. It was the magic linchpin that held it all together and would prompt them to read like no sterilized, monotone, boring textbook ever could. It is what is called the "taboo hook" in the excellent book *Teach Like a Pirate*. When students feel they are being treated like they are adult enough to handle mature themes, they respond with renewed enthusiasm for those subjects.

Scandal and violence are what teens love. Luckily for me, history is filled to the brim and running over with it. I have often thought myself lucky to be a history teacher. Once I was at an in-service with other history teachers only. Some were complaining about kids not liking the material, thinking it was boring, and not being interested. I stood up and said, "What are you all crying about? We could be teaching math. Imagine what the math teacher is thinking: 'Those history teachers get to talk about wars, heroes, murder, mayhem, fires, floods, gold strikes, the Wild West, Indian raids, atomic bombs, and rock and roll. All we get to do is balance equations and solve theorems.'" They all just shut their mouths and nodded in agreement. It is great to be a history teacher, and if we present the right material, kids will love it, and even love to read it as well.

After some thought, I came to the conclusion that all subjects are fun, and filled with scandal and violence. My good friend, who also teaches, once told me a story about Albert Einstein always answering the door naked when young female interns came to his house. I was told Einstein said, "Usually they run off screaming, but sometimes, they come in." That is funny and risqué. Who knew math had sexually explicit stories? What about Archimedes, who was nicknamed "the Greek Streak?" He was taking a dip at the public bath and got so excited about his theory that he ran all the way home to test it, stark naked. Now that is some interesting math that kids would love to read. Science, you say? How about Pierre Curry getting so irradiated that he walked out of his office, fainted in the street in front of a passing horse and buggy, and had his head crushed like a grape? I have even used the World War I poem "Dulce et Decorum Est" when teaching about chemistry in my physical science class. I ask them who killed the man in the poem, and they never get the answer right. It was science that killed him, mixing harmless elements together into a lethal chemical concoction that killed and maimed scores of thousands. What about English? Please! They have the Scarlet Letter and Shakespeare, without even getting into the lives of the authors themselves, which are quite provocative. If you look hard enough, you can find interesting stories about every subject that often deal with scandal and violence. It goes back to the old analogy; there is no such thing as a boring subject, only a boring teacher. Bring out the exciting stuff in your subject, find or create a reading about it, throw out that dry old text book, and watch something amazing happen.

Many people get uneasy when I tell them what my readings are mostly about. They say that I am perverting the youth (possibly the reason Plato was killed), I am making them sexual and violent, and I am just going for shock value. I hate to break it to the world, but kids are already reading sexual and violent content every day. Kids love to read Facebook, they have to text the juiciest gossip, and they love reality TV and tabloid journalism. Whether they see it in my class or not, they are going to be reading it. I might as well make it about my subject. Many will still argue that scandal and violence have no place in school. I disagree.

The place for it is in school. Why do we have sex education in school? After all, the students will hear about it on the bus, from their friends, and on the internet. Why do we teach about drugs in health class? Students could learn about those from the local drug dealer, in the bathroom, and on the street corner. Why is there driver's education in school? They could learn to drive themselves, from their friends, or even their drunk uncles. The reason we teach these subjects and many more in schools is because they need to hear the truth in the proper setting, from an adult with both wisdom and knowledge that the students can trust. That is exactly why I should teach these difficult subjects in my class. They can learn about violence from a video game, but who is going to come in with the proper perspective? They can learn about assaults from watching TV cop dramas, but who is going to distinguish reality from Hollywood? They can watch movies about war with their stylized violence, outrageous language, and ridiculous special effects, but who is going to separate the fact from the fiction? I am.

When I talk about these subjects in my class, my students get to ask questions of someone who knows. We get to read the accounts from the other side and see it from different angles. We understand why it happened, and what it caused afterwards. We get to understand that these are real people, and not just images on the screen. We get to have the veteran come in and tell us about what it was like instead of taking some Hollywood director's word for it. When we learn about sex and violence in my class, it is not fun; it is serious. It is not abstract, it is real, and it is not glorified, it is "historified." If there was ever a place for the scandalous and violent events of the past to be discussed, it is in my classroom; if I don't talk about it, I leave it up to their friends, video game makers, screenwriters, bigots, racists, and closed minds.

I was in my college classroom on September 11, 2001. The class was buzzing with chatter when the professor entered the room. We talked about it for a few minutes at the beginning of class, then decided to proceed with class. A few minutes into the class, an announcement came that the school would be releasing. The rest of the day seemed like a blur. With so many tiny pieces of information swirling from so many sources, it was nearly impossible for my mind to process it all. There was one piece of information that seemed very wrong to me when I learned it, however.

A friend told me that many of the local elementary schools had stayed in session, but did announce that parents were welcome to pick up their children if they desired. Most parents did not come early to get their kids, obviously because they were working, but that that is not what bothered me. I heard that nearly all of the class rooms were watching the news of the event live, when announcements came for teachers to turn the TVs off and not discuss the events. I later learned the decision was made by school directors to do this, because they were worried about scaring the children. I was outraged! I just remember thinking about how the day of most of those young students progressed. They heard of the terrible events at school, saw a small portion of it on TV, and were ordered not to watch it the rest of the day (obviously, it never left their minds). Then after school they went home to an empty house, as their parents (or in most cases *a* parent) would not arrive for a couple of hours—then curiously watched TV coverage of the events alone. The children will learn of the events in today's modern world somehow, whether the teacher allows them to watch TV or not. Cell phones, Facebook, radio, internet, and myriad other technologies assure that.

Schools have an obligation to teach. Often schools think they can control the smallest details of the curriculum. I believe the best schools and teachers realize they should not try to control the entire curriculum, instead focusing on the teachable moments. Some of my most memorable lessons have come after a student at our school has died in a car crash. The discussion my classes have about decisions, life, death, etc. will never leave my mind. Once when the housing/ financial crash in 2007 was beginning, I was standing in front of the class to begin my lesson when I got a very honest question. A young lady asked me what was going on with the economy, and if people struggling to pay their mortgages would get to keep their homes. In hindsight, I think what she was really asking was if her family would soon be homeless. You could tell she needed an answer from someone, but either had not found the right person to ask, or had not found the right answer from anyone she had asked so far. A question not answered well never goes away. I was teaching biology at the time; what business of mine were financial questions? I soon realized that it did not really matter what I said the rest of the class. If this young lady's mind was not set at ease, she was not going to hear anything else I said anyway.

She needed to hear an answer from someone who understood the economy, loans, mortgages, and housing. I am not an expert on those topics by any means, but I know enough to help teenagers of families struggling to pay their mortgages understand that they will not be on the streets when they go home that afternoon just because Bernie Madoff, Freddy Mac, and Fanny Mae made some very poor choices. School is where the important questions students have should be answered, by adults who have more wisdom than themselves. It should not be a place where young people have such troubling questions that their minds cannot focus on the lessons that the curriculum has deemed important. Yet often no one will help them comprehend what is happening that is important to them. This is what upset me about the entire prohibition in some schools of TV news on 9/11. These young people needed answers to very complex questions, and had many experts in place to help them, yet a very valuable learning opportunity was wasted.

Schools have an obligation to the students to discuss the difficult subjects that arise throughout life. Schools and teachers cannot just ignore something as earth-shattering as the September 11th attacks, carrying on as if they did not happen. Instead, teachers and schools should grasp the moment—no matter how difficult—to help students understand the world in a rational way, instead of leaving these difficult topics to the minds of children. If teachers refuse to address these questions, they will still be asked by the children through texts, Facebook, on the bus, at the lunch table, on the playground, and on internet message boards. I remember one person telling me that a student in their class was very upset because another student had told them during class change that their school was in danger of a terrorist attack, because it was close to Oak Ridge, Tennessee (by close, I mean about 100 miles away). Someone had told them that Oak Ridge's importance to the nuclear weapons program in our country (where the nuclear fissionable material for the first atomic bombs was produced) would make it the next likely target, and when all that nuclear material exploded it would kill everyone with hundreds of miles. The student was understandably scared and upset. The teacher told the child that was silly, then just proceeded with the day's lesson as if nothing else in the world was happening.

That teacher missed a wonderful opportunity to handle difficult subjects in the proper manner. If I think about my school now, we have so many experts who could have shed the proper light on that tragedy as it was happening. We have an aeronautics class, with a teacher who was a professional pilot for decades. We have historians who could put the whole Oak Ridge scenario into the proper context and alleviate student fears. Our school has numerous veterans who could discuss the Middle East, groups wanting to hurt America, etc. There are health professionals who can describe how to stay safer in emergencies like these. Our school right now has a retired Marine who was a chemical and biological weapons expert. Why would a school not use these experts to help children get the answers they need from the proper channels, instead of allowing rumor and hearsay to run wild? More important are the adults who are there to listen, comfort, hug, and cry with the students instead of ignoring them and sending these latchkey children to cold, dark homes where mom or dad may not be home for hours, to watch these scary events by themselves and let their own little imaginations roam free.

What this one example, which may seem like it has nothing to do with not reading textbooks, shows is that teachers cannot just ignore certain subjects because they are difficult, uncomfortable, or sordid. For the same reasons, teachers cannot just say that we are not going to discuss certain subjects because they are violent, sexual, or drug related. We cannot just stick our heads in the sand of the textbook and only address the whitewashed, bland, and boring material that the high priests of education have deemed safe for the masses. These difficult (and wildly interesting) topics must be addressed by the teacher. Do not think for a moment that if they are ignored by the teacher, they won't be explored by the students on their own. When they do go delving into these topics, who will they ask? And what kind of insipid, juvenile, and ignorant answers are they likely to find on the back of the bus, in popular culture magazines, in Facebook replies, on internet gossip sights, or on bathroom walls? As teachers, we must finally own up to our responsibilities to teach important life lessons, whether they are in our sanitized state or national curriculum or not.

We don't live in the 1950s anymore. When kids go home from school, they do not have Aunt Bea waiting for them with milk and cookies to talk about their day. Most of them do not interact with their fathers to get that *Leave it to Beaver* advice they did not get at school. Many children today do not even have meaningful conversations with their mothers, either; their moms may work two jobs and come home late, or be exhausted, addicted to drugs, busy with their newest boyfriend, or a million other reasons. I recently saw a survey reporting that parents spend an average of two hours per day interacting with their children. When they actually put cameras in the homes to record how much time was actually spent, the results were shockingly disparate; only ten minutes per day. It is more important than ever for teachers to not shy away from the meaningful questions asked about real topics that kids will not discuss with anyone else outside of school.

If teachers do not delve into subjects that sanitized texts gloss over—and many parents today are not involved enough to tackle these difficult topics—it leaves the students only interacting with other people in their own age group. Now, there is absolutely nothing wrong with children associating, talking, and discussing things with their companions; but there is something wrong if those are the only people they are talking with, especially when the issues are the difficult ones in life that could really be more thoroughly dealt with by the wisdom of a more experienced, wiser elder. Children spend most of their time talking to people who are just as smart, or dumb, as they are. When they only discuss things with their friends, they do not receive the wisdom of the group: the accumulated opinion of the herd, the experiences of the grandparents, the discipline of the parents, the guidance of uncles, the knowledge of the ones who have been there, studied, and suffered the consequences of poor decisions about the very subjects of which they ask. Our students today do not sit, as I often did, around the supper table discussing and even listening to grown up topics. They do not sit with their parents on the couch, watching the evening news as I did after supper every single night. The kids have their own TVs and smartphones, and they get to control their media by playing on their computer or game systems, texting on their phones, and watching TV designed for their own age group. If teachers do not let them read the truth about subjects in school, where we can select the proper readings that allow them to achieve wisdom from others, then from where will this wisdom come?

When I used the Wilfred Owen poem "Dulce et Decorum Est" to teach chemistry in my freshman physical science class, I wondered if anyone but me was enjoying the poem. I thought it was so different from many other boring chemistry lessons that many teach every day, but you never know if the kids are going to enjoy it. I figured a few of the boys would like it, because they always get into the war poetry a bit more than the females. The next day a female student came up to me as she entered the room. She put this book right in my face and said, "Look what I got! I made my mom drive me over to the bookstore last night after supper." It was a book with all of the collected poems of Wilfred Owen. I was amazed. Not only did she enjoy the poem, she wanted to read all of his other poems as well. She did not want to wait; she had to read them that day. That is what not reading from the text has the power to do.

I must give a word of caution, because if you stop giving out textbooks and let kids read interesting things relating to your subject, there will be those who get upset. Other teachers may be threatened by your teaching. Your readings may cross lines into other subjects, and for some reason many so-called experts in your school will start to ask questions like, "What does that have to do with *your* subject?" This is obviously ridiculous, but when you read things about your subject from the real world, these topics will naturally cross over into other realms of study. That is how you know they are from the real world. About the only way to make a subject not interact and bleed over into other areas of study is to use the sanitized version of a subject found in a textbook.

I assure you, other adults in your school will get nervous when you start reaching into other subjects and making them interesting too. The teachers of those subjects will often feel threatened when they realize kids are liking what you are allowing them to learn about a subject that is supposed to be someone else's dominion. If you are willing to trust the students enough to allow them to learn the interesting aspects of a subject, when the teacher supposed to be in charge of dispensing knowledge about that subject will not let them, then those teachers will feel threatened. When that happens, the students will let those other teachers hear *all* about it. Some kids will go and demand to know why that teacher never allowed them to learn all the cool stuff. Then that teacher will feel embarrassed, and come down on you for outing them. You will have exposed them for what they are; people who destroy the love of learning their subject in the next generation, by hiding the most interesting points of the very thing they are supposed to be teaching students to enjoy. Instead of being praised for teaching across the curriculum, or being a teacher of life and not just one pigeon-holed subject, you will be ridiculed for "doing someone else's job" or "sticking your nose" where you are not the "real expert" on the subject.

Other teachers will see you reading things that at first do not appear to go along with the curriculum, and think you are just wasting time. Maybe we are studying rock and roll lyrics form the '50s and listening to the music, watching the videos, and even having a live performance of a few of those songs by a real musician. Neighboring teachers will hear the commotion, walk by, look in, and say to themselves that you are only using tricks and ploys, and not doing real teaching (by which they mean boring lectures and worksheets). You will know who they are, because after your class is over they will just *happen* to come by your room and nonchalantly ask what you were talking about that day. When you tell them, they will look down their noses at you as if to indicate you are not a real teacher of authentic curriculum deemed appropriate by the state. What will really give those people away is because they always give the same loaded answer when you are finished telling them what you were doing that day: "Oh."

People will say that letting kids read about scandal and violence is just a way to catch their attention with the gross-out factor, not real learning. "It is like giving in to the out-of-control media that only focuses on the shock value of sex and violence," they will say. That is not true. Yes, it does grab their attention; however, the ultimate goal is not just to entertain like the media, it is to inform, enlighten, and educate. Again, when adults with more wisdom and perspective use this tactic, it is not the goal to just to create a chance to discuss risqué topics. The purpose is to use it as an attention-getter, to encourage talk about the real issues that are underneath the surface. Sure, other teachers will look down their pedagogical noses at you for not being a "real" teacher who uses "appropriate" teaching methods; but in the end, their methods will not get the kids to read or think. So what good are their methods anyway, and whose techniques are really superior? The answer is obvious.

I am challenging teachers to not only get away from the boring textbook method that has damaged generations of potential learners by boring them into a life of non-reading, but to also use interesting written sources outside of those textbooks. Yes, some of those interesting sources may contain material that is difficult, risqué, sexual, or violent; but if it is not addressed by the teacher in an appropriate classroom setting, the topic will still be addressed by the students in ways that often lead to misinformation, wrong thinking, and actions—with dangerous consequences. Sure, other teachers in your school may feel threatened when your students begin to enjoy your subject, and maybe even aspects of subjects they teach. True, boring teachers will not like you when you expose them by showing the students that your subject can be fun, and the kids begin to ask why their class or subject is not. However, it is time for teachers to realize this is not just a good idea, but *imperative*: we need to search out things that are interesting to read, yet answer the great questions about our subject that people have asked for centuries. In other words, it is time to stop giving out the textbooks and start allowing young people to learn to love to read again.

CHAPTER IV

LET YOUR STUDENTS DO WORK THAT IS WELL BELOW THEIR GRADE LEVEL

A s I stood there leaning against a wall in a first grade classroom, I had to secretively brush a tiny tear from my eye. I was witnessing one of my proudest moments in teaching. I was watching a young lady, whom just about everyone in our school had given up on, summon the amazing courage to deliver a very moving rendition of *Mary the Missunderstood*. Just to see that young lady in front of the class reading that children's book was amazing. She was not the only student reading that day, but knowing where she came from and what kind of courage it took for her to do it changed the way I thought about education forever.

It all started a couple of weeks before, while driving to school. Sometimes I just cut the radio off and drive in silence during my fifteen-minute commute to work, letting my thoughts wander. I am amazed sometimes by how productive those fifteen minutes can be. That morning, I was pondering a couple of things happening in my educational life that led me to a breakthrough as a teacher. I had a student who told me at the beginning of the semester that she did not like history. But as the course progressed, she really started to get into the class. I asked her one day if she was actually starting to like history, and she responded, "I guess so." When I asked her why she was previously convinced that she did not like history, she told me it had always been all about the dates in classes she'd been in before; but in my class, she learned it was all about the story. I could not hide a prideful smile, as that is what I strive to teach in my class. Indeed, everyone loves a good story. Luckily for me, history is full of them.

I was also thinking about how kids get turned off by the formalized educational system before they even get to my class in high school. Kids excitedly go to kindergarten, loving their teachers and ready to learn. It stays that way for a few years. Before long, they see school as drudgery and cannot wait for summer breaks. I often wondered exactly how our educational model was able to kill something as powerful and intrinsic as the desire to learn, experiment, and have fun. Kids all over the world loved stories about people, both past and present, and real or imagined. Somewhere between kindergarten and high school their love of learning about history, which is just stories about real people doing amazing things, was being extinguished. As I silently drove down the road, I thought about stories, the love of learning, and my student who had just rediscovered her passion for something previous years of school had destroyed. That is when it hit me.

Instead of letting kids learn to hate history and then having to try and undo all of that built-in disgust years later in high school, I needed to do something about it in elementary school to stop it from happening in the first place. What I needed was an academic preemptive strike. It all came to me in a flash. *How about children's stories?* I thought. My two sons, ages four and six at the time, loved stories. They begged me to read to them every night before bed; when one book drew to a close, they tried to persuade me to read another, and another, and another. I eventually had to put a limit on the number of books we could read before bed. My boys loved books. What were children's books, anyway, but stories about interesting things that happen to people (or sometimes animals)? I had my great idea. I would have my high school students write their own children's books about some stories from history and illustrate them. Then we would take them to a local elementary school and read them to young children. After the story, we would tell them our books were based on real history, and history was fun because it had such neat stories.

Instead of waiting for those tired, boring teachers who were mailing it in every day, getting ready for their retirement ten years from now, to destroy the children's love of history (not to mention their love of learning) with their drill and kill worksheets and their bold words, we would intervene to save their love of history before it was too late. I think we all know some teachers who have really retired years before the paperwork was actually signed. I completely understand the burnout that comes with being a teacher, but educators must fight that slide into lethargy and complacency. Many did not have the will to fight the ever-changing standards, increased paperwork, and constant bombardment of morphing curricula. They let it get to them and break their spirits, and it is ultimately the students who suffer. It is easier to train up a child than repair a broken man. It was time for my class to do a little intervention, on the first-grade level. Maybe it was even more than an intervention; possibly we would get to them before they ran into *that* teacher, the one who was almost certain to destroy their little historical minds. One day, if they ever did meet that teacher who tried to bore them with dates, bold words, and maps, convincing them that's all history is about, somewhere in the deep recesses of their minds they would cry out "No! There is more to history than that! What about the great stories they read to me as a small child?" It was time for us to grab opportunity by the throat, when kids were not yet jaded by the system, to nourish that love of the story that all children (and I believe all people) have buried deep inside of their souls.

I started the discussion that morning by asking my students to go around the room and tell everyone which story they liked best from the course that year. There were many answers, and several repeats. I then let them in on my plan, and immediately they were excited. Next, I told them to think about their favorite stories and decide which ones they felt could be easily adapted into a children's novel. Immediately a hand shot up. I was more than a little surprised when I spun around and saw whose arm was attached to that hand.

Sitting there with upstretched arm was Brittney, a girl whom many teachers would consider a disciplinary problem; some would go so far as to say she was "low functioning." I did not know the history of the girl, and how she had been caught doing everything from fighting to cursing to threatening. I just laid down the law on the first day, and held everyone to my high educational and disciplinary standards (it works for the Marines, after all). She had always responded well in my class. She was always on time, shared with the class, did most of her work on time, and performed decently with her grades. I had even grown to like the girl, and to be honest, by this late time in the semester, she was probably my favorite student in that class. I try not to play favorites and I never tell the students if I like them, but there was something about this girl, who had obviously lived a very rough life, responding and growing academically on par with any other student in the class. Maybe I liked her because she encouraged me, and reminded me why I became a teacher. Possibly it was that she was an example of how teachers (including myself) cannot let our expectations (or lack of them) force us into thinking that some students just cannot learn. If it was not too late for this student to care about history, then it was not too late for any other.

I taught Brittney's older sister a few years before. She was a very nice young lady, but she also struggled in school. Since her graduation, I often saw her working at a local restaurant. She always spoke to me, and she was so kind. One day when I ran into her at the restaurant, she said, "Hey, Mr. Campbell! You've got my sister in your class. I don't understand it. She loves your class, and Brittany doesn't love *any* class." I am not sure why she enjoyed my class over the others. Maybe it's because I tried to do more hands-on activities and less textbook reading, which may have caused her more frustration academically. However, even when we conducted deep readings of primary source documents (like an excerpt of *Mein Kampf* during our World War II section) she was the first one to really break down that text and decipher its meaning. I recall vividly when she was reading the part about how Hitler felt the Jews were in too many prominent positions and controlled money and banking, she sat straight up in the totally silent classroom and said out loud, "So that's why Hitler hated the Jews. They had the power, and he wanted it." That was brilliant analysis, and simply stated so that everyone could understand it. I figured if there was one thing that girl from a troubled life understood, it was power: who was abusing it, and who wanted to take it. Soon, she even began to do well on more academic tasks. I guess sometimes all you can say is a teacher's personality and style just mesh with certain students. Not every teacher will really be able to reach every student every day, but it has always been my objective to really affect at least one student's life per year in a really meaningful way. I figure if each teacher could do that, in our school that would be forty lives changed each year, and 160 over a four-year high school career. That means 160 kids have been saved from prison, a life of crime, or drug addiction. All I can surmise is Brittney was just my student for the year. I am not saying that she was destined to become a CEO, political leader, or Rhodes scholar, but possibly she would learn she was not as dumb as the standardized tests had told her, was not as much of an outcast as many of the students treated her, and not as hopeless as the world had convinced her she was.

When she started to really respond in my class, somewhat to my surprise, I began to ask other teachers how she had done or was doing in their classes. One of my friends said she had really struggled to even stay awake in his class, which she sometimes did in mine as well; I learned it was because she worked so late every night. He also told me something that was much more revealing about the life she led away from school. As my teacher friend was working bus duty one morning, Brittney's mother pulled into the drop-off lane and let her out. When the door opened, Brittney's mother was spewing a swear-filled dialogue at the top of her lungs. Brittney turned around and hurled her own raw diatribe back at her mother, then slammed the door so hard it shook the car from side to side. Her mother then squealed the tires as she screamed out of the parking lot. This young lady had her struggles, and I am sure that on too many days, the importance of something like balancing an equation, diagramming a sentence, or the causes of World War I was the furthest thing from her mind. For some reason she was responding in my class, and I could not squander the opportunity.

When I asked her what story she wanted to do, she actually picked a local history story. There is a town about twenty minutes from ours that is rather notorious because an elephant named Mary was hanged there. The huge elephant was part of a circus, and an inexperienced trainer poked her in the wrong place (prodding a severely infected tooth, it is said) with his sharp stick—Mary killed him (stories vary on the specifics). The next town on the circus's schedule told them they could not bring the dangerous animal into their town, so the circus owner decided to kill it (as they say, "the show must go on"). They considered several options, like shooting and electrocution, settling on hanging as the best course of action. As the town was a railroad town, they had a large crane and thick chain. They decided to do it in the railroad yard, where many onlookers gathered to watch the spectacle. Mary was eventually hanged, but not before the chain broke, slamming Mary down and breaking her hip during the first try. This is the story that the girl wanted to weave into a beloved children's bedtime story.

I did not discourage her, even though I knew the story would need to be handled with some maturity to make it suitable for the children. I said, "Great choice! You will be the project manager for that book." Not giving her time to protest, I quickly looked over the rest of the class, asking who would like to join her on that project. As my eyes scanned the room, not a single hand went up. "Anyone?" I asked, trying to hide the desperation in my voice. I was a little worried that no one would want to work with her, thinking the others would say her idea was a bad one for little kids, or think she was just too dumb to be over a project with her limited English skills and atrocious grammar. I made my way back across the room, desperately scanning for at least one hand; yet it was no use. At that exact moment, I heard Brittney say, "I don't care to do it by myself." I was a little shocked by the air of confidence in her voice. Maybe I shouldn't have been. Her life had been a struggle since the beginning; she was used to trying to overcome obstacles, and she was also used to being a social outcast. I did not know whether to be proud of her for taking the leadership role in a daunting academic task, or to feel sorry for her that no one else deemed either her or her idea interesting. Either way, the educational die had been cast.

Undeterred, she began writing the story. By the time everyone in class had settled on a project, another student agreed that he liked Brittney's elephant story best, and the next day a student who was absent joined in as well. I felt much better that she would not be alone, but she still found herself in a leadership role of writing a book. I figured it had been a long while since the students had read a children's book, so I brought in some of my sons' favorite children's novels the next day. The students passed them around, seeing how many words were on each page, what is a good length for a book, how many illustrations they needed, etc. After a couple of days, the books were really taking shape. As I examined what Brittney's group was doing, I was stunned.

As Brittney and her group stood to present their story to the class, they revealed how they had crafted a story about Murderous Mary; they had put a very unique twist on the tale. Her group decided to call their book *Mary the Missunderstood* (yes, that misspelling of misunderstood was actually in the title). Even though the mistake could easily be made out from my chair in the back of the room, I decided against interrupting and pointing out the problem with the title immediately. I thought about how hard they had worked, how a girl who didn't care about most classes or even school in general, was in the lower quartiles on all of her tests, and had a rough home life, had taken the leadership role. I did not want to discourage her by pointing out flaws in front of the entire class the very first thing. An old saying I'd heard from a teacher friend of mine began to roll through my head: "Praise publicly, correct privately." I held my tongue and decided to be quiet, settle in, and hear how their story unfolded. I am glad I did.

They had crafted a story about how the elephant was often treated badly because she was so big. In fact, her circus managers and owner billed her as a monster to attract people, but she was really a very kind animal, inside her massive body. Once she had come up to a young boy to make a friend, but he was frightened; he had thrown his food at her and run off in terror. Mary went off by herself and cried. Later that night during her performance, a mighty wind came through and snapped one of the tent poles. Poles, tent, rope, and all began to collapse onto the panicked crowd, who were running for their lives. There was the boy from earlier; he was directly in the path of a huge, falling tent pole that would surely crush him. Just as it was about to thunder down upon him, it stopped. Mary had thrust herself under the pole, catching it on her massive back, and pushed against it to buy the boy time to make his escape. Just as he did, Mary collapsed under the strain, and the entire circus tent crashed down. After the ordeal was over and all was safe, the people began to rummage through the wreckage. The boy began to frantically dig, and eventually uncovered Mary lying under the tent pole, unconscious. The boy started crying, and told the elephant how sorry he was that he had judged her by her outward appearance. The boy managed to croak out these words between his sobs: "I didn't mean it. You are my hero." A tear slid down his cheek and dropped onto the elephant's massive shoulder. Mary awoke, and despite a few scrapes and bruises, she was okay. The boy leaped for joy and came back every night to see his hero perform until the circus left town. Each time he came, he brought Mary a bouquet of flowers, a big bag of peanuts, and a hug. I sat in the back of the room speechless, fighting back tears.

You have to understand what Brittney had just been through. She had only been back in my class for a few days, following a suspension for fighting. It seems someone was calling her names and making fun of her lower socioeconomic status. The one thing I learned about her is she did fight, but as far as I could ascertain, she was never the aggressor. She would fight back like a wild cat, but she never started the trouble. When she returned to class, I did not even mention the fight. Instead, I just welcomed her back and we returned to work. Knowing what had happened to her over the last two weeks, the story she chose to write stunned me. Here was a story about an animal many people considered rough and dangerous, inspiring fear in some small, weak people. She was teased and taunted, but instead of responding with violence, Mary slunk over to a quiet corner and cried by herself. Later, when the person who had been so cruel to her (albeit out of fear) needed her help, she did not hesitate to risk her own life saving her former bully. This plot line gave me a very real insight into the soul of a troubled and tortured young person. Something screamed out to me as the story was read; although she appeared tough to many, and had been picked on, inside it hurt her—yet she wanted to forgive. Had she learned to forgive like the elephant in the story? No, but something inside of me felt that deep down she wanted to, and there was hope that one day she might learn. If she had been born to different parents under different circumstances, maybe she would be able to forgive more readily. For now, she just had not found the power to do so.

My surprise continued as the two other groups revealed the stories they had written. Besides *Mary the Missunderstood*, there was also *Billy the Buffalo*. Billy was a buffalo, growing up on the plains. Later he found out that all of his friends were gone, never to return. He searched and searched; however, Billy was only able to find one other buffalo friend with whom he could share the rest of his life. The story was essentially about the destruction of the buffalo on the Great Plains during the Indian Wars of the later 1800s. The final story was another local history topic, *Paul and the Two Little Pencils*. It was about a man considered by many to be the strongest to ever live. His name was Paul Anderson, and he lived in our small town for a time in the 1950s. He was very poor, small, and sickly growing up. A bully once broke the only thing his parents could afford to buy him for school that year: two little pencils. He swore to himself he would never be taken advantage of again. He began to exercise and play every sport he could, never mind his heart condition. He went on to win a gold medal at the Olympics in weightlifting, and eventually established a home for troubled boys that he funded through Christian evangelism.

I contacted one of our local elementary schools, and the librarian suggested the first graders would be ideal for our story presentations. I announced to the students the next day that we would be attending four first-grade classes. As I read the names of the teachers of each class, I heard Brittney say, "Oh no! I can't read to her class. That woman hates me!" "What are you talking about?" I asked. "First grade teachers do not become first grade teachers because they enjoy hating little kids," I countered. "Well, she did," was Brittney's reply. "How do you know she hated you?" I asked. "What did she do to you that was so bad?" I prodded. "Well, I can't really say, but I could just tell," was her only reply. "It's been ten years. She probably doesn't even remember you," I offered. Brittney did not say any more, but she was obviously only half-buying my story.

For all I knew this woman could have been the Wicked Witch of the West, but I had to take up for the teacher, and try to calm Brittney's fears. I wanted her to present her story, and I could not chance her becoming frightened or intimidated into giving up before we even got to the elementary school. Brittney never said another word, but I had a feeling those thoughts were still ingrained in her mind. I had no way of knowing, however, just what kind of learning experience this whole episode would be when the day to read the books finally came.

As I often find, when you try to do something with your students that is unconventional, there's a ton of red tape to work through. I had a time securing a bus to transport our students, because everyone kept wanting to know where we would get the money to pay for the gas for the arduous two-mile trip. One administrator at my school even proposed the idea that I charge the students a couple of dollars each to offset the cost. "No way!" I replied. I was not going to charge my students to read to children; that was absurd. If it came to that, I would pay for the trip myself, out of my own pocket. Finally, a reasonable person heard what my students were using the bus for and said she would find a way to pay for the small trip out of educational funds. "Surely if we have money to go to every sporting event in the world, we can let some kids go read stories that they created themselves to elementary students," she said. I could not have agreed more.

Finally everything was approved, and I even received the principal's approval to miss a few minutes of the next period's class, since we would most likely run over our ninety-minute time slot. As we filed out of the room and into our bus that morning, I was a little surprised to discover my students had planned some special activities to ramp up the involvement of the first graders to whom they would read. The group presenting *Paul and the Two Little Pencils* decided to bring two unsharpened pencils to give to each student. After reading their story and dispensing the pencils, they would encourage the students to give those pencils to someone who was having a bad day or was being bullied, since their story was about a young boy who was bullied. The *Billy the Buffalo* group brought along a stuffed buffalo so the kids could hold him and pass him around during the story, since some of them may not know what a buffalo looks like. We were loaded onto the bus and ready, and the kids were more excited than I had ever seen them. They had worked hard, and seemed to really enjoy the chance to do something different from normal schoolwork. The students learned that helping someone else enjoy learning is a difficult, but enjoyable task.

When we arrived at the school, we were met by the school librarian who coordinated our efforts with the first grade teachers, and she offered to show us to our first room. As we walked through the hall, I looked at my young authors; they were more than a little nervous. Most had never presented anything like this before. It was really outside of their comfort zone, to stand up and teach a lesson to such small students. I knew they were going to do well, though, because they had prepared so well and worked so hard on their stories. As we arrived at our first room, I was startled by which teacher answered the door. It was none other than the teacher who Brittney believed hated her.

When we walked into the room, the teacher was so pleasant. She greeted me cheerfully, and allowed me to introduce our group. She began to talk to my students, and quickly saw several that had been her students over a decade ago. She remembered their names, hugged them, and patted their backs. As she moved to the final student, Brittney, she froze. "Oh, Brittney" she said, "I remember you." With a big smile on her face, she gave Brittney a huge hug. Over the teacher's shoulder I could see Brittney's surprised, yet relieved, face. In an instant, all of that worry and trepidation melted from the young girl's face. As a teacher, I have seen many instances where students think I do not like them or harbor some type of grudge against them. I am not sure how or why certain students come to this conclusion, but it is most often completely erroneous. I do not think I have ever hated a student. Some of them drive me crazy, frustrate me, disappoint me, and make me fear for their future; however, I do not believe I have ever hated a student. Matter of fact, I am almost sure that if anyone ever decides to go into a profession designed to help kids, that person cannot make themselves hate those same young people. I knew that, and most adults knew that; but now, a teenage girl knew it as well. The misconstrued feeling she had carried with her for over a decade was now revealed to be false. However, I would not fully understand the ramifications of that moment until much later in the day.

All of the groups did a masterful job reading their stories to the kids. The students read slowly, allowing the kids to take in the pictures on each page. The first graders were glued to those stories. The final story in the first classroom was *Paul and the Two Little Pencils*. After it was over, the student reading told the students it was a real story about a boy who lived in their hometown, many years ago. He also told them how the tiny and sickly Paul grew up to be a very strong man, winning an Olympic gold medal, and then went on to found a boys' home to help needy children. I was so proud of my students, and snapped a few pictures with my cell phone as they read. I did not get a picture of Brittney, however, as she chose not to read to that first class.

As we waved goodbye to that first group, we made our way through the hall toward our next destination. As we walked, I asked who would be reading in the next room. I wanted all of the students to take turns, so they all got a chance to read. I looked over at Brittney and asked if she would like to read the story of *Mary the Missunderstood* next. "Oh no!" she replied. "I can't do that. I get too nervous to speak in front of people," she insisted. I even saw her neck area begin to get red and splotchy, just thinking of the idea. "You know, you really should think about reading it," I insisted. "After all, the story was your idea." She looked down silently in thought as we walked, but I decided not to push the idea any further.

The students continued to do well and wowed audiences in the next three rooms. The kids loved the stories, my students loved reading them, and I loved seeing them encourage the next generation of students to not loathe history, but love it for the stories that the subject contained. We were on our way to the last class, and as we walked I gently reminded Brittney that this was her last chance if she wanted to read. "I just can't, Mr. Campbell," she pleaded. Then she kind of hung her head in silence as we walked the rest of the way to the room. As fate would have it, the other groups read first, and for the grand finale *Mary the Missunderstood* would be read. I was kind of doing the emcee work between each book, and as I introduced that last story, I tried to hide the disappointment I felt knowing that this great story about forgiveness would be read for its final time without the girl who had been the impetus behind it. I finished my introduction, but when I turned around, I was in for a very big surprise.

Standing behind me, with her book held in front of her like a protective shield, was Brittney. She looked sheepish, but there she was, ready to deliver her story her way to the final group of children. I turned to the students and said, "We have a very special treat for you. This is Brittney, and it was her idea to write this story about Mary." I then stepped aside as Brittney settled into the chair in front of the students. She did an amazing job, reading with passion, although she rarely looked up from the book in her nervousness. I noticed the same red splotches creeping up her neck, but she surprised herself as she read. By the end of the story, she seemed like an old pro. We said our goodbyes and exited the class. I told all of the students how proud I was of them and of their amazing job on this project as we walked toward the bus for our return to our own school. I did not really single Brittney out in front of the students, but I was mentally preparing to let her know later how proud I was of her. About the time we were loading the bus, one of my students remembered that we had a bunch of extra pencils left from our *Paul* story. He asked if he could run them back to the first class we spoke to, and leave them for the kids there. Little did I know, that one simple act would change the entire day from a great one to one of the most influential days of my teaching career.

We were sitting on the bus waiting on the student to return from his pencil errand, so we just started talking about the day. The kids were so excited, and their thoughts ranged from, "I was so nervous," to "those kids were so cute," to "that was so much fun." After a few minutes of talking, I began to wonder if the student who took the extra pencils inside was ever going to get back to the bus. It seemed like he was gone way too long, just to walk to that first class and back. After a few more minutes, I saw him come out of the front door of the school with a smile on his face and a spring in his step. He bounded to the bus, leapt onto the top step, peeked over the top of the first seat, and announced, "You all have to come with me. You're not going to believe this." For a moment we hesitated, but we could see the seriousness in his face, so we followed him back into the school. After I saw what was going on inside, I was glad I did.

We walked into that first classroom and there was a buzz of activity amongst the children. Some were working hectically on some type of craft project; another six or seven were crowded around a couple of computers pointing, and walking to meet us was a smiling teacher. "Let me show you something," she said, motioning for me to follow. "After you left, my kids were really excited about the story about *Paul and the Two Pencils*," she said. The students demanded to look him up on the computer when they learned that he once lived in their home town. As we arrived at the computer station, we saw that the students had pulled up pictures showing him winning the Olympics, lifting cars, setting world records, and standing in the classic strongman pose while letting women hang from his biceps. The kids were so excited they did not even notice us; they only kept looking for more pictures on the internet.

We followed the teacher to a couple of tables, where some students were surrounded by glue, leather, string, and scissors. When we arrived, she explained how one student *loved* the two pencils she received as part of the story to remind her about bullying. She refused to put them away after the story. She just kept holding them in her hand and could not do her other work. The teacher implored her to put them in her pencil box with her other school supplies, but she would not turn them loose. "But I don't want to put them down," the girl replied "I'm taking them home, and I'm going to tell my whole family that story and show them my pencils." The teacher showed great wisdom, asking the girl if she would like to make a pencil holder to place around her neck so she could hang them close to her heart. They would still be within sight, but she would have her hands free to do the rest of her school work. The little girl's eyes glistened and before the teacher knew it, a dozen children surrounded the table and began to make their own pencil pockets.

I must admit my head was spinning while I tried to take in the bustle of activity that surrounded me. I was amazed by how a few stories had sparked further research efforts and creative ideas. I had fully expected those young students to want to hear the stories, gladly take the pencils, and hug the buffalo; I had not expected it to light an educational fire in them that took over their school day. Honestly, I had been thinking more about what this assignment would do for the educational development of my own high school students. Sure, I thought the smaller kids might eventually look back on that day and remember a few cool history stories, but to inspire them like this was nowhere on my radar. This incident really showed me the power of turning students into teachers. I have heard so many people say that a person actually does not understand a subject until they are able to really teach it to others. I guess that saying was right. My students had learned so much researching, finding pictures, and creating their own children's books that they were transformed into real teachers who changed the lives of their new little students.

The other thing that really encouraged me was the astuteness of the teacher in this classroom. Sadly, I feel that too many teachers would not have responded the same way to the desires of the students to do further research or start a craft project. "But we have standards to cover," or "We have to prepare for the test," maybe "That's not in the curriculum," or even sadly, "That's not real learning. Here's a worksheet," would have been heard in far too many classrooms. Not this teacher. She saw the excitement of the students, and seized the opportunity to use their enthusiasm to piggyback off of the lesson provided by my students, allowing for these extension activities. I was so encouraged to know there are still teachers who have not been stifled by standards, crushed by curriculum, and turned off by testing. I saw real learning, in both my kids and the first grade students; it might not have been quantitatively measurable, but it was real.

The teacher thanked us again, and told us to come back any time we wanted. As we filed back to the bus, we were all smiling and talking about what we saw. It was an amazing day, and it was obvious the students loved their time sharing their books with the children. I sat there watching and realizing that school did not have to be boring, teaching did not have to take place only in the students' classroom, people learn more when they prepare to teach, lives are enriched when people of different ages mix together, and high school students can learn so much from children's stories. I had anticipated some of this. However, I had no way of knowing the impact that this day was having inside the heart of Brittney.

We returned to school a little late, as my first period adventure bled over into second period. That was my planning period, so my room was still empty. Before the students all grabbed their book bags and headed off to their next class, I told them how proud I was of them one last time. The last student to get her things together was Brittney. She stood up near the front door, and I was in the back at my desk. I called to her, "Brittney!" I said, "I thought you said that mean old teacher hated you." I prodded further, "It looked to me like she liked you after all." Quietly, and still somewhat stunned she said, "Yeah, I guess so," while shaking her head as if still trying to make sense of it. Then I added, "You were amazing. I thought you said you couldn't do it, but you did. I am very proud of you today." Immediately she put her head down to hide her tears. She paused a moment and took a couple of deep breaths before saying, "Thank you," in a voice cracking with emotion. Then she quickly slung her backpack over her shoulder and hurriedly disappeared through the door.

I sat quietly in my room, just letting the events of the past couple of hours swirl in my head. The activity was a much bigger success than even I had ever envisioned. The students had learned so much more than a little bit more about history. We had done more than make a preemptive strike against historical apathy. I saw the residue of a ten-year-old, hurtful belief vanish from a girl's face in an instant. I saw a teacher exhibit wisdom that is rarely seen. I also saw a girl cry because she heard the words, "I am proud of you," for what was likely the first time in her academic career. If we had done a worksheet, would she have had that opportunity to overcome her fears? If I had given a test, had them write an essay, passed out the ACT, proposed an IQ evaluation, or looked at

GPAs, would Brittney have had the chance to be on the same level as everyone else? Sometimes we have to forget which students are considered the good ones and which are called the bad ones. We should just create an atmosphere where everyone can excel in real-life activities. "But what if those low-functioning students cannot handle it and embarrass themselves?" some will ask. The real question should be, what happens when we let our struggling students out of the confines of structured in-class academic pursuits, and students (even the struggling ones) find out they can do things they never imagined? What kind of impact will that have?

As I began to think about those simple words, "I'm proud of you," and the impact they had, I came to realize that they were more than academic. It was not just about hearing that someone was finally proud of her for something she did at school, but I feel that was most likely either the first time she'd ever heard it from an adult in her life, or it had been a very long time. How did I come to that assertion, when I did not know what was going on at her house? It was the reaction she had that convinced me. After that day, she would always make a point to say "Hi," to me if she saw me in the hall, on bus duty, or in the cafeteria. She came up to me one day and asked me what other classes I taught, because she was designing her schedule for her senior year, and she wanted to take my classes if she could. She was able to secure a spot in one of my elective history classes; she came to tell me as soon as she registered, and she was beaming. There was one day, near the very end of that school year, when she stayed after my class to tell me some news that would leave me the one who was in tears.

In our state, certain core classes have what is called an end of course exam (EOC), which is mandated, created, given, and scored by the state. I never fretted much about the test, as I figured if I was teaching hard while the students were having fun, engaged, and learning to genuinely like history, they would be fine on that test. My strategy had worked so far, and my class scores were good with little to no test preparation. I never made it a point to tell kids they had to do well, my job was on the line, it looked bad on me if they did not perform well, etc. I never much cared for educational scare tactics. I know the students did hear it, though. The most failed EOC in our state was Algebra I, and those teachers were really under the gun. Many of those teachers talked about it ad nauseam, gave practice exams constantly, reviewed for weeks, and basically told their students that the sky would fall if anyone made below their predicted score (one way our state measures how effective the teacher is). Whether I said it or not, students had been indoctrinated with the importance of standardized testing since elementary school. Never was I more aware of how much impact this had on the students' idea of their academic self-worth than the day Brittney stayed after class to talk to me.

Those state EOCs always come near the end of the school year, and the last couple of days before school is out, we get the score. Sometimes there is such a rush to get the scores back before the students leave for the summer that the students receive the scores before I do. This year, they did receive them before I did, and they told me at the start of the class period that they had received their scores. I did not even ask them what their scores were, because to me, it was of little consequence to my thoughts on how their learning had progressed. I had been with them every day, and had seen how amazingly they performed real learning activities (like the children's novels). I did not need some quantitative data divorced from reality to cement my opinions. However, as the class ended, I noticed Brittney was lagging behind and realized she wanted to talk to me. As I walked to the front of the room, she said, "I'm sorry, Mr. Campbell." "Sorry for what?" was my immediate question. She pulled a folded piece of paper from her book bag and shoved it into my hands. It was her results from her U.S. history EOC. I did not even look at the numbers. "What about it?" I said. "It's my EOC score," she said impatiently. "I scored one point less than my predicted score," she said, becoming more frustrated with my lack of interest. Her voice was rising, and I could hear the tension. "I don't need a test to show me what you learned. I get to see you every day, and I *know* you learned," was my answer. I placed the results back in her hand. "But look," she said. "I scored one point below my expected score. That means it looks bad on you, right? It looks like you didn't teach me like you should." I finally got it. She was not mad because her score reflected negatively on her. She was used to making poor grades in school, and could quite frankly care less what some educational suit in the state capitol thought about her. What she was really upset about was that the test results said that I had not done my job. It was at this point that I really began to understand what kind of damage standardized tests do to the students.

"I'm sorry. Sorry I made you look bad," she said, nearly in tears. I told her to look me in the eye, which she did with some effort. Her eyes were glistening with tears yet uncried. For most of her academic life, she went to school but was not really involved. What she learned was mostly a result of a passive role in school; just sitting there, doing what she was told. For once, in my class she had engaged in being her own teacher. She had accepted a leadership role and taught herself; more importantly, she'd even taught others. For possibly the first time, she'd really learned. Her spirit was crushed; for once she had made a connection with a teacher in a class that made her want to really work for an education, and some person with a big degree and an important job in the capitol (who must be an expert on real learning) told her she had not really learned. The test score said the teacher had not really taught, and her efforts had been wasted. What kind of rational person who says they care about the development of children will let some multiple choice test, taken one time a year, represent the entire educational worth of a human being? Brittney may not have been an A student, but she was smart enough to learn through her years of indoctrination that her score meant her entire year had been wasted according to some, and both she and I were failures.

I looked her straight in the eyes, and gave her the greatest pep talk my mind could summon. I told her that a multiple choice test cannot quantify her learning. I argued that a snapshot of learning on only one day cannot measure what she had done the entire semester. I said that some filled-in bubbles could never tell the story of her overcoming her fears and reading in front of those first grade students. I told her that those "experts" in Nashville did not care enough to come to the school to see her take charge of the children's novel she was inspired to write; they could only sit in their offices and look at some numbers on a sheet of paper. I convinced her that the first graders would not know or remember her score, only the story they heard that changed their lives. Then I took the paper from her, crumpled it in my hand, threw it into the garbage, then reached onto my desk and pulled out my personal copy of *Mary the Missunderstood*. I said, "This is all I need to look at, to know what kind of a student Brittney is!" I then gave her my handkerchief, told her to wipe her eyes, straighten her back, and walk proudly to class. She never needed to worry about what she had done to me because of her score, because she had given me one of my greatest teaching moments. A hint of a smile graced her face; she wiped those tears, grabbed her backpack, looked me in the eye, and laughed that nervous laugh you let out when you are trying to keep from crying. She said "Thanks, Mr. Campbell," and walked to her next class proudly.

This entire event would never have happened if I would not have committed the educational sin of letting students read below their grade level. There is so much talk of finding a student's reading level, then only letting them read at that level or slightly higher to encourage them to grow as a reader; people would have lost their minds if they heard I was teaching children in high school with books intended for first graders. If they had seen me lugging those children's books into my class for my students to read and use as research, they would have died an educational death. If they had known I let a sixteen-year-old student leave a misspelled word on the cover of a book she wrote, they would have demanded my teacher's license. Yet because of this risk, I saw the most amazing growth in one of my hardest-to-reach students. My high school students had obtained a real education (not only in literacy, but also in the functional literacy of presenting to others to aid their learning), and younger students were inspired to do their own research and create their own artwork to extend the lessons presented. This concept, breaking the newest fad to never allow kids to work with text below their reading level, is not popular in today's educational climate. If you really want to reach kids, use it wisely (educational experts' opinions be damned) and watch something amazing happen in your students.

I was so inspired because of how well this activity worked that I began to look for other ways to let my kids read below grade level to develop their learning. I was so encouraged that I wanted to try something I had never done before; read a complete novel in my classroom. The school administration gave me a content reading class as a history elective. I knew this was the perfect opportunity to try out my plan of reading a novel in class; now I just had to find the perfect one. I scoured my book case at home, looking for the books I loved as a high school student. I reread several novels, and even bought a few new ones looking for the perfect book. Finally, I found it. It was the classic *All Quiet on the Western Front*, by Erich Maria Remarch. I had just returned from a three day summer in-service about using texts in class and they had preached ad nauseam about Lexile scores. The Lexile score is one of several ways to evaluate the reading level of texts. You can simply copy a segment of the text on your computer and then paste it into their website's tool and it will automatically tell you what grade level the reading is. Out of curiosity, I did just that; however, I would be sorry I had.

The result of the Lexile analysis said the novel was on a fourth-grade level. I was stunned. It was one of my favorite history books, and I was 34 years old and had a college degree in history. What did that say about my intellect? Also, how could a book that dealt with many of the most powerful human emotions like life, death, revenge, pain, suffering, love, loss, guilt, and depression on such a deep level be a children's book? A teacher at my school told me she had stopped teaching the book because it was too powerful for her to deal with every year. She said she left school depressed every day for months, sometimes in tears, while her classes read through the book. She told me the emotional wringer was too much for her, anymore. How could a book with that great of an emotional impact on an adult be below the level of a teenager? Finally, how could one of the biggest selling war novels of all time, loved by millions, assigned to me in college, praised by critics, and loved by generations, be nothing more than a kid's book unworthy of reading in high school?

I decided that a teacher with real world experience and over a decade of classroom wisdom who had spent five years in college reading and understanding history had more wisdom than a computer program. I became determined to teach that novel, and I am so glad I did. About a quarter of the class had never read a book in its entirety. I am glad I did not choose some boring book that was on grade level to be their first (and most likely last) book. I was glad I did not pick some book just because it was on grade level, cementing the idea that books were boring and they had been missing nothing their entire lives by skipping reading. That year's students devoured that novel. They loved the human stories; we discussed it in class, with several students always willing to volunteer their personal feelings and analysis of each section. Because of that book, I had something happen to me that I have never heard any teacher say happened to them in any other class, in all my years of teaching.

After four weeks of teaching the novel, a student was transferred out of my class and into another class that was supposed to better prepare her for the ACT test. She had just received her last ACT score and it was low, and being a senior, the counselors felt that studying to score better on a multiple choice test would benefit her more for this college readiness test (college and even life in general) than reading one of the most powerful novels of all time. A friend of hers, who was also in the class, brought me her copy and told me she had been transferred out of the class. A few days later, I saw her in the lunch room and went to talk to her. I told her I would miss her in the class, and she said she liked the class and would miss it as well. Then she said something to me that I will never forget. "I would like to keep reading my book," she said. "Is there any way I could get it back and keep it, even though I am not in your class anymore?" she begged. "I would be willing to read it on my own time" she promised. "I just love it so much, and I am right in the middle of it. I have to know what happens," she confessed. I could hardly believe my ears. How many teens want to read books assigned in their classes, much less agree to do it on their own time outside of class? I immediately thought, *What if I had let the Lexile score deter me from assigning that novel?*

A friend of mine told me that he read Dr. Seuss's *The Butter Battle Book* to his U.S. history class. I checked out a copy from the local library, and was amazed. That children's book is all about two groups of people who hate each other, but the only real difference between them is which side of their bread they butter. They forget how much they have in common, instead focusing on how different they are and thinking about ways to isolate one another and prepare for each other's destruction. Basically, the book is about the Cold War between America and Russia. It made sense to me, being a history teacher, but I was curious what my students would think of the children's story. When I read it in class, I got about halfway through the book before hands went up. "Is this about the Cold War?" they asked. Amazing, how fast my students got the hidden message. I wasn't even to the part about the wall and the missiles yet. I wondered how many adults had read the book to their children, yet never picked up on the fact that this book was a history lesson.

Sure, the book was way below their grade level for reading, but it was not really about having them read words that were at their functioning level or slightly beyond. The real point of the activity was to get the students to look for underlying meaning, similarities, anecdotes, and comparisons. We were able to use that book as a springboard to other stories with a historical meaning. We soon compared *The Wizard of Oz* (in movie form) or *The Wonderful Wizard of Oz* (in book form) to the Populist movement (a political movement of mostly farmers in the late 1800s). My son read *The Wonderful Wizard of Oz* in kindergarten, so I know it was way below their level, but my students really enjoyed trying to compare the different characters in the beloved book or movie to characters in a political movement. It really got their minds working when they had to compare people from different time periods and stories to one another.

We also used the largest grossing movie of all time, *Avatar*, to compare to the Indian Wars of the late 1800s on the Great Plains. The students were amazed by how the heroes and villains of a historical event could flip roles by a simple retelling of the story and moving the setting to an alien planet. Soon we were discussing *E.T. the Extra Terrestrial* and its similarities to the story of Jesus Christ. My students were blown away when I broke the movie plot down for them. He arrived on earth in an old building out back, in a small, out-of-the-way place; he befriended normal people; he healed the sick; he did miracles for his followers; the government wanted to capture him, but he escaped; and finally, he went up into the sky while those who loved him stood around and watched. "Jesus," my students said immediately. These type of activities do not stunt the educational growth of my students, as the educational elite predict. Looking for deeper meaning in stories is something that serves them well throughout life. They begin to make connections between all kinds of different genres, and see relationships that escape the average consumer.

I took the children's novel to a whole different level after several years of experimentation. It was the week before our state-mandated EOCs, and I decided on the controversial idea that I would do *no* review before the test. I had been keeping meticulous data each year; my class scores were getting better as I did less and less review. I decided to try no review at all, to see if my scores climbed even higher. It was risky, but if I trusted my gut (and the three years of data I had collected) it was the only logical decision. Many teachers were doing week-long reviews (some even month-long, and I knew one teacher who started review after the Christmas break), but I just kept teaching interesting topics, reading about scandalous and violent American history stories, letting my students have fun, and letting them learn to love the subject. The day before, I promised my students a surprise: a Dr. Seuss novel. I pulled out the author's final book. Actually, Seuss had died while writing this final novel, and two men had to come along and finish the book for him. It was titled *Hooray for the Diffendoofer Day*. The book is an amazing tale of a small school that is full of very odd teachers. They teach such unusual subjects as smelling and yelling. They just kind of do their own thing at that school, but the kids love it because all of the teachers are eclectic and interesting. One sad day, the principal announces there is a big test that they have to take immediately, and they have not prepared. What is worse, if the students do not do well on the test, they will be forced to go to the Flobbertown school. Flobbertown is a dreary place, with tons of homework, where all the teachers are the same: boring. Everyone panics, but once the students begin the test, they realize the test is easy because although the school did not teach the information on the test, they learned something better. The teachers trusted their students to have fun and enjoy learning, and encouraged them to think. All of the students did well, and they got to stay in their weird little school that really taught them how to love learning. My students picked up on the analogy immediately. "Yes, I am weird," I said. "We have not really done much with standardized testing," I confessed. "Many times you have probably asked yourselves, 'What does this have to do with history?' when we started some new project. But in the end, I think I gave you something that maybe you would not have gotten if we had just prepared for a test," I informed them. With near unanimity, the class responded, "How to think!" The next day, they took the test and I had my highest scores ever. Is it not amazing what letting teenagers read a bunch of text way below their grade level can do for them?

Are there children's novels out there for other subjects that could really help students understand a variety of disciplines? I assume so, but I have not looked. The teacher is only limited by their ability to be creative in finding books that will bring out some intended aspect of their subject. I am sure there are books that use mathematic principles to organize the numbers of pages, the graphics, etc. I seem to remember Scarecrow in the *Wizard of Oz* mumbles something about triangles and geometry when the Wizard gives him his diploma. Maybe math students could watch that clip and discern if he is actually right. I know there must be certain literary techniques and devices used to make the wording of books more effective. Maybe a language arts class could explore why so many children's novels rhyme, or adapt more complex books to an age-appropriate rhyme scheme. Students who are artistically inclined can illustrate books, act out skits based on themes and situations found in the book, or develop craft and extension activities to go along with the story.

Having students interact with literature not in their targeted developmental range, with the sole purpose of getting them thinking about how to interact with people on different developmental levels (which we have way too little of in our society), is an excellent way to develop new thought patterns. Some people say that grade level mixing is not as productive as isolating students of the same age into separate classrooms, but I disagree. Observe high school students interacting with people much younger or older than themselves, and watch magic happen. Send students of any age to read to elderly residents of nursing homes and watch intergenerational relationships blossom. Send older students to read books they have developed to younger students, and see connections be made in ways you never expected. People may say grade mixing can't possibly work, but it has for thousands of years and it will continue to pay dividends when used properly. If you need a modern day example of this idea that is succeeding on a monumental scale, just think about the Special Olympics. They mix people of different developmental levels together, and no one is arguing that either the participants or the people who go to help are having their educational experiences downgraded from the interactions. Everyone learns in new ways they just cannot when they're isolated among people their age and their developmental level. Mixing reading levels, developmental levels, and age groups can pay huge dividends to the teachers brave enough to challenge the status quo and use their imaginations to springboard the education of their students to new levels.

I know many of you are saying that this tactic worked well for my history classes, but it cannot work in other subject areas such as math and science. I disagree. I feel that any subject that needs a preemptive strike against the disdain and even vehemence that often accompanies it as the years pass could really benefit from using text that is well below grade level. I know that studies show math is the most feared and loathed subject by high school students. Math is a just a subject, like any other. It has no inherent detestable qualities. Kids pick these ideas up as they move through the early grades, when teachers convince them math is boring by giving them nothing but worksheets and fake problems that divorce the subject from their reality. Also, the focus of testing on so many math skills is helping convince many kids that they are no good at math—after all, the tests *prove* it. If so many kids are learning to hate it in grade school, teachers must take matters into their own hands.

Teachers should find the interesting topics in math (there are plenty), and use it to convince kids that math is fun and they can be successful at it. I think of all of the interesting people who have contributed to the body of knowledge in math: Newton, Einstein, Leibnitz, etc. Teachers could easily put their students to work on children's novels about those mathematicians, which could be read to younger students to show them that the stories in math are interesting. A couple of years ago, the Mayan calendar (or at least the ending of it) was all the rage. Could we use mathematic principles to address how the Mayans created their calendar? How about the rate of the spread of infectious disease tied to zombies? That would be a hit with younger students today. When my boys were in kindergarten, they had a book about Newton that read like a comic book. There are so many kids into comic books that those could be used to great effect, as well. Students could develop their artistic and writing skills while creatively developing stories to teach math to younger students. I am sure that a variety of topics would be considered interesting by younger students if teachers would just get creative, and let their students write books about them for younger kids.

Interesting biographies can be used by teachers of every subject to make their subjects more interesting. Have students research important people or events in specific subjects. For example, we talk about Jonas Salk's development of the polio vaccine. Once students do their research, challenge them to write an essay or research the topic on their high school level. Challenge them to teach it to a middle school class, then an elementary class. This project forces the students to not just write about the subject, but also to think about the most effective attention span, literacy level, sentence structure, words per page, book length, illustrations, and wording for their target audience. "But they are not experts on the subject!" many will cry. No worries, just bring in a few books from each level and have them read them and compare. The students will soon have it mastered. It really is not that difficult when you allow students to use their own wisdom.

No subject should be off limits to using text below grade level or Lexile score to get the students interested. There are many books that teach the basics of math. How about using books like *What Is the Name of This Book?* Or *The Lady and the Tiger?* I'm sure that if you plugged those books into the Lexile calcula- tor, you would find that their scores are well below high school level; yet those books are obviously high school level and beyond. When I worked through *The Lady and the Tiger*, I think I made it to the third puzzle before I got stumped. Not that I am a math genius, but I believe it is a significant challenge even for adults. I even tried it on my home room period one time to see if they would find the critical thinking puzzles as interesting and challenging as I did. They were hooked, and even started begging me to give them more. They loved the challenges so much I decided to turn every Friday into word puzzle day in my home room. How many math teachers have students begging for math puzzles to solve? I would assume very few, because they are trying to get their students to the next level of mathematical proficiency, instead of finding interesting text to read—even if the curriculum says it is below what they *need*. Trust me, if you had students who could work their way through those books, they would be pre- pared for any type of problem the world threw at them that required problem solving skills, pattern recognition, and the principles of mathematics.

Remember that grade levels are made up any way; they are figments of some educational expert's imagination. Who can say on what level a five or seven year old should read? There are children reading adult novels, and adults reading children's novels. There are adults making millions off of comic strips and cartoon characters. The American colonies had a literacy rate exceeding 90 percent, with most children learning how to read with the easy-to-follow children's book, the *King James 1611 Bible*. Today we have millions of children's books and many adult novels in the world adapted to the easy readability of children, yet there is a plunging functional literacy rate. Who is to say what level of reading benefits people the most? Of course, I am not going to try and push the reading level of a high school senior with a board book for babies, but I think educators must ask themselves what the purpose of the reading is. Depending on the answer, the difficulty of the book can be selected to determine the outcome. For example, if the goal is to understand the change in complexity of sentence structure between preschool, elementary, middle, and high school books, it's likely that may be a great reason to let an older student read literature aimed at younger readers. In other words, there are many reasons to let students of all reading levels explore different difficulties of text. It should be at the wisdom and discretion of a teacher who knows the students and goals best, not some hard and fast rule dictated by some educational administration suit who threatens your job if you dare use a reading level that is not deemed appropriate by a computer program.

I hope you have seen that the wisdom of the teacher when choosing material to use in the classroom is much more important than what some expert, curriculum, or computer program determines is effective. The tool created by a person should never be used to replace a person. We should not throw out the wisdom of the teacher for the knowledge of a program. Teachers must know their students, both strengths and weaknesses, and use this wisdom to make the appropriate educational decisions when it comes to reading level. If children's novels, comic books, puzzle books, or any other reading can suit the goals of the teacher, inspire students, or facilitate learning, it is the responsibility of that teacher to find a way to incorporate these into their instruction. The next time you need to find something to inspire your students, instead of going to the college prep section of teaching materials or test prep workbooks, think about going backwards in the developmental difficulty of the material. If used appropriately by the right teacher, this option can lead to a gold mine of educational opportunity.

CHAPTER V

MAKE ENOUGH NOISE
TO BOTHER EVERYONE ELSE

I t was one of the most surreal events that ever happened in my classroom. The whole class was full of kids laughing, lying on the floor, doubled over holding their stomachs; a few were even crying. I was lying in the floor curled into the fetal position, sucking my thumb in total shock. I had never expected this scene to play out in my room, not in a million years. At the door of my classroom was a hapless teacher's aide from across the hall, standing there in terror, holding a roll of paper towels. This one-time event became an educational lesson that would be etched into my memory forever.

We were discussing a unit on phobias in my psychology class. I was trying to demonstrate the difference between a fear and a phobia. I spoke of spiders, heights, and public speaking, but the kids just could not quite put their fingers on exactly where a fear ended and a phobia began. I looked around the room for something to help me get my point across. My eyes landed on a very safe and non-threatening roll of paper towels (you know, the brown kind that schools always have that don't absorb anything). I decided that I could use them as my object lesson. After all, what could go wrong with an innocent roll of paper towels?

I asked the students, "You see this roll of paper towels over here? It might be natural to have a slight fear of getting a paper cut or maybe even an aversion to work." I continued. Then I prepared for my acting debut as a real life, walking talking "towelophobe." I bent over so I could peer directly into the seated students' eyes, I then whispered, "But no one would walk by paper towels and say..." Then I bellowed the rest, complete with bulging eyes, protruding neck veins, and waving arms, "PAPER TOWELS? OH, NO! NOT PAPER TOWELS! KEEP THEM AWAY! PLEASE, NOT THE PAPER TOWELS!" I then curled up into a ball on the floor and began to suck my thumb like a three-year-old preschool kid begging for his mommy. All of the students were shocked at first, but then the smiles began to spread across their faces. They were beginning to understand the difference between a rational fear and an irrational, paralyzing phobia. As I looked up from my thumb sucking, I noticed the students were beginning to laugh heartily. Sure, it was funny, and the students were having a good time, but nothing could have prepared us for what happened next.

As I lay there peering up at the students' smiling faces, and they looked at me wondering if I had lost my mind, the door flew open with such force that it banged against the wall. The teacher's aide from across the hall burst through the door at the front of my class and leapt into the room. Evidently, she had heard my screams about paper towels, and in her mind she was convinced that someone had hurt themselves in my class. I also taught biology in that room, and in her mind, no doubt, she saw a kid who had nearly severed his arm on a scalpel. Dancing through her imagination was blood spurting forth with each beat of a child's heart while I rushed back and clamped the artery with both hands, and couldn't leave the student to get the paper towels because I had to control the bleeding. As she snapped herself from her vision, the aide knew what must be done, and jumped into action to save the day. She quickly returned to her classroom and grabbed her paper towels, then she darted across the hall, threw that door open, and screamed, "I've got the paper towels!" There was nothing but silence...for a while.

She stood there hunched over, with knees bent and eyes alert, her head on a swivel scanning the room. She was ready to pounce in the direction of the severed artery and save a life. Instead, she saw me staring up from the floor in shock, and my stunned students' heads swiveling around to see who nearly tore the door off the hinges. Despite this chaotic scene, after she screamed, there was not a sound in the room except for the aide's heavy panting. After about five seconds, the students burst into laughter that nearly shook the foundations of the school building. I soon followed. The only one not laughing was the thoroughly confused aide. She stood erect, her muscles relaxed, and her bulging eyes momentarily receded back into their sockets.

After we stopped laughing (in about five minutes), we explained to the would-be first responder what we were doing. She laughed too, although she was not as amused as we were. It was in that moment that I learned the power of making noise. I did not know the aide was in the hall. I couldn't have known she would come bursting in to save the day and give us all the laugh of our lives. Had I not been yelling in my room, that moment would never have happened. Now, over a decade later, I sometimes see students from that class. They still ask me if I remember that time the aide burst into the class with paper towels. Of course I do, but then I ask the next follow up question, "What were we talking about that day?" They always remember: phobias.

The first time this happened it was accidental, but now that I have learned the power of disturbing others by making loud noises, I plan them, create them, orchestrate them, and even fantasize about them. I think about how I can use the element of surprise in my lessons: how I can shock them a bit with a loud noise, or how I can end my lesson with a proverbial bang. The kids sitting in my classes do not know whether my outbursts are planned or not, and it does not really matter. All that matters is that I use this tool to help my students remember. It takes some practice and experimentation, but eventually a teacher can learn to use disturbing noises to change the educational outcome of the students.

Later that year, I decided to use the power of the loud noise again. In my psychology class, we were studying operant conditioning and the "Little Albert and the White Rat" story. If you are not familiar with it, a scientist was trying to see if fears were learned or innate. He took a baby, unbeknownst to the mother, from the workplace daycare. He used the boy to see if the little tike was afraid of the color white. He gave him white fluffy animals and other things to play with, allowed doctors to come into the room dressed in white lab coats, etc. Baby Albert was not afraid. It was time to for the doctor to ramp up the sadism!

Every time baby Albert saw something white, the scientist would bang a huge bell behind the baby's head and scare the devil out of him. Of course, the baby cried every time. It wasn't long until baby Albert would just start crying and looking behind him for that stupid bell every time anything white came into the room. I could tell my students of this experiment to serve as an example of operant conditioning, but this story had a loud noise in it, and I had already learned the power of the loud noise used to disturb people. If a scientist could use a loud disturbing noise to become famous, why not me?

That day, I had some notes already on the board when the students came into the room. I told the students I would give them a few minutes' head start on copying them down, since there were so many. The students all swiveled to face the board and began to concentrate on their task. There was this very polite and nice young lady named Bitsy, who sat right near my desk. I had a metal trash can right between my desk and hers. I slid a hammer out from under a piece of paper that I used to conceal it on my desk. I could hardly hold in my laughter as I slowly moved the hammer toward the trash can. I felt like I was in Edgar Allen Poe's "Tell-Tale Heart," inching myself further and further inside the door to have a peak at the old man's buzzard eye. Finally I was ready to give my students a lesson on operant conditioning they would never forget, but I could never anticipate the shock I (not just my students) was also about to receive.

As I pounded that trash can, it rang out a peal that could wake the dead. Bitsy dropped her pencil and used both hands to clutch her heart as her mouth opened wide, yet no sound escaped. Of course, all of the other students stopped what they were doing and quickly snapped their heads around in terror. Some dropped pencils, some screamed, some had their eyes bug out like some type of demented cartoon: all of them were scared out of their minds. The funny thing was, as they looked toward me to find out what the sound was, they saw me staring at the quiet student beside my desk, waiting for her to start breathing again. She had gasped and was just sitting there in shock, clutching her heart with her face frozen into an expression of terror, but she was not breathing. The students followed my gaze to the quiet girl, and soon we were all just staring at her with our own breath held, waiting for her to decide if she would pass out or resume breathing.

Finally, when it seemed she could hold her breath no longer and we were nearly mad with anticipation, she gasped and the color returned to her face. You cannot imagine how relieved I was that I had not killed one of my students. We all had a great laugh out of it, and eventually we got calmed down enough so I could explain what I was trying to teach them about operant conditioning. It made perfect sense to them. When I finished my explanation and told them to write down the next note from the board, every student was looking at me, then the trashcan, then the hammer. Then they would dart their eyes to the board for a moment, then back to the hammer, then scribble a few words, then back to me. It even went on for the rest of the semester. When taking notes, the students would constantly be looking for the huge trash can gong to scare them out of their minds.

I realized that the trash can hammer beating had done so much more than I ever imagined. Yes, I thought it would startle them and then we could better discuss the connection between operant conditioning, baby Albert, themselves, etc. I had no idea that just one loud noise would stick with them for the rest of the semester, so well that they never forgot the lesson. No matter which student in the class I asked or when I asked it throughout the semester, students always remembered baby Albert (and even felt sorry for the little fellow), operant conditioning, and the theory of learned fears. What is even more amazing is that from time to time I will see one of those students from that class. They always start their conversation with, "Remember the time you almost killed Bitsy?" Of course I do. I will never forget it, and neither will they. After all, was that not the whole point?

There have been many times when I have disturbed the students in my class as part of the lesson, to great effect. What really bothers other people is when you are so loud that the noises escape your classroom, creep down the hallway, and invade their sacred space. It soon became a running joke in the school that teachers would offer their condolences to those unfortunate enough to be placed in classrooms next to mine. My first year in the second school where I worked had me floating from room to room each class period, as we had more teachers than rooms. This was tough on the entire school, because there was literally nowhere to hide from my loud noises. As I moved from pod to pod around the entire school, my voice rounded every corner, my music assaulted every nook, and my beating and banging scared literally every student and teacher in the entire school. It even became a humorous affair when a substitute was in a nearby room. A huge crash, bang, or yelp would escape my room, and the substitute would jump and run to the door, expecting to see a herd of stampeding wildebeests invading the hallway, only to have the students laugh and tell the substitute that all was well. "It's only Mr. Campbell."

I soon had to start warning new teachers who moved within earshot of my classroom. Once I had an office next to my room, and they moved a principal out and moved the transportation director in. I thought it was only proper to warn my new neighbor before the first day of school that he might hear some loud, strange sounds coming from my room. He said, "Okay," and smiled, like he thought I was joking. Well, about three days into class we were reenacting the beating of Charles Sumner (by Preston Brooks on the Senate floor) in my classroom. I placed a CPR training mannequin in a seat and dressed him up in a coat, tie, and name tag identifying him as Charles Sumner. When the kids entered the room and saw the dummy in the front of the room, they knew something crazy was going to happen. When the bell rang, I quickly closed the door and recited the very speech Preston Brooks had given to Sumner. Then I proceeded to beat the dummy Sumner with a galvanized pipe about four feet long, three ways: fast, hard, and consistently. I had tested the beating a few times to make sure all was safe before the students arrived, but I guess in my historically-inspired frenzy I was just enjoying myself too much. The first hit landed with such force on the dummy's face that his head snapped back and the pipe crashed into my Smartboard with such force it detached the electronic pen tray, and the pens went flying all over the room. This was no time to be timid; after all, I had a story to tell. I hit the dummy again, and it fell out of the chair and into the floor. The final blow landed on the chest of the mannequin with such force that whatever hard plastic material it was made of shattered into a million pieces. I tossed the pipe down and left through the back door (just as Brooks had done), trying to conceal the smile on my face from a job well done.

I usually stay outside of the door for about a minute, and it is always the same. As I stand listening through the door to the room, the first few seconds are utter silence. Then I begin to hear some nervous laughter, and finally the kids start chatting. "Did you see that?" they ask. "Who is Charles Sumner?" they demand. When the kids begin to get feverish, I return and explain it all. They never forget that day. What I did not know until after class was that my new neighbor would never forget that day, either.

After class, I went into the hall to watch the students during class change and the transportation director immediately threw his door open and came up to me. "What in the world was going on over there?" he wanted to know. I recounted the whole story of Brooks and Sumner to him. "I thought the worst fight in the world had broken out over there! I thought they were coming through the wall. I just heard bodies hitting the floor, and things being torn off walls, people shouting, and banging. It nearly knocked me out of my chair!" he said, with a bewildered look on his face. "I even jumped up and came running to your door to help, but all I saw through your window were students sitting dumbfounded, in stunned silence, while a dummy lay destroyed in the floor!" he recounted. "I was just about to head in to help, when I remembered you told me that you were really loud and I realized it had all been part of your lesson." He said this with an air of exasperation in his voice. I did my best to apologize for frightening him, and we had a good laugh. That event helped me realize something I had never even considered about my teaching by using loud noises (besides the fact that scaring the wrong person badly enough could be detrimental to the longevity of my teaching career).

Even people outside my classroom want to know what is going on in my room when they hear the noise. The transportation director might have hated history, but when he heard and partially saw what was going on, he immediately came to me after the class wanting to know what was happening, who Preston Brooks and Charles Sumner were, why they were fighting, and (of course) who won. It is in our nature to want to know what is going on, especially if it is something wild, exciting, or passionate. It is why rumors spread so quickly, Facebook has exploded in popularity, and people have gossiped for centuries. If it is something exciting, then people get passionate, scream, yell, throw things, and even fight. Making noise in your classroom will get people interested in what you are doing, whether they are in the room or not.

Once, my method of making loud noises to reinforce the lesson even spawned a retaliatory attack. I guess I had been making noises from the beginning of school, and it was approaching the end of the first semester. I was floating from room to room that year; during this particular class period, I was teaching in a classroom that had a wall between it and the next one over. It was not a block wall like the ones in the rest of the school; this one was only a metal wall that could be moved. I guess it did not insulate sound as well as a regular wall, and lots of my loud noises had made it to the other side. My class and I would soon find out just how loud we had been.

As we sat quietly working in December, there came a loud banging from that wall that nearly shook us from our seats. It was not just one loud bang but dozens of them, all over the wall that adjoined our room to the one next door. It was not just banging, there were yells and screams as well. I instantly looked up, expecting a car to come crashing through the wall or something equally catastrophic. Instead, I actually saw the wall shaking and pulsating from the furor of the pounding. All of my students whipped their bodies around to face the back wall. I actually scanned the room for another Bitsy, clutching her heart while trying to catch her breath, but there were none this time (I guess I was a little bit traumatized by the whole operant conditioning experiment, as well). Just as it appeared that we could recover from our scare, the door sprang open.

The door that joined my room to the one next door nearly crashed through the wall as it exploded from its moorings, and in pounced dozens of screaming children. These were not your normal high school students; they were armed. The intruders began to hurl paper wads at every one of my hapless students. My kids were ducking under desks, taking cover behind each other, and running away to the far sides of the room. Then, the teacher of the class next door leaped through the door, looked straight at me, drew back his cannon of an arm, and let fly a paper missile that was heading right for my head. If not for my ninja-like reflexes, combined with my youthful and graceful gazelle-like movements, it would have nearly decapitated me; however, I ducked out of the way just in time. As my students and I lay crouching and hiding all around the room, it got very quiet. The intruders stopped yelling and throwing things, and that is when they said something that my students and I would never forget.

"PEARL HARBOR! DECEMBER SEVEN! NEVER FORGET IT!" the intruders cried in unison. Then, just as quickly as they had come, they departed back to their side of the wall and shut the door behind them, never to return. "What was that all about?" one of my hapless students muttered. I looked down at my watch and saw the date, and that is when I realized the teacher next door had used my own trick to help both his own class and mine. It was indeed December 7th, a day that all history buffs should know; a day that Franklin Roosevelt said would live in infamy. The teacher next door had heard me and my class making all kinds of crazy noises all year. He realized this was his chance for a little payback, for all the mischief we had caused, and also a golden opportunity to use my own tactic against me.

He asked the students at the beginning of class if they wanted to pay me back for all of my auditory assaults on his class's peace and quiet. His students naturally said, "Yes." Each kid made two paper wad bombs as they waited for the perfect time to attack. They had planned to wait until halfway through the class, when my side of the wall became very quiet, then launch their devious assault. They did just that. I am sure the neighboring teacher probably wanted payback more than anything, but he had to also know that he was borrowing my tactic and using it against me. What I quickly realized is that he not only allowed his class to do something they will never forget, but because my class was the target, it allowed my kids to piggyback off of that learning experience. For once, I got to experience what it was like to be the class next door to the loud disruption, and it was a tremendous learning experience for my students as well. I actually took the few minutes after the attack to teach my kids what he was talking about. I still have kids talk about it today; they have not forgotten. Disturbing other people not only works for the class doing the disturbing, but also the class getting disturbed. After class we talked about it, and agreed that it worked as such a great teaching tool for both classes that we now arrange to attack each other's classes on purpose, and we even choreograph which class will attack each period (unbeknownst to the students, of course).

One year I was teaching in a classroom that was formerly used for administrative purposes. My room and the one next door actually had a wooden door between them, with a glass window and about an inch space under the door. To say that it was a barrier to the sound would be to highly exaggerate its effectiveness. To make matters worse, the only electrical and internet connections for my computer were right beside that door. Not such a big deal, until you realize that is where my speakers were. I love to use music and sound clips, and being right beside that door allowed nearly all the sounds I made to escape into the room next door.

I apologized in advance to the teacher who moved into that room adjoining mine that year. I felt sorry for the fellow teacher, once I got to know the guy better. He was a very quiet person, and I feel it would have been much easier for a louder person to handle all of my disruptions. They would have not only understood more what I was like, but also their class and voice would have been louder—so mine would be less of a distraction. We agreed if he ever needed a period of silence, I would work very hard to coordinate my lessons with him. When I returned from Christmas break that first year, he had installed some foam board and blankets on his side of the door to deaden the noise. Unfortunately, they had minimal effect.

We had become good friends by then, and he told me the story of fixing the door over Christmas break. He said he had decided to do it after asking that the door's sound-blocking ability be enhanced by the maintenance department—three times. He decided to take matters into his own hands. When he told his wife where he was going that morning as he went to buy the materials to fix the door, he said his wife responded with something very interesting. "Why not just go next door and tell that loudmouth to teach more quietly?" she half asked, half told him. His response to his wife let me in on a little secret I had never before considered.

My neighboring teacher told his wife that it was not a teacher problem; it was a facility problem. We were teaching in rooms that were never designed to be classrooms. Although they were being used as such, they had never been properly adapted to adequately perform that job. He went on to say to me that he also told his wife, "He's probably the best teacher in the school. His class is so fun, and the students learn so much," he added. The part about me being the best teacher is highly debatable, but it made me consider something I had never thought about previously. I used to think that my class was fun for my students, but I worried that teachers around me thought I was just goofing off and making noise to be silly: that I was not really serious about my job. I even *knew* that some teachers felt that way, but I also realized that the ones who had to teach beside me day in and day out (at least one of them) realized there was a method to my madness, and sometimes my madness worked.

I was teaching biology in my early years in the classroom. There were not enough lab rooms for every lab teacher to have their own, so we rotated to the lab rooms when we taught lab classes. First period I was in another teacher's lab room, and my kids were always so sleepy. Being a first year teacher, I thought that after a good night's rest, teenagers would be ready to go to their first period class. Boy, did I have a lot to learn. I soon found out, after some prodding, that they did not get a good night's sleep. As the teenage zombies filed past me into first period yawning, sleep still matted in their eyes, hair not fixed, moving like automatons, I would sometimes ask them why there were so sleepy if they slept all night and just woke up. I always got the same answers. "I stayed up until four a.m. playing video games," they would say. Maybe it was, "I was texting my boyfriend until two in the morning." Or the ever popular, "Our team didn't get home until midnight, and I couldn't calm down enough to go to sleep until three a.m." I knew I could not go home with them and make them go to bed earlier, so I needed something to be their educational rooster, waking them for another fascinating day of learning. Some really loud noises sounded good to me, but they could not just be annoying; they also had to be fun.

As I was pondering this dilemma, I walked into the lab class one day and I saw the answer to my problem. The teacher who taught in the classroom most of the day had brought in a decorative brass bell on a wrought iron frame standing about two feet tall. I immediately asked the teacher if I could ring her bell. "Of course, any time," she said. When class began that morning, I started with a few review questions. I like to refresh the students' memory, call on every one of them, let them know I can see who is there, and likely give them their first adult interaction of the day (beyond a grunt and shrug). When I asked the first question, the student got it right. What did I do? I ran up front and grabbed that bell, held it high above my head like a championship trophy, and said, "THAT WAS ABSOLUTELY RIGHT! THE BELL OF KNOWLEDGE TOLLS FOR YOU!" I rang that bell with all I had. It was pretty loud and a few of the students winced a bit, but they also smiled. They sat up straighter in their chairs, they wiped the drool from their chins, and every one of those sleepy eyes were now on me. As we went around the room asking questions, the bell rang many more times that morning. I rang it, the students rang it; some rang it softly, some rang it loudly, some rang it with a head butt, some tapped it with their pencils, but that bell rang often. By the end of my formerly three-minute pedestrian review, we had transformed it into a fun wake-up call. This would become our new signal to start the day, but to some the bell became much more than that.

I found out a few days later that one student was very sad she had not answered a question right yet and received her chance to ring "the bell of knowledge" in front of the class. She was not the most studious member of my class, but there was something about ringing that bell in front of her peers and showing that she was smart just like everyone else that motivated her. I told her to look over her notes in the classes after mine when she had spare time; glance over them in lunch; maybe even take them home and look at them for a few minutes and be prepared the next morning; she would get the first question. She was the first one in the door the next morning. She hopped into her seat, whipped out her notebook, and reviewed the material from the day before. When class began, I turned to address the class with the bell of knowledge in hand. Her eyes were locked on the prize.

I called her name, announcing to the class that she would receive the first question and therefore the first chance to ring the bell. She was on the edge of her seat with anticipation. Before I could even get the question out of my mouth, she blurted out the answer, and before I could even affirm her answer, she leapt from her seat, sprinted down the aisle, and gave that bell a furious ring that not only woke our class, but probably a few others around us as well. She had a smile on her face all class long. I realized that it was not really the chance to ring a little bell that a teacher had bought at a yard sale that was so important.

It was really about the confirmation of that student's worth; an audible display that she was smart. Other students would know when she rang that bell that she was a good student, that she knew her material, that she was learning, and that she was every bit the person that every other student in that class was. She rang the bell many more times that year, but I will always remember the look on her face the first time she earned the chance to do so. I quickly realized how hard some students would work for the opportunity to ring a silly little bell that many teachers, and even myself, might have dismissed as childish or too gimmicky to be effective.

I will also remember that day for another reason. After that class when the not-so-studious student earned the right to ring the bell for the first time, I was feeling pretty good about myself, the student, and education in general—until I stepped into the hall after class. Another teacher came up to me and said, "I was in the teachers' workroom, and I heard that dang bell ringing." She was obviously upset. The teachers' workroom was a good thirty yards from the class. The pealing of the bell had to pass through two heavy oak doors as well as make a couple of ninety-degree turns in the hall way. I was a bit shocked that the bell's sound had carried so far. "It was the bell of knowledge," stumbled out of my mouth (half expecting her to understand). "The what?" she spat back. "It's a little tool I use to praise the students for getting right answers in class," I returned. She was not impressed with my new education gimmick. "Well, it's loud, and annoying, and you can hear it all over the school!" she finished as she stormed away without even waiting for me to answer.

It was in that moment that I realized many teachers had not learned the power of making noises so loud that it disturbed others. *If she could have just been in the room, and seen the student's face when she was able to ring that bell for the first time,* I thought. However, she was not in that room, and it was obvious she would never create that opportunity in her own class. I had stumbled upon this little trick; after I saw its power, I was not going to stop using it. I had been so proud of myself, at least until I stepped into the hall that day. I became a bit discouraged, but I had to ask myself a question. *Do I keep doing what works for the students, or worry about some other teacher on the other end of the hall?* It was simple for me to see that I had to do what was right for the students. What kind of teacher would I be if I stopped doing something that worked so well at encouraging and even inspiring students to work at school, learn the material, and get that much-needed affirmation that likely never came in any other class, on a ball field, or even at home? As a matter of fact, I became determined to keep letting that bell ring in my class, keep waking up those students, keep inspiring young minds, and keep giving those young people something many of them were not getting anywhere else; the chance for a student to stand up and say, "I am smart, I am worth something, and I want the whole class, maybe even the whole school, to notice," was too valuable to squander.

Once, there was a student who was in an adjoining classroom who was also a family friend. Often I would see her as she left the neighboring classroom, but I also saw her and her family outside of school. Once I asked her if she planned to take my class the next year. She said she was not sure if she would sign up for my class or not. I have the reputation of being more strict with my students than most teachers (no leaving for the bathroom during class, no food or drink, if you are tardy you have to do the tardy choice assignment, and so on). I told her not to worry about the exaggerated stories about how tough my teaching style was. Then she said something to me that was very profound. "It's not like you really teach, anyway." I was speechless. In my mind, I tried to reason what she was really trying to say about me. Had she been listening through the wall all year, and become convinced that all we did was make loud noises and goof off? I could see how some people might get that impression walking by my class once, but to be beside me all year and really be convinced of that was almost hurtful. I had to prod her to tell me more.

"What do you mean by that?" I asked. "You don't think I'm teaching over there?" I inquired. Her answer is what really amazed me, on several levels. "I didn't mean that you don't do anything or that your students did not learn. What I meant to say was, all that I hear going on over there is the students doing activities, building things, having competitions, tournaments to find out who the greatest inventor was, you telling stories, and listening to music. I don't hear you giving out worksheets, having the students read the textbook, or looking up definitions," she responded. I realized that although her original statements seemed like an insult at first, it was really one of the greatest compliments I'd ever had.

When she thought of teaching, the only thing that came to her mind was what many teachers do: give out worksheets, have the students read the textbook or look up definitions, etc. What she heard me doing through the wall was something completely different. It was the opposite of teaching, to her teenage mind. She knew the kids were still learning, but I was not doing what others teachers did. I began to think on this concept. Maybe I was not a teacher in the regular sense. Maybe I was something else, a conductor on a ride to self-education, a facilitator of education, a fellow traveler on a trip through time—or maybe even a ringmaster who presented the strongmen, bearded ladies, and freak shows that are American history. Whatever I was, she was right. I was no teacher, in the sense of the word that most high schoolers thought of it. I was something else. When I look at the way many of our teachers try to force students to learn—by doing the most boring and mundane of activities that have no relation to real life and are obviously fake learning—I will take her comment as a compliment. I'm not that kind of teacher. I am something different. And what gave this high school girl sitting on the other side of the wall for a year that idea? It was the loud and distracting noises that came through the wall from my room. Without them, to her I would have been just another boring, regular, run of the mill teacher, which is something I never want to be.

I even once had a teacher tell me that he had to rearrange his room, due to my loud noises. Again, it was when I was a floating teacher without a room, and I was teaching in a room with a metal wall that did not block sound very well. It seemed my loud voice was carrying through the wall. I guess some of my stories and activities sounded interesting, not only to the kids in my room, but to the ones on the other side of the wall as well. The teacher in the adjoining room would have the kids bored to tears with worksheets, outlines of the chapter, bold words, and chapter review questions. While they were supposed to be working on this drudgery, the ones near the wall would often be distracted by the mysterious sounds coming from my side of the wall. Soon, the entire row nearest the wall that separated our classes was listening to the Village People, and me explaining what their song "YMCA" had to do with the Gilded Age. Or maybe it was Metallica's "One" video that was pounding through the wall, as I tried to show how the video depicted the terrible destruction caused by the industrialized warfare of World War I. Possibly, it was me running through the room yelling, "Exercise!" in Japanese at my students-turned-American POWs, as we studied excerpts from the book *Unbroken* and learned about the story of Louis Zamperini. Whatever it was, it was infinitely more interesting than the other teacher's drivel; his students were side-tracked, and I was to blame.

After class one day, as we were standing outside our doors watching the students change classes, the teacher next door brought his problems to me. As he explained about his students near the wall that adjoined our class rooms, it was clear that he was blaming me for the problem. I could not help but feel that the *real* problem was his boring teaching style. I couldn't help that the metal wall wasn't a better barrier to my classroom noises. What did he want me to do, be quiet and boring like him? I signed up to educate my students to the best of my abilities, using every tool and trick in my arsenal, and I was going to do it. I think what the other teacher was really saying was that the kids wished they were in another room, any room, other than his. Instead of him upping his game, he wanted me to sink down to his mundane level. I cannot do that and I will not do that; I will *never* do that. I can try to be quieter, I can ask to teach in a different room, but I refuse to stop using methods I've found that help kids learn.

So, there you have it. Making a lot of noise and bothering other people will help your students learn, when planned into your instruction. It might even help other students and teachers in other classes learn, especially the ones who are being bothered by your loud noises. I know that it can help your students remember important events, make connections with their teacher and other students in the class, and even make connections with students and teachers in other classes. Additionally, you can help to create moments that many of the students will never forget.

Many teachers rattle on about all kinds of things that seem important to us teachers, but the truth is that unless we find a way to *connect* what we are saying to the kids, they will not learn it anyway. In ten years, what will the students remember? Ask yourselves what *you* remember about high school. You will probably remember very little subject matter from any one teacher. I cannot recall more than a couple of distinct lessons from even my best teachers. What I and others do remember are those moments when outlandish things happened. These moments will take place in and outside of the classroom without planning. It might be the time the kid laughed and blew milk out of his nose at lunch. It might be the time the kid in the front of the line on the football team slipped and fell as he ran onto the field, and all of the other players fell over top of him. These crazy moments will happen, so you might as well plan to use them to your benefit. So in twenty years, when people remember those crazy things that happened at school, at least they will be things that happened in *your* class, and they will be helping them remember things you wanted them to know.

If you read this chapter and are convinced that using loud noises that bother others is a viable tool to use in your classroom, *do not think others are going to like it.* Some teachers, usually the ones who are loud and outlandish themselves, will understand what you are trying to do. I had a principal who would walk by, hear something crazy going on in my class, pop into the room and just lean up against the wall for a few minutes and take it all in while smiling. I would ask if he needed anything, and he would just shake his head and stand there, watching. I was a young teacher, and it made me a bit nervous. One day, he called me into his office and said, "I love stopping by your class. I miss being in the classroom and having that personal interaction with the kids. Sometimes I just walk the halls looking for something interesting going on in a classroom. I stop in and enjoy just for a moment the interaction I miss about being a teacher." He got it, but there have been many other colleagues who have not.

There have been many neighboring teachers who gave me dirty looks, as I leave a classroom beside theirs after such lessons. I have had secretaries and office workers make remarks to others in front of me (obviously for my benefit). They've let me know they have a hard time concentrating on their paperwork because of the loud noises coming from my room. Once, I even went to the principal when I was stationed beside one of these people who liked peace and quiet all around them. I knew there could be problems. I asked the principal what I should do, if a conflict arose about my noise level. He told me to tell that person I was teaching, and they should go back to their room. He got it, but I have also had people complain about me to the principal. I have even had a teacher walk down to my room and slam the door during one of my quieter lessons (I always close the door on the louder lesson days). I even came in to school early one morning and saw a note taped to my door complaining of my noise level. I know I make so much noise in my room that it can bother everyone else, but I must remind myself why I do it. It works, and I highly suggest you try it immediately.

CHAPTER VI

Let Your Students Play

As I walked over to the table that had the beverage station, I could cut the tension with the knife. It is one of those feelings when you know another person has something against you, and they know you know it, but both people are afraid to speak to one another and clear the air. I was the teacher; I had to be the bigger person and speak first. She was pouring her tea, so I walked up behind, gathered my courage, and spoke. "Congratulations on being in the top ten percent," I said. Without even turning or looking up from her glass of tea she said, "Thanks." "I don't guess that incident in my class kept you from this nice banquet after all," I said, half asking. With that she turned, met my gaze, and forced a pseudo-smile. "I don't guess so," she said, "but I am still mad about it." "That's okay," I told her, "when you play the game for real, sometimes it gets messy and personal." "I guess so," she continued, now turning around to actually talk to me for the first time in half a year. I could feel the ice melting on our frigid relationship. "You know that ten years from now, I am still going to remember that, right?" she asked. "Maybe so," I said, "but you have really given me a great compliment." "What is that?" she asked. "Well, in most classes if they do something that is remembered the next day, that is good. If you remember it for ten years, I feel that I did an excellent job at teaching that lesson." She smiled, looked down at her tea, and prepared to walk back to her seat. "Thanks, Mr. Campbell," she said, and walked away.

I remember standing in front of my sociology class the second day of school and teaching the definition of sociology. "The study of humans in groups," I said. I had taught that same definition five times before, but this time, something jumped out to me about it. I was teaching about how people act in groups and I was in the middle of a huge group. We have almost a thousand students in our school. We have them separated into four groups according to age. We have dozens of classes going on simultaneously all over the school. We have dozens of sports and clubs, of nearly every type imaginable. There are cliques, groups, subgroups, cultures, subcultures, and countercultures embedded throughout the school. What I realized is that we were actually inside of one of the greatest human experimental laboratories for studying human behavior, yet for some reason I was standing up and talking about people in groups. All I really needed to do was stop talking, sit down, and simply create an environment to allow my students to study these different groups and see what kind of sociology was going on around them every single day.

I wanted to create some type of situation that really showed students the elements that develop in groups within society. How leaders are made, who the followers will be, how unified groups end up splitting, why people backstab and sabotage, etc. I could talk, give notes, create worksheets, write tests, and give out study guides about it, or I could create a real situation in my class where kids got to experience the group dynamic. I could make the learning experience so real that they got to live all of those things and witness them in real life in a way that they would never forget. By the time I concocted my scheme, I felt silly for ever trying to teach about how people act within a group any other way. I looked to one of the greatest examples of a sociological experiment ever conducted, the television show *Survivor*.

I was in college when *Survivor* debuted. I remember seeing all of the commercials for the show and thought it looked very intriguing. A group of people dropped off on a tropical deserted island surviving for weeks on their own, and only the strongest surviving. It sounded great. However, I never had time to watch it as I was so busy with school, work, and recently being married. Imagine my surprise several years later when my wife got into the show, and I realized I had been fooled. I remember the first time I actually sat down and watched an episode, realizing it was not about the strongest surviving in the uncharted wilderness. It was more like a game of free-for-all lying and backstabbing. It seemed that often the strongest person was voted off by the weak people, because the feeble players felt threatened by the stalwarts. I was appalled and turned off immediately, and since that fateful day when my eyes were opened to the deception, I have never enjoyed watching the show *Survivor*.

I had a friend who was a total *Survivor* nut. He tried every season to get on the game; he analyzed every challenge at home meticulously, and he and his wife debated the outcomes for weeks after it was over. I told him I never really liked the show, because it seemed the weak people got together and voted off the strong people and it was totally not real life. That is when he keyed me in on a few things. First, he told me that it was not real survival in the jungle. Nothing was going to eat them (the producers would make sure of that). It was about survival in the game. Second, strong people are not really strong in this kind of setting if they cannot keep from getting voted out of the competition. And finally, what is so appealing is that you cannot tell who will win at the beginning, no matter how strong a player they appear to be at first. He made his points, and I reluctantly listened; as I drove home, I ruminated on his revelations.

Maybe I missed the complicated beauty of the entire show. Maybe it was more like real life than I imagined. We do not live in a society where people are going to get eaten or fall over waterfalls. We live in America, where we have to worry about things like not getting a job, not making the boss happy, disappointing our spouses, losing our reputation, etc. Most of our challenges in America are not physical but social. Second, strong people in America are not always those who are physically strong. Maybe the strong people of America are those who are strong spiritually and/or emotionally, with an indomitable will to succeed, or the ones who understand the power of delayed gratification. Just because you can physically outduel another person in a challenge does not mean you will be successful. It cannot be predicted who will win in America from the beginning: which company will become the dominant one ten years from now, which team will win the Super Bowl at the beginning of the season, or which presidential candidate will win at the beginning of campaign season. Maybe *Survivor* had more to do with modern American society than I initially believed.

I did tons of research on the topic. I felt I already knew about *Survivor*, so I also watched a show I found very interesting that had a season run on the Discovery Channel called *The Colony*. It was supposed to represent what it would be like for a small group of people to start civilization over in an urban setting, after a major catastrophic disaster. The show started its participants with a few days of isolation and sensory deprivation before they were released into an abandoned part of New Orleans after Hurricane Katrina. They had to survive a few months on their own in close quarters. I think it was even more of a sociology experiment than *Survivor*, because they intentionally created scenarios to test their little society, such as having invaders come to take their things, bringing in a small group of people to beg for supplies, having a couple of people ask the group to take them in, etc. They even had a couple of psychologist/sociologist/ anthropologist types comment on what happened in the show. Slowly, my idea of our own *Colony/Survivor* experiment began to take shape in my mind—complete with tasks and challenges that would be used to show the students the sociological elements I was attempting to teach in my class.

Next, I designed the challenges to incorporate a variety of learning styles in my classroom. I always tried to hit as many learning modalities as possible, but I, like most teachers I know, always struggle to fit in many of the modalities of learning into my lesson. It seems that the kinesthetic, 3D spatial, etc. learner is always left out the most. I feel that modern industrial style school is just not set up to handle these types of learners effectively. This was my chance to use relay races, singing competitions, dance-offs, drawing, problem solving, building, creating, etc. in my class and also make them fun, challenging, and competitive. Often, the type of student who excels in the average public school class is the verbal-linguistic learner. The ones who always prosper in our system are the people who are good readers, writers, and spellers, and know how to answer written test questions, ask questions in class, and respond in written format. Most classes never give the kid who can build a machine, sing a song, or create a dance the chance to be the smart kid or star of the class. I envisioned a class where the verbal-linguistic kids would fight to get the students who could balance well, solve a riddle, and analyze a problem on their team. If done correctly, this experiment would help all types of students learn to use their unique gifts and skills in a way that most classes never would.

I also purposefully created challenges that would strain ties within the group. This was a sociological experiment, after all. I used all of the aspects that we learn about in sociology (in group, out group, leaders, followers, group speak, sociological imagination, sociological perspective, role conflict, role strain, etc.) and tried to make sure they became part of the game, so the students could experience them first hand. It started the very first day, when I nominated two students to be the team captains. They had to pick their teams by making alternating choices. It was really interesting to see the different leadership styles. One leader was very outspoken and basically chose the members himself. The other captain was very soft-spoken, and basically allowed the rest of the team to tell her who to pick. It was also very interesting to see which students were picked and in what order. Was it popularity, a previous relationship with the captain or other members, intelligence, etc. that determined the choices? I told each team to pick a name, hand sign, and celebratory chant or cheer. They were both creative (and we all had a good laugh), and when they were finished, I told them to go back to their seats. The thing I remember most about that day was, as they were walking back, this one boy looked over at the other team and yelled, "You all are going down!" I was amazed at just how quickly people can adapt to roles. It had only been a couple of minutes and we had all been one happy family for weeks before the game began, but since we had chosen teams, the competition factor escalated and split the class almost immediately.

After the students picked the teams, we all sat down and discussed what we learned just from picking the teams. We had a very interesting discussion about leadership styles, popularity, and outcasts. I purposefully created games that strained ties within a group. I planned some games where certain segments of each team had to be left out of the challenge, while others got to participate just to see how that would happen. How would the teams choose who participated and who did not? Would this create tension? Sometimes I would exclude certain people from being eliminated if they did not participate, forcing the group to think about sitting out the "weaker" members of their team. Other times, I would let teams choose to select someone from the other team to exchange for their own player to see if the player who moved to the other team would still feel ties to their original team. I wanted these teams to feel every emotion that a real group could feel in a real life situation, and I finally had an idea that would allow me to do that.

One aspect that did come to my mind, that had to be effectively dealt with, was the fact that people could get their feelings hurt in a game like this, especially emotionally-charged teens. What if a certain element of the team was cruel to a certain person? They could easily gang up on them and vote them out, always make them the whipping boy, or make them feel unwanted and worthless. I took special precautions to remove the vindictive element from the game. For example, I decided not to allow people to be voted off of the game. Instead, when a team lost, they would lose one of their members. The winning team would huddle around a fake fireplace I made just for the game. I would pull up a random number generator from the internet, have the members of the losing team number off, and let the generator decide who left the game. To make the winning team feel like they had some power, I would give them the choice of accepting the number of the person that came up on the first try with the generator, or the winning team could decide to run it one more time to try and get the number of a person on the losing team. This way, there would be no voting off someone because they were not liked, had performed poorly at a challenge, were unpopular, from a lower socioeconomic status, etc. It was completely random—almost.

As soon as we began playing the game, I realized the power of it and needed a few more controls to make sure that the game was a bit emotionally safer for the students. I underestimated how quickly and totally the students would become engrossed in the game. I tried to have games where the individual winner of challenges was selected or singled out, not the losers. This would keep people from feeling poorly about themselves, like they had let their team down and were being punished for it. I also tried to pick games that would allow the unpopular students to do well. If the less-popular students had certain gifts or proclivities, I would use them in a challenge. It might be drawing, paper/rock/scissors, making up rhymes, etc. With enough creative thought, I felt I had a game that would allow everyone at times the chance to succeed, insulate people from vengeful retribution, and focus on the positive aspects of the people and groups, not the negative.

After each session of the game—and many of these became very emotionally charged, passionately embroiled, and even hilarious—I had the perfect opportunity for small talk at the end of each session. This would bring out what sociological things we saw. It was so easy. I would just consider the task for the day (maybe it was a relay where each had to balance a book on top of their head) and ask them who decided who would go first, which team member they thought would be the best at the challenge, which team thought they were going to win, how unified each team felt they were, etc. I found it was so easy to get the students to engage in these discussions. They wanted to tell what they saw, what went on inside their team, and what they noticed about the other team. It was much better than any discussion about a worksheet or a reading, because these students got to discuss what they had *personally* experienced. My room had been transformed from a schoolroom to a real-life, self-contained, sociological laboratory.

In the back of my mind, I heard some stuffy bureaucrat from our state capitol. I could see him looking down his nose through his reading classes perched at the end of his proboscis demanding, "But how will you evaluate the students' learning progress?" Ah, yes, how would one evaluate something like this? It was going to be difficult. I considered that if we played the game once or twice a week, and it took an average of thirty minutes per day, this could potentially take up eighteen hours from the semester. That is quite a bit of time; much like an entire unit. I remember the words of John Taylor Gatto. He said that when real learning was taking place, it was easy to see that it was occurring—it was just difficult to say exactly *what* was being learned. How was I going to really tell how much was learned, what was learned, and which students learned it?

I made one of the best decisions of my teaching career when I decided not to really care about the evaluation. I allowed the talk-back sessions to allow me to guide them—to make sure they were understanding what they did witness and experience real sociological aspects in the game. I let the fun they had tell me the students would remember. I allowed the creativity they displayed to show me they were using parts of their brains that were often repressed in school. I let the excitement in their voices, the nervousness in their eyes, the pursed lips, and their body language guide me to realize that they were learning more than any textbook, worksheet, or test could ever teach them. However, I decided to have one formal summative assessment at the end of the game.

An essay entitled "What I Learned from the Game" would be the culmination of the experience. This is where I would allow the students to write to tell me what they had learned. With an activity like this game, no multiple choice, true/false, or matching test would do, because I did not know what to expect from it. I had no idea what exactly would be learned. I hoped they would learn about cooperation, leadership, team work, social pressure, groupthink, and so on, but I could not be sure they would actually learn those. And what if they learned other things which I had not anticipated? I did not want to shortchange them on what they could learn. Also, when I went on hikes, read books, or went to historical places on my own time, because I wanted to, no one ever gave me a test, quiz or worksheet to make sure I learned. In a way, those type of artificial assessments tend to dampen the experience. Since my sociology class was an elective, I decided to treat my students like adults who were doing something on their own time for their own gratification, because they enjoyed it. Paper or hardcopy assessments would only prove to them that I did not trust them to learn while being fun and creative. A few talks after each installment, their actions within the game, and one final essay would be the only assessments they received in this game.

I will never forget the first day of the game. When I saw all of my preparation come together, I knew I had something special. I decided to start the first day as they do on *Survivor*. Each team would make a flag (to be carried to each competition), a team logo (to decorate their flag), and team buffs (to be worn by each member). I bought two different colors of fabric and two different colors of paint, borrowed some scissors and paint brushes, and let the students have at it. It was amazing to see them working together, dividing up the tasks, creating logos, designing buffs, painting, and cutting, all in a sociology class. Of course, they got paint on the floor, paint soaked through their flags onto my table, and there were strings of cloth on my floor when they were finished; sometimes real learning is messy. At the end of the period, I had two groups of students standing with their flags, wearing their buffs, happy and smiling to be part of their group. I felt the game was off to a great start, but there was nothing that could prepare me for what would happen the next day.

It all started as the students came in the door. As one kid settled down into his desk, another walked through the door with excitement written all over his face. "What are you so happy about?" the first student asked. "You don't remember?" came the reply. "Oh, yes! It's game day!" he piped. They were both smiling and looking at one another, practically rubbing their hands together in anticipation. That is when it hit me. I have never experienced an exchange like that between students on days I had announced a test, quiz, worksheet, or even a guest speaker. The students were genuinely excited. With each new student that came through the door, the anticipation only grew. "Do we get to play the game today?" a student asked. "Can we play the game at the first of class?" another begged. "What will the challenge be?" yet another wanted to know. And all of this happened before the bell even rang to officially begin class.

After I took attendance, I said, "It looks like we are all excited about the first day of the game." A girl said, to my astonishment, "That's all my friend and I could talk about in our last class." I was stunned. When I thought about it, the whole premise was very simple. All we did was pick captains and choose teams. That takes place in playgrounds and backyards all over the world, every single day. I did not feel it was earth-shattering, but the students could barely stand the wait, they were so excited. They had been so excited they pretty much ignored their last class, because they were too busy thinking and talking about this one. I kind of felt bad for the previous teacher, like I had negated his or her entire class period with my silly game. On the other hand, I was encouraged that something this simple created so much excitement. I wondered what took me so long to think of it. I began to wonder what the students were going to do when we actually began the game.

The first challenge would be to compete in a relay against the other team while balancing a book on their heads. It seemed so simple that I felt it was a good way to start the entire experiment. Each team would simply get into a line beside one another, walk from the starting line down to the turnaround line, then make their way back—all while balancing a textbook on their heads (I finally found a good use for a textbook, after all). There was a caveat; each team would select a member to find the middle page of the book before the other members could start the relay. This would put tremendous pressure on just one team member to quickly get it right so the rest of the team could proceed. There was not as much pressure on the students in the relay portion because there were many of them and obviously the blame could easily be defrayed. Both teams picked what most teachers would consider the smartest students on the team; the students who made the highest scores in classes and standardized tests.

I demonstrated balancing the book on my head as I walked and gave the instructions: "Just put it on your head, walk down, and come back. If you touch the book with your hands or it falls off, you must return to the start line and begin again." All of the students nodded their heads with understanding. I gave them a minute to decide the order the students would go. It seemed such a simple first challenge, but I was not expecting the turn of events that convinced me I had discovered the Holy Grail of sociological education.

As the game began, it was pure joy for me to watch. The focus on their faces, the arms held out as if a tightrope act in the biggest circus ever was being executed. I yelled, "Go!" The two smart kids raced to the book and began flipping pages feverishly. The first girl to bring me her book, actually the vale-dictorian of her class, pointed to a page while anxiously awaiting my verdict. "Wrong," I said. She was stunned and hurried back to the chair to keep looking. In the meantime, her competitor brought me her book, successfully finding the middle page, and her team was allowed to begin the relay. They screamed with excitement and patted her on the back, high-fived, and slapped each other's backs with approval. Conversely, the valedictorian was at the chair struggling with her book. Again she returned, and again she was wrong. Two more times she came to me for affirmation, yet two more times she was wrong. She looked distraught, running her hands through her hair and spasmodically tearing through the book looking for the clue she missed. Finally, she came to me with the correct page.

The task was not as easy as it first appeared. Not only were there numbered pages, there were several blank pages at the beginning and the end. There were also pages in the introduction that were numbered with Roman numerals and a section at the end that was numbered separately. All of these needed to be assessed by the students before they properly determined the center page. It was not as easy as seeing there were 151 pages and telling me the middle page was 76. For the rest of the game, the valedictorian glared at me with vehemence. I knew that not getting it right the first time and costing her team precious moments really bothered her. I soon found out just how much.

Meanwhile, I enjoyed watching the game. The gasps when the book shifted on their heads and the cheers and shouts when the book fell to the ground were all such a treat for me. It was then that I realized that I was also having a lot more fun than when I gave a worksheet, a quiz, or a test. One team accumulated a lead as the contest drew down to the final competitor. The last member of the leading team was nearly down to the turnaround when the final competitor of the trailing team was handed the book. It was a very daunting task, but when I saw what he did, I was simply in awe.

The boy opened the book and placed his head into the gap between the pages, as it sat with the spine facing up and the edges of the pages nestled snuggly near his ears. The other team saw it immediately, and their faces all dropped. The boy from the trailing team took off at a very quick pace, while the leader walked slowly and methodically toward the turnaround line, none the wiser. The trailing student caught up to him quickly, and zoomed past to win the race. All of his teammates swarmed him, and they hugged one another as they jumped up and down on the sidewalk. The losing team could only look on, knowing they had been outwitted. It was a sight I never saw before in school: a group of kids so excited that one of them had solved a problem. They looked like they had won the Super Bowl. Now that the first challenge was over,

I came to realize that this game could have far greater implications than even I dreamed.

After the celebration of the come-from-behind victory, we all re-entered the classroom with the shocked and dejected losers trailing in, their eyes glued to the ground. The losing team could barely believe they'd seen their impressive lead evaporate before their very eyes, because of the critical insight of one player. The losing team would have to confront the realities of the game's first loss; they were losing a member. The winning team gathered around the tribal council fireplace and the random number generator was brought up on the overhead screen. The downtrodden members of the losing team numbered off and awaited their fate. When the number came up, all eyes concentrated on the unfortunate soul as she awaited the decision of the winning team to accept or regenerate the number. The winning team decided to regenerate, and one member's relief turned into another's terror. When the random number generator was done, another student was selected. The losing team looked at their exiled member with melancholy. They all gathered around the convicted and hugged one another, promising never to forget them even if they were in exile. They fabricated elaborate tales of how they would try to win her back from exile, if they had the chance. They encouraged her to not lose hope, the game was young, and she would always be a member of their team. I merely looked on from my corner of the room, touched by the outpouring of emotion that I had only hoped for, but I would soon come to expect as the game became more and more emotionally powerful with each challenge.

After class, the valedictorian was waiting for me. She went and grabbed the book that began the challenge and turned through the pages again. She argued with me as to why her first answer was right. We discussed it and she was wrong, but did she ever try to convince me! She seemed oblivious to the fact that despite the late start of her team, they still won. It appeared to me that what she was upset about was being proven not to be the smartest person on her team or in the class. Not only had the other team's member beaten her to finding the middle page, but another member of her team received the accolades for being witty and saving the day with the open book balancing trick. It was as if her GPA was a fabrication, and although she appeared like a strong player to the others while buoyed by the false confines of school, her strengths quickly evaporated in the very real world of the game. Maybe I should have given *Survivor* more credit after all.

Instead of that first challenge being an aberration, each challenge proved more exciting and enthralling than the last. One of the next challenges was putting together a puzzle. I had some of my boys' jigsaw puzzles at home; sixty-piece puzzles designed for ages 5-8. To make the task more intricate, I had the team divide into two groups. One group would study the puzzle pieces, but could not touch them, and then estimate how long it would take the other half of their team to actually put it together. They did not reveal their prediction to the other team. The team that put the puzzle together the fastest won the challenge, but there was one small caveat: the team that was the closest to their predicted time *received a time bonus*. I did not reveal how much of a time bonus would be awarded for the closest prediction; I only wrote it down on a piece of paper at my desk. This way, no matter which team finished faster, they would still not know who won until the predictions and time bonus were revealed.

Once again, it was very interesting to watch how each team divided itself into the group of time predictors and puzzle workers. It was also amazing to watch the two teams put the puzzle together. The first team used everyone on the puzzle working group to concentrate on a different part, and it took them nearly double the time of the other team. After watching the first team struggle, the second group decided that too many cooks spoil the soup and just let two of their members work on the puzzle. By using less students, they finished much faster. It was really a case of too many people trying to use the same resources, and they actually inhibited one another. This was a very valuable lesson for the teams: that more people do not always mean a better result. By looking at the faces of the predictors, it was also plain to see that the stress was on the group that could do nothing about the puzzle. We discussed how many times in society those who cannot really affect the outcome of an event feel more stress than those that are actually involved and can affect the outcome (sports fans versus actual players, coaches versus athletes, directors compared to the actors, and those nervous parents versus their children). No matter the challenge, the students received lessons from the real world and were having so much fun playing the game. The students began to demand a theme song be played each day they entered the room on a game day to signal it was time to get ready. I decided on "It's Time to Play the Game" by Motorhead.

Another challenge was making paper airplanes to see who could throw them the farthest. Again, the teams had to separate themselves into two groups. One group would do the folding of the planes and the other group would do the actual throwing. There were ten people on each team, so five folders and five throwers were chosen, respectively. The two teams had very different strategies, with one team choosing to have each folder create their own unique plane while the other team chose their best plane folder and then had him create five identical planes. I found the use of two such different strategies fascinating. While one group tried the time-tested "five heads are better than one" strategy, the other team rested their entire success on the mind of one student whom they perceived to be an intellectual giant. The team that chose only one person to make all of their planes won. Yet again, this was another example of how not using all of your people could be an advantage. Not only did the single designer from the winning team feel successful, the whole team experienced a sense of accomplishment because they shared in the decision to use the risky strategy. I could see that my students were learning so many real-world lessons from the game.

These were the type of scenarios that I envisioned when I first created the game. It seemed like no matter what day or challenge, if I created the right learning atmosphere, amazing things happened. Teamwork went through the roof. Each team had their own style of leadership and membership, and each had their own style of selecting people to do different tasks (like intentionally leaving people out of challenges). These are great leadership lessons for the real world. Having too many managers trying to do too much can actually inhibit productivity. People who micro-manage do not always get the best results. Having more people does not mean you naturally have an advantage for getting things accomplished. These were amazing skills and knowledge that could not have been learned if I had given traditional lectures and worksheets. This type of learning had to be experienced. The students must have the freedom to experiment, use trial and error, and even fail. There is no other way to learn in the world, so why would educators even try to use fake teaching in the confines of a classroom?

Each group was very different in how it operated, thus allowing the other team to see various ways of accomplishing the same tasks. Sometimes, the teams learned a better way from the other team that they adopted in later challenges; other times they saw that their way was superior, and they should not always try what others did. They also learned that the only real way to see if something works is to actually try it in the real world. Sure, they always chose the tactic they felt was going to produce a victory, but they never really knew its success until it went into practice. Sometimes they were dreadfully wrong. Sometimes they were exceptionally right, but still there was this anticipation until the completion of the task. What a real life lesson for them! When the president pushes his new agenda that sounds so good, no one really knows how it will actually work until it is implemented. When that new multi-million dollar college coach lays out his plan for getting his team back on top, it cannot be proven successful until his strategy and team hit the field. When that retirement investor promises tremendous yields, a person can never be sure until the decision is made to put the money into the plan and see what happens.

In the fake world that schools often create, it is as if the ending is always pre-programmed. We know what will be created at the end of the chemistry lab if all of the directions are followed. We know what kind of craft will be created if we follow the directions in art class. We know that each student in woodworking will create a bird house at the end of the project. Somehow, we are supposed to know that if every student follows the same present group of standards that each student will achieve a successful grade on some prefabricated standardized test created by bureaucrats and psychometricians in some far away capital city. Teachers need to allow students to break free from the safe confines of prearranged schooling and run wild in the sometimes scary, but always unexpected, world of real life—where they are free to create, plan, devise, succeed, and even fail.

Not only did predicting, critical thinking, and decision making explode in my classroom, but I also tried hard to find ways to incorporate all of the different learning styles of my students into the game. I remember having a couple of students who liked to doodle and draw. When the teams got down to three players each, we had a competition. After it was over and we had a winning team, instead of using the random number generator, I allowed the winning team to be the judges of an art competition. The loosing team had to draw a self-portrait in three minutes. The winner got to stay in the game, while the two whose portraits were not selected left the game. The stakes were high.

I could tell immediately that some of the students were at a loss, with limited art skills. I did not feel bad for them, though. There were many times when artistic kids felt the same frustration as they walked into class and were only allowed to use reading, writing, and lecturing to learn. Most of their tests were verbal-linguistic. This would give them a chance to be appraised on something in which they could excel. It gave those that were not artists a chance to struggle at a school task. It also gave the team of art critics a chance to learn as well. They had to consider what made a good picture, how accurate the picture was, and how all of the things they learned in art class helped create a pleasing portrait.

When time was up, and the students presented their self-portraits to the judges, something very odd occurred. One girl began to laugh at her own picture. I do not mean a nervous giggle; I mean a full blown knee-slapping, side-bursting, belly-rupturing laugh. She could not even bring herself to talk. She just handed the picture over to the judges, and allowed them to look at it for themselves. The artist's good friend was on the team that was judging. She too began to laugh. The artist, if this was possible, began to laugh even harder. She eventually stumbled over to the wall and landed with her back against it, propping herself up for support. She then slid down the wall and settled onto the floor where she covered her face and kept laughing. By this time, everyone in the room was laughing, even those who had not seen the drawing. Every student was begging to see the drawing, so they could fully appreciate what was so funny. I even felt myself begin to chuckle, although I had no idea what was on the paper. I had to move over to that side of the room so I could get a glimpse. I was surprised by what was on the paper.

The portrait was not that bad. She was no great artist, but she had tried to draw herself accurately. For some reason, however, the artist had made a very large and asymmetrical bulge on one side of her head. The students began to call this large protrusion the knot, tumor, and goiter. They even made up nicknames for the nicknames; a few days later, I heard them referring to the "goit." It was not long before the student's laugh infected the entire class. Immediately, a thought ran through my head about a conversation I had with a colleague of mine a few days before. He said his kids never had fun in his class, and school was not supposed to be fun. I whipped out my cellphone and took a picture of the girl in the floor laughing with her face in her hands. I snapped another photo of her friend, laughing equally hard. For a moment I thought I would text him the pictures to show him that school could be fun; then I decided that was too self-serving. I decided to just keep the pictures for myself, to remind me that school could be fun; it was up to me to figure out how. Now, after a really hard day in the classroom, when I wonder if I really accomplished anything at all, I will take out my phone and scroll through the pictures and re-live some of the educational triumphs that have taken place in my class.

Just when I thought that the laugh-in was about to end, it happened. The friend who was on the judging team was finally able to stop laughing long enough to squeak out a few words between gulps of air. "I think I peed on myself!" she gasped, her words trailing off into another fit of hysterics. What fleeting chance the class had of regaining its composure was gone again, as the room erupted into uproarious guffaws. As I sat and laughed too, a very striking thought went through my mind. "When was the last time the students ever had this much fun in class?" I wondered. I doubt the students had laughed that hard in a long time about anything in school, or out of it, for that matter. The more amazing part to me was that it was an art assignment that prompted this fit of joy. When was the last time anyone had this much fun in an art class, whether they were the type of students who enjoyed art or not? What was the current educational environment doing, as it sadly curtailed so many arts programs and concentrated on math and language only? The students were being robbed of intellectual (and social, spiritual, and emotional) growth by restricting their access to the arts. This one task in the game (and many more like it to come) convinced me more than ever that art classes deserve a very important place in America's modern educational system.

After the class, as I reflected on the entire situation, I fell into a melancholy stupor at my desk. I thought about what high-stakes testing was doing to our schools. Because these tests mostly focus on math and verbal linguistic skills, classes like physical education, art, drama, and music were being whittled to the bone. A friend of mine is an art teacher in a neighboring system, and she traveled between several schools; each art student only received thirty minutes of direct art instruction per week. I remember speaking with another friend of mine who told me his school had to share an art teacher with another school, and they only got him after the Christmas break. How sad it must be for many of those kids to have to wait from August all the way until January, just to receive their chance to create art. I saw how much fun my class had with the project, even if they were not artistically inclined, and realized that the chance of that happening in most schools, even mine, was fading fast. How many more art programs must die, drama classes converted into extracurricular clubs, and art teachers fired and replaced by reading coaches—just so schools could massage the numbers of the test scores to prove to some number cruncher in a faraway office that they are actually doing their jobs? I left that day with laughter in my heart and a smile on my face about what happened in my class, but there was also a frown somewhere tucked down inside at the realization that these type of scenes were disappearing from the American school system.

I returned to the class, undeterred as we continued the game. I noticed that in the coming weeks, the intensity soared. Activities that were always reserved became very intense when placed in the confines of the game. Jenga is a game we play at my house. It is always a bit unnerving, as you're wondering whether the tower will fall or not on each player's move. When I made Jenga one of the game challenges, the intensity was so thick you could cut it with a knife. As each student removed their piece, you could feel the tension mounting. To add to the pressure, I added a time limit to each round. We started with thirty seconds, then dropped to twenty-five, next to twenty, and so on. The students were nearly frantic. Some shouted support to their teammates, and others spewed negative words at their opponents. People were wiping their sweaty palms on their jeans before they took their turn, students were standing up on desks to get a clear line of sight, girls took off their bracelets to make sure their adornments did not knock over the tower. Finally, after about the fifth round, when we had a break between attempts, this girl turns around to me with her hands clutching the sides of her haggard face and said, "Mr. Campbell, I don't know how much more I can take." I laughed a bit as I thought to myself, *These students are really getting into this challenge.*

When the simple game of rock/paper/scissors was placed as a challenge in our version of *Survivor*, the innocuous and innocent game of children turned into a tension-filled room of nervous energy. The day we did rock/paper/scissors as a challenge, it was intense. Students were trying everything to win. They were staring each other down with intimidating faces, refusing to look each other in the eye, boasting, shouting jeers, and singing praises. The students who did not have their turn at the time were sitting at their desks in rapt terror waiting to see if their team would win or lose. Individuals would talk strategy with their teammates before they went up. Some stared, watching other players' tendencies and plotting strategy. It was unlike anything I had ever seen.

After the challenge was over, we had a fascinating discussion about it. Students started asking if it was better to throw one hand sign over another. A girl responded affirmatively and then started talking about some mathematical tool they had learned in advanced math that would predict which hand sign would be the best to throw. Another started talking about they were watching how often each gesture was thrown, and trying to calculate which one was most often used. Another said that their team should have counted each one thrown and plotted out which one would be best to use. I thought the students were using advanced mathematical principles, statistics, and analysis like I had never seen. What would happen if a math class started their day with this activity, allowed the kids to think about it, then played the game over again? Would the kids be able to better their results by implementing mathematical principles? Think of all the different topics the math teacher could address or demonstrate for to the students to try, and improve their results from such a simple game.

One day, I had the brilliant idea of letting the kids have an old-fashioned duel with Nerf guns. The kids stood back to back, took two paces, and fired. If they missed they had to go again, and this time, take only one pace. If they missed the next time, they only took a one-foot pace and fired. If both duelers missed three times, then they were both out of the game. The person who was shot first had to leave the game immediately. I could see the nervousness in their faces. As each student stepped to the line to duel, their hands trembled, their voices shook, and they wiped their sweaty palms on their pants. They were so nervous that one small mistake could send them out of the game. The students were also very focused on holding the gun, placing their feet, and aiming their weapon. I must admit it was probably the best challenge we ever did, because of the intensity and suddenness of leaving the game.

As with all of the other challenges, this one really started the creative juices flowing. I was not really expecting the students to analyze every aspect like crime scene investigators and engineers, but they did. Some took giant paces to increase the distance, while others took tiny ones. One student put on his oversized jacket, hoping he would appear a larger target than he really was. Others checked out the gun trigger, weight, sights, firing mechanism, trigger pull, etc. Some asked if they could fire the gun first to test it out. Other groups watched the previous duelers and then plotted strategies—like whirling around quickly but not shooting, to force the other person to make a hasty and errant shot. Students laughed, screamed, and jumped up and down; but most of all, they cared. I know they cared, because just as one girl was about to begin her paces, she bent over, placed her hands on her knees and stared at the ground. I thought she was going to pass out or be sick. When I asked if she was okay and ready to begin, she said, "I think I'm going to pee on myself."

This student with the weak bladder was not done surprising me that day. She lost; however, it was what she shared that was so amazing. When the dueling was over and we walked back toward our room, I found myself walking beside the dejected dueler. I asked her how she felt, and she replied "I think I'm going to cry." Now remember, it was one of my goals to not have kids get hurt personally or let the game become vicious. I was a little hurt by her answer, and asked her why. "You see, Mr. Campbell," she began, "I was voted off at the very beginning, and I had just earned my way back onto my team last week. I was so happy that I was back with my friends, but then the very next week, I had to leave them again." I could see she was being honest; the look on her pale face and the emotion in her voice left no doubt. I was a bit hurt that I had allowed the game to get too personal, but I also realized that she was not mad because someone had blamed or degraded her, held a personal vendetta, or tried to have her voted off through treachery. She was upset because she loved her team, worked hard to be reunited with them, and now had to leave them again. If a student was going to cry in my game, I was glad it was because they were learning a very important aspect of sociology: *there is a powerful need to be part of a group.*

When we returned to the room, we prepared for our talk-back session. I allowed her to go first, now that she had a few minutes to compose herself. She began to tell the class what she had related to me. As she continued, I heard the emotional strain return to her voice and it began to crack. I saw the tears welling up in her eyes. When she paused, I interjected, trying to save her from crying in front of the room. She put her head down and deftly wiped her tears. It was the beginning of the best talk back we ever had about a challenge The kids could really feel what I was trying to teach. When the bell rang for lunch, I walked down the hall with the girl who was moved to tears. I told her that she made my day, maybe my whole teaching career, because I had never felt that a student was so involved in the class, connected to what I was trying to teach, and so emotionally moved. She countered with, "Yeah, maybe, but I feel like a dummy. I cried in front of the whole class." I had cried several times that semester talking about sick friends of mine who had terminal diseases, my children, etc. I even told them the famous quote from Jimmy Valvano (who was dying of throat cancer when he said it). "If you laugh and you cry, then you've had a full day." I just told her that I saw her laugh and I saw her cry and she was the only student lucky enough in my class to have had a full day so far. She managed a smile, said "Thanks, Mr. Campbell," and walked quietly toward her lunch table.

I heard for years from principals that the secret to being a great teacher was incorporating the three Rs: rigor, relevance, and relationships. I think I discovered this accidentally, by incorporating the game into my sociology class. It is really easy to make something rigorous. All you have to do is make it really intellectually demanding. A teacher can easily add tons of reading, homework, details, personal projects, research, outside of class assignments, etc. I am not trying to say that those type of things are bad, but if you miss the other two, then I have found it is pretty evident those things either will not be done by the majority of students, or kids will go through the motions to get the grade they want. Many students who are intrinsically motivated will just ignore them. Early in my career, I made the mistake of having rigor without the relevance and relationships, and I had a tough class with many kids failing. The students would love my stories and jokes, and even go home and tell their parents about them, but the students were not motivated to do the extra work. I was missing two thirds of the equation.

Adding the game instantly contributed the other two aspects of the three Rs. The relationships, which were a struggle for me (and I would say many other teachers as well), were instantly embedded into the lesson. Many times, people had presented the relationship part of it as a connection between teacher and students. Yes, it is important for students to feel that their teachers care genuinely about them as individuals, but a teacher must remember that if you have thirty students in a class, there are a lot more interpersonal relationships than just those between the teacher and the students. Do not miss those all-important connections between each of the students.

The students learned so much from one another. They made friends they had never made (and possibly would never have made, if not for being placed on the same team to work together freely). They learned to trust one another when they had to rely on their teammates during challenges. Stereotypes broke down when their preconceived notions of certain genders, races, cliques, age groups, etc. exploded, due to possibly the first meaningful interaction between themselves and these groups. Some of them may even have gained one of the most important things in life, one of those things that people often say are so rare that you can usually count them on only one hand—a true friend.

I would dare say that the students learned more about themselves and their fellow students than they did about me. I am not ashamed to say that, because who says that the relationship part should only be between student and teacher? I am not the only person from which a student in my class can learn. People have the right to learn from many people in their lives. Sadly, too often in school, we try to make it about the teacher, but we should realize that the relationships between students can have a greater impact than relationships between the teacher and the students. After all, I will not be going with them to college, returning to their high school reunions, traveling with them to other classes, playing on their sports teams, becoming their lifelong friend, or becoming anyone's future spouse. Our society freely admits that the hidden curriculum of friends and peers are a major theme of public schools, yet we doom many of those relationships. How? Relegating them to a superficial and superfluous depth, by only allowing individuals to get to know each other on a surface level. Just because someone sits beside another student, is forced to be someone's lab partner for one day, or walks in a line with them to lunch does not mean that a real, true, and lasting relationship will ever develop. Teachers must give up some of their control to create situations where students can really learn about one another, and discover the importance of meaningful relationships.

Relevance is the final factor in the equation, and again the game makes incorporating this aspect very easy. It is very difficult for teachers to relay this message to students through our classroom studies. I am sure so many math teachers are tired of hearing the age old-complaint, "When are we ever going to need this?" That can be heard in so many classes, whether it be English, foreign languages, science, or art history. I have even heard it in my elective classes, like sociology. Why would learning the difference between intrinsic and extrinsic motivation be on the top of any teenager's list of most important things, much less types of leadership in groups and out groups, or the Iron Law of Oligarchy? However, when the students played the game, they discover these principles for themselves, saw them in action, and became engrossed in them because they did determine their outcome within the game. They saw how they actually were and it was very relevant to their lives, both in the game setting at school and outside of school. Instead of teachers repeating that the things we teach will be important, if we really believe it, then we need to create situations that allow the students to discover for themselves how these aspects can be important.

Because school is often conducted away from the real world in fake classes doing fake worksheets about things that usually do not matter, it is easy for kids to wonder what the connection is between what they are told is important to learn in a school and what is going on in their real lives. I remember seeing a poster hung on the wall of my high school math class, titled, "When Am I Ever Going to Use This?" Underneath those words was a chart of the forty most common jobs in America, and it had a dot under a list of mathematical principles that a person needed to do that job effectively. I remember it vividly, because beside stay-at-home mom there were about 25 dots that correlated to things like finding integers, trigonometric functions, matrices, and a bunch of other things that I did not understand. I do not know if that is true, but I felt it was false because no one ever proved it to me. I had a mother who stayed at home until I was in the third grade. My wife is a stay-at-home mother now. I would say that neither my wife nor my mom, or just about any other mother I know, can actually do the things that poster claimed. What I am trying to say is that just because a poster says it, does not mean a child will internalize it as true, see the relationship, and dedicate themselves to learning it because it is important.

I once had the English as a second language teacher for my school in the class beside of mine. He was working with two students who were born in America, but had lived in Mexico for most of their lives. Our school (and city) has an extremely small population of people who can speak Spanish. They knew almost zero English. I remember thinking that their English proficiency was growing so quickly, and they never asked the teacher why they needed to know this. They did not have to; it was evident to them they needed it. How would they communicate with their teammates in soccer? How would they talk to people at lunch? How would they text a message to a friend? How could they ever go on a date? It was obvious to them that what they were learning was going to help them every day of their lives, and they worked hard to learn as much as they could, as fast as they could. We need to make our subjects that real and relevant to our students. If we truly feel that they use math and English every day, then all we have to do is teach it in a way that they understand they will need it every day, and they will be begging for it.

If teachers are not willing to demonstrate what we teach is relevant to a student's everyday life, then we should stop saying it. The students see what we are saying as a lie and just tune it out. Belief is important because whether true or false, people act on it. As they say, "Perception is reality." To most of our students, when we say things like "Music is not important and math is, because math is what will get you a good job," no one is listening. Any teenager can think of every person they know who works with music (singers, producers, band directors, etc.) and compare them to all of the professional mathematicians they know (probably none outside of the people in school telling them how important math is). They do not believe that math is more important than music. As teachers, we must let them see it for themselves; no longer will students be left asking that age-old annoying question. If you teach it the right way, you will never have to hear that question again; if you do hear that question again, you had better start teaching differently.

"But I teach math," some argue. Sure, some subjects can be more challenging than others, but it is very easy to make those subjects relevant. Let kids get automobile accident data from the police department for the previous month and let them analyze it. They can determine the most dangerous intersection in the town, and then write up a summary and put it in the newspaper. Launch a five-part series with one article each week counting down the top five most dangerous intersections. I bet people would read that in the paper. Get data on all of the sexually transmitted diseases from the health department. Have the students analyze the incidents of the different ones and if they have the data on age, look at that as well. Have the students see which one affects kids the most at their age. Are there mathematical principles that improve the odds of winning at card games like poker or black jack? If students should ever end up on a game show and be offered a cash trade for what is behind the door, should they take it? Is health insurance worth the expense? Are lottery tickets worth the risk? There are a million creative ways, no matter the subject, to allow students to see why using the things you teach in class are important to their lives now.

"What about English?" you ask. Give them a code and ask them to break it (that can be used in math, too). Design the code where knowing the parts of speech and punctuation are helpful. You could create some text messages that made the recipient mad or confused. Have all of the punctuation removed, and then let them put the punctuation in that changes the meaning of the text. No teen wants their girlfriend mad at them over an innocuous text because they forgot some punctuation. Possibly a contract for a multi-million dollar deal between a celebrity, sports star, or musical talent could be created, in which independent and dependent clauses are of great importance. Have the students figure out which clauses depend on the others, how much the base salary will be, how much incentives change the pay, and which ones depend on others happening first. I do not know every subject as well as those who teach them, but if you are creative, anyone can create lessons that show students how what they are teaching is very important to them.

I guarantee that teachers hundreds of years ago did not have to tell children the importance of their subjects. If you did not learn how much food to feed your farm animals, the animals died and then your family went hungry all winter. If a child did not put enough nails in the barn, then it collapsed and killed all of your animals, and your family starved. If you sewed your shoes wrong, then they came apart while hiking through the woods in the snow, and you got frostbite and lost your toes. Those results were easy to understand for those students. Sometimes, in our modern society, it is harder to see the relationship between what we are teaching and the end result, which may only come years or decades after the lesson. It is educators' jobs to make sure we teach in a way that the students will know *why* they are learning our subjects.

When I was a child and our family bought our first dog, I read a manual on how to train him. The one thing I remember from that book was that if a dog does something either good or bad, it is the trainer's job to either praise or punish immediately. If you wait days, hours, or even seconds (because the dog is a puppy and has a short attention span) he will not know why he's being praised or punished. The trainer must make the consequences of their actions immediate. Teachers must do that for our young students. If you just say to a child, "Well, don't worry about it now, but in forty years you will see why it is important," you will have already lost the ability to teach the students. It is okay to say that there will be implications on down the road, but you must make some *immediate* application for the student at that point in his or her life. If you are teaching health and there is a student killed in an alcohol-related crash, teaching math and someone predicts the apocalypse, or teaching English and kids are interested in Elizabethan verbal cut-downs, use these opportunities as a place to teach related topics that tie in to the specific subject. When the teacher presents the subject matter in the right way, the students will make the connection.

It did not matter what kind of challenge we did, whether it was mental, physical, artistic, group, or individual; no matter which one it was, the kids had so much fun, really got into it, and learned more than I could ever have imagined. The most important part was the fact that they were having some type of challenge that sparked their competitive sides. Many experts say that competition in the classroom is a bad thing. To the chagrin of many a utopian dreamer, competition is a major part of human drive. Being a sociologist, I actually teach about experiments and examples from societies around the world in which competition amazingly produced enhanced results. One of the classic examples of this is called the Robber's Cave Experiment, conducted when boy scouts went to camp and were divided into teams. They competed for everything, including who would eat meals first. One group would even stand and taunt the other for finishing second, and having to wait along the wall while they received their food first. This does not sound exactly like the atmosphere I want to propagate in my room. However, the ending of the Robber's Cave experiment is the big surprise.

One day, those running the experiment turned off the water to the camp. Hurriedly, they gathered all of the boys together and told them there was another camp of boys on the other side of the mountain, and the counselors were sure that boys from the other camp had sabotaged their water supply on top of the mountain. Both groups of boys in the camp decided to march up that mountain, find the water source, and fix the problem. As they marched up the mountain the previous divisions disappeared, and the boys melded into one cohesive unit intent on accomplishing their goal. After they fixed the water problem (created when camp counselors stuffed the water pipe full of rags), the students came back down the mountain exhausted from their mission and thirsty. As they stood in line for a drink, many kids, regardless of previous team affiliation, demanded members from the other team drink first, since they had worked harder than themselves and deserved it. There is a way, like in this experiment, for a teacher to create a competitive atmosphere in the classroom that does not create academic winners and losers; instead, it only creates a scenario where the students are competing to overcome an obstacle.

Instead of focusing on making the students hate each other, I try to focus my competitions on defeating a task. Whether it was how to make and throw the paper planes, how to pull out the Jenga pieces, or how to draw a self-portrait, the real challenge is within each student or group. How will they plan to defeat the task, divide their labor pool, and struggle to overcome their own deficiencies becomes the real focus of the tasks. Using things like the random number generator, talking to them about how they accomplished their tasks after the challenge is over, and setting up the challenges so one person is not made to feel like the one that caused their team to lose, are all important aspects to making sure that both teams are unifying not against *each other*, but against the challenge itself. The game is not really about defeating one another. The game is about defeating boredom, not conquering the other team but conquering a challenge, and not about building a better plane, but building a better learning environment.

I began to brainstorm about how the element of game challenge could be incorporated into my other classes or even other teachers' classes. My math teacher friend and I devised a game that he could use in his algebra classes. He creates teams (complete with names, slogans, etc.), has them compete at different challenges throughout the week, and then rewards points that accumulate throughout the semester. He has reward challenges that allow members to switch teams and be taken off of other teams. This way, weaker teams can gain stronger mathematics students that can help them be successful. He gives more students to some teams to help them overcome mathematical deficiencies, and designs games around mathematical principles that still allow students with lower math functions to be successful at the game. Once, he even staged an epic rap battle between teams using mathematical terms. No matter how good a mathematician a student was, he or she could find out what the terms meant and work them in to a free-form rap that would win the student the title of "Epic Math Rap Master" and therefore points for their team.

Another geometry teaching compatriot of mine needed to create some relevance for his course. Zombies and doomsday prepping were all the rage at the time. It seemed that every TV channel had a show about surviving an end-of-times disaster, or a roving undead horde looking to eat some human flesh. He decided to divide his class into teams and give them a challenge each week that they needed to do in order to survive a zombie apocalypse. Sometimes, they had to find the area of their space they had chosen as their compound to defend against the zombies. Other days, the groups had to use a certain amount of money to build a perimeter around their compound, with various kinds of materials that cost different amounts of money. Another time, they had to figure out how much rain they could collect by using objects of differing surface areas. They had to calculate the rate of infection as it spread throughout a population. No matter what kind of challenge he used, it always related back to surviving the zombies. Throughout the semester, the teams accumulated points for how well they accomplished their tasks and by the end, only one team would survive the zombie apocalypse. My teaching friend found that his students worked harder, had more fun, and related math more to reality because of this project. They competed in their zombie survival game every Friday, and the students easily admitted that Fridays were by far their favorite days of the week in his class. This concept worked in my class, worked in other classrooms, and will work in any classroom *if* the teacher puts in the work to get the intended results. The only limit to the application of this concept is the teacher's imagination.

Many may be thinking how this simple game could get a teacher in trouble, or possibly even fired. Why would learning, creativity, and excitement ever be considered a bad thing in the classroom? Well, just wait until the teacher beside you figures out you are spending 20–40 percent of your class time playing games. Wait until some parent asks why you are playing games instead of reviewing for tests. What happens when the principal comes down to your room and demands to know how you are going to accurately appraise the students' learning from the game, to make sure they all receive the appropriate grade? How will you react when one of your students leaves your class, goes into their next one and asks a teacher, "Why is this class so boring? Why can't it be fun, like my last class?" Those are all things that can and will happen. It can create tension between a teacher and their administration, parents, and other teachers. The real question that a teacher has to ask himself or herself before implementing a game structure into their class is, *What is best for the students?* As long as that is the guiding principle, it is easy to discern what should be done in the classroom.

Once, I watched two students in front of the class agonizing so badly that I almost felt sorry for them. It was obvious how nervous they were. I saw red splotches on their necks, sweaty palms being rubbed together, eyes darting here and there across the room, and fingers rebelling like ten idle brats that could not be held still. Finally, the last student rose and addressed the class. "Please don't send me home," he pleaded. There was no emotion in the rest of the class. They just stared coldly at the quivering student, then took their slips of paper and began to write. After folding their papers, I collected them, walked to the board and begin to unfurl the pieces of paper and read the names on each. As I read the names, I tallied them on the board. The boy who had just made the impassioned plea nervously watched my every move. Heading into the final piece of paper, he had the same number of votes as another one of his nervous counterparts. With the final paper, I could feel every eye in that room burning a hole in me, while they waited anxiously for the name on that final ballot to be read. After pausing a few moments for dramatic effect, the first syllable of the name on the paper escaped my lips and the class went crazy. The boy who had just begged for his life slumped in the chair, a broken and spent soul. Another student leapt from his desk and began to pump his fist while the rest of the students cheered, laughed, groaned, and even banged their fists on the desks. That day was the one when I realized the ultimate power of turning my class into a game.

The victor came to the front of the class and stood graciously, accepting his applause and waiting for the gift, for which he had competed so well, to be bestowed upon him. Before he accepted his reward, he embraced the other student who had finished runner-up. They both smiled as the second-place boy raised the hand of the winner triumphantly, while a smile finally graced his lips. I reached down into a magnificent wooden box to retrieve the prize. The students all looked on with excitement. I never told them what they were really playing for, and truthfully, I don't think it really even mattered to them. Playing the game, having fun, being creative, laughing, learning, and making friends was enough for them. Since I promised it, however, the students longed to see for what they all had been competing so feverishly. As I pulled the prize from the box, everyone began to laugh, except the winning student. Even though it was only a mere cardboard crown from a local fast food establishment, he stooped low to accept its regality like any deserving knight of bygone days. He stood tall and proud and allowed the rest of the class to see his victor's crown and received a standing ovation. Any other kid in the school would have considered such a worthless trinket laughable, but not this student. Everyone in that room knew what it represented, and this young man was proud to wear it. Imagine my smile when I walked through the lunch room later that day and something colorful and out of place caught my attention out of the corner of my eye. As I turned to look, there was the winner of the game, sitting tall and proud, his cardboard crown almost sparkling in the fluorescent lights. As our eyes met, he peered back at me with a proud smile.

So, what of the angry girl at the beverage table? Well, she did not win the game, and she never got over her failure to her team in that very first challenge. I have no doubt she will remember me, my class, and that challenge for the rest of her life. She may not remember anything else I ever taught in that class, but that day will never escape her mind. A friend of mine is fond of saying, "Students may forget what you say, but they will never forget the way you make them feel." That is very true. My ultimate goal is to make my students feel something, and I know the game does exactly that. The feelings may be fear, anger, competitiveness, friendship, nervousness, or hilarity, but they will feel *something*. That student remembered that day, because she was faced with a challenge, came up with the wrong answer, went back and kept reevaluating her problem-solving process, and eventually got the right answer. Her team even won the challenge. If that is the worst experience she ever had in her educational tenure, I can live with that. I think what really happened was that she faced a real problem for the first time in her educational career, and it was so different from that which she was accustomed to that she was not prepared. The game sometimes gets messy, creates real relationships between people, and makes students care. I will wager that my students will never forget the lessons they learn from the game in my class as they begin their adult lives. In the words of our theme song by Motorhead: "It's all about the game, and how you play it. Now, it's time to play the game."

CHAPTER VII

Brainwash Your Students

As I stood in the back of the class, I knew it had to end. All of my students were facing the front of the class with their eyes locked on the Smart Board. Each held their right arm with the upper part parallel to the ground and the forearm perpendicular to the ground with their hands clinched in a fist. The tension in the air was as tight as the little fingers in their hands. Their mouths, in perfect synch with one another, all echoed the same haunting words. Where three days before we had all recited the "Pledge of Allegiance," today something more sinister had replaced it. The amazing part to me was that no one complained when I threw out the "Pledge of Allegiance" for this cheap imposter. I was saddened by how easy it was to take time-honored traditions of our culture and replace them simply with a few fancy words. That is when I knew I had to stop it before it went too far, before someone got hurt.

It was only my second year of teaching U.S. history, but I was already looking for new ways to keep the class fresh and exciting. I have never taught a class the same way twice. My brain just needs new challenges and stimuli, and I think the more I am excited about the class, the more the students are as well. I was researching that summer for something different to do the next semester, when I began to have an interesting thought. If I really wanted students to understand history, I needed them to experience it, not just read about it or memorize it. I needed to find ways to really make history come alive by putting kids in situations as close to real life as possible, so they could experience the same emotions, dilemmas, pains, and joys as those who actually lived it. Many teachers work on their weakest, least interesting lessons and units to make them stronger first. That is an excellent strategy, and the one that I had adopted over the last few years of my own teaching career. The lesson/unit that really caused me problems was often the part of history that many of my students said they enjoyed the most.

Many people will say that the Holocaust needs less work than most history subjects, because it is so emotional, interesting, shocking, and memorable; I found it to be quite the opposite. It never failed that when I talked to students about the Holocaust, they always said the same thing, "How could those Germans go along with that?" It was a valid question, but as I tried to explain the sociological mechanisms at work, the students always had the same answer: "Well, if I was alive then, I would not have gone along with that. I would have stood up and said something. I would have saved every Jew I could." I tried repeatedly with each new class to explain that there were good people back then, just like themselves, yet barely any tried to help. They just went along with everyone else and tried not to make waves. No matter what examples I used, they always disagreed with me and made it out like they would run up to those camps and cut the wire with their teeth, if necessary, and lead all of the Jews to safety—German police dogs, Nazi bullets, and jackbooted thugs be damned. I knew I was not getting through, and I had to think of a way to let them experience what was going on in Nazi Germany so they could really see how they would react.

As I scoured the internet for help, I came upon an experiment that a teacher conducted with his class several decades before. He called his experiment the Third Wave, and it changed the lives of the students who participated. This teacher tried to get his students to experience what it was like to live in a totalitarian society and feel the social pressures of the group to do what they considered wrong, according to their personal morality. His experiment caused quite a stir, and he stopped it long before its intended ending date: the kids became too engrossed in the structure of it, and it threatened to do permanent damage. It sounded like a good way to get fired (which he was, the following year). I was only in my second year at a new school, so I had no tenure. I knew if I tried it, I might end up with the same fate as the originator of the experiment—fired. In other words, it sounded like something I *had* to try.

I did not want to copy what someone else had already done, just use the aspects that I needed to create an experience the students would never forget. The Third Wave experiment (later turned into a series of articles, a book, and even a stage production) was basically a way to implement some of the social manipulation the Nazis used in Germany in a high school class. This allowed students to experience many of the same things, to see how they would react if they were really in a totalitarian state. I began to wonder if I could take children in such a hyper-individualized state as modern consumer-driven America and get them to so easily shed that independent thought process, adapting to a group mindset, as the originator of the Third Wave said. He bragged that it only took one day for his kids to become totally engrossed. But it was done decades ago, in a big city in California. Could the same principles work in a small-town high school in Southern Appalachia? There was only one way to find out, so I dove in and begin to identify the major components to a successful switch to a totalitarian state.

When one looks at how Hitler duped a nation of educated, civilized, and sophisticated people into giving up so many freedoms, one can see that his methods were quite simple; yet he achieved amazing results. Hitler tapped into feelings that every person and group of people possesses. Hitler enjoyed a wicked acumen for the social sciences, and applied them with deadly effect. *He knew the inner desires that motivated people.* The understanding of how people behave in a group was also very important to his rebirth of Germany. He knew just how to identify, reinforce, foster, then perpetuate the exact behaviors that he desired. When I finished my research into Hitler's rule of Germany, I felt the most important factors to emphasize during the experiment would be the feeling of being special, belonging to the group, self-improvement, multi-layered surveillance, group rewards, and personal gain.

I noticed that every appealing program often has an ear-tickling ring to it. I decided on the STRONG program (Students Together Reaching Outstanding New Goals.) They would be part of a program that made them academically and socially strong. I made up membership cards that had the phrase on them, and every kid would have to sign one on the first day. They were to keep those cards with them at all times, to show their pride at being selected to be in such a prestigious program. I also built credibility by creating a packet of paperwork from the originator of the program, a letter from the director of curriculum, and testimonials from teachers and students who participated in the program previously. I began to build excitement the week before by telling the students I had big news, but was unable to tell them about it until the next week. I talked about it every day, and acted very excited. The kids were tantalized each day, and were salivating by the time the next Monday rolled around.

Everyone loves to hear that they are special. People have used flattery to connive others since the beginning of time. Think back to Adam and Eve; all it took was a few words of how Eve was smart, and could be even wiser if she would only eat of the forbidden fruit. That is how people today get us to vote for them, date them, and work for them. It was a simple, time-tested tactic, and it had to be included in my repertoire. I decided to tell my students I had been working to get accepted into a foundation that used best practices acquired from many of the elite private schools to enhance learning. I told them I had been submitting samples of their work and my rigorous curriculum for several months during the application process. Luckily, we had been accepted to participate in this prestigious program, and no other school in our entire state had been selected. My class was a special group who had proven themselves worthy of high praise, and even more elevation in the eyes of respected experts. They were the chosen ones of the academic world, destined for greatness.

To emphasize group superiority and belonging, I decided to no longer give individual grades. Every grade would be determined by the group. I created a list of rules, such as everyone had to come to class with their work done, be on time, feet on the floor, eyes toward front, back straight, and bottoms of feet on the floor. If that was done, then everyone received a 100 for the day's participation. If anyone did not do one of them, the entire class grade went down to ninety, and continued to drop by ten points for each infraction. Many students liked the idea, especially those who were struggling academically. They could get a 100 just for being on time and sitting up straight? That sounded like a good deal to them. My better students were a bit unsure, but after all, they had been well conditioned by their parents and eleven years of formalized public schooling to believe I was the expert and knew what I was doing. After all, if it was done in elite private schools, it had to be effective at developing great students.

To emphasize self-improvement, I decided to create five mini-lessons, each dealing with one of the core values (which I created) of the program. The first day was self-sacrifice, the next hard work. Then we covered dedication, followed by leadership, and finally unity. I would take just the first fifteen minutes of class each day to teach that lesson, full of examples from history of how these core values helped individuals and cultures achieve amazing heights through the application of those attributes. Yes, it would mean extra work for the students to have to learn not only U.S. history, but also these additional lessons; however, if they put these lessons into practice in their lives, they would become better students, citizens, workers, and leaders. It was their pathway to use the insights of others, to develop themselves into an unstoppable juggernaut that gave them a special advantage over the rest of the population.

Hitler was also a master at giving the same job to multiple people, and then having those people report directly to him. It is how the paranoid dictator monitored everything to make sure everyone was doing exactly as he directed, and no one was plotting against him. Each of the students received a special wrist band that I ordered in our school colors. They were to wear the wrist band at all times to show their relationship in the illustrious group. If any student saw another student not wearing their wrist band and told me personally, the entire class would have ten points deducted at the next class meeting; but the person who told me of the infraction would receive ten extra points. The students were also taught the salute and told that when they met each other in the halls (this even applied to other classes, and the students would be easily identifiable by the wrist bands), they had to salute one another. To not salute a fellow member of the STRONG program would result in another deduction of ten points from the malefactor's class's grade, and the informant would receive those ten points personally. I did not need to roam the halls to make sure all students were obeying my rules; I could just get my lackeys to scour the school and do the work for me. The most amazing part was that all I had to offer them was a few measly points on a daily grade.

I also encouraged the students by promising them group rewards. I told them this was an elite program, in which few were selected to be a part. The fact that they could tell their friends, wear the bracelet, and graduate this program would be a huge reward for them in the eyes of other students, teachers, schools, colleges, etc. They would also receive something special for completing each part of the program. A class party would be held after the first week, when they completed the first five mini-lessons. Other students had parties for Christmas or Halloween, but they would receive a party because they had achieved a special academic task that no one else even had the opportunity to try. You should have seen their eyes light up when they realized they would receive such a special treat in my class. I was notoriously known for never having parties in my class. In fact, I always made a pact with my students that we would not have homework, but we had to work very hard in class—with no free time and no goofing off (of which parties were included). The students were a bit shocked and amazed, but you could see the determination in their eyes to earn the group reward.

The personal gain also enticed many of those students. All of the students were juniors and many had begun to think of their post high school futures, with many of them considering college. I told the students that when college admissions officers saw that they had completed this prestigious program, it was almost a given that they would get into the school of their choice. I even cited some data on the fake letter I handed out that 90 percent of students who complete the program get into their college of first choice. *That* got their attention. Just to be able to have an advantage supposedly reserved only for elite private school attendees was a huge draw for those college-bound students. The ability to get a leg up on every other public school student gave them the heady feeling of being elite. The big surprise for me, however, was which students really got into the program the most.

I figured the students who really cared about their grades would get into this new curriculum in order to keep their grades high. I could just imagine them going around and making sure everyone was doing their work and remembered to sit up straight and keep their feet flat on the floor. The first day of the new program, however, something very different took place. The students who always made good grades acted like their normal, grade-conscientious, teacher-pleasing selves. They wanted good grades now, just as they always had before. Basically, there was no real change in them. As the students entered that first day of the STRONG program, I saw something amazing from another group of students in my classes.

There was this one boy who was not a discipline problem in my class, but had his struggles. He had been suspended for a week for an incident on the bus. He was not disruptive and in general he was nice to me, but he often did not turn in his work and made low test scores. Basically, this boy did not like school, probably would not have been there if not for the compulsory school law, and was bored with the entire process. This morning, however, something was very different. He got in the class early, sat in the front desk, and waited in rapt attention, anticipating his first assignment. When the bell rang, all my students were there on time and ready to learn. The principal came over the intercom for the daily announcements, and when they were over he announced it was time for the teachers to lead the students in the pledge. I told the students we would do our pledge in a moment, but we needed to take our first STRONG program quiz. Their first assignment was to write the STRONG pledge on a piece of paper, word for word, as they had been instructed the day before. All of the students were working on it, but this young man was done with blazing speed and slapped his pencil down onto the desk with a loud smack as if to announce, "Look at me, I am the first one done!" I took up the papers and everyone had written something very close to the pledge. The very eager young man's paper, however, was word for word—perfect. A few students had missed a word here or there, but I figured it was pretty good, getting kids to write something that was totally bogus. I would deal with that later. It was time for the true test.

I announced it was time for the pledge, and in unison, without any dissent, every child stood to say the new pledge that morning. The struggling male student in my class was the first one out of his seat, leaping to attention. All of the others students followed. This time, instead of facing the flag in our class, we all faced the Smart Board. I had the STRONG logo up there flashing in front of the students. Every single one raised their arm in the new salute and they all had their bright orange wrist bands on to identify them as STRONG members. I was more than a little shocked that I could just make up some new curriculum, tell them a bunch of good-sounding lies, threaten them with their grades, and completely resocialize my class in one day. Just think, these students had started their day with the pledge to the flag since kindergarten, and now I could just say we were going to pledge to some fictitious program—but not one single person would say anything about it?

A very amazing thing was not only taking place within the students, but also within me. I had expected it to be a mind game I would play on the students, but as I stood in the back of the classroom and watched those students move like automatons through whatever task I put in front of them, I had a strange feeling down deep in my gut. The most amazing thing was not what was happening to them, but the feeling I was experiencing. I began to get a sensation of great power. *This is what Hitler, Stalin, Pol Pot, and any other great dictator must feel inside when they see people conform like sheep to their sinister plans,* I thought. I could understand the dark power that comes with people following your every order, no matter how silly, contrary, or sinister. To me, it was almost repulsive. A shudder went through me; I wanted to get that power out of my hands, but I decided to press on to prove my point. After all, it was for the kids.

Through the rest of the first day, the students stayed at attention in their seats with feet flat, eyes forward, and backs straight. The students earned a 100 for their behavior in class, but after I graded the pledges, they received a ninety for their work, as a few students had not known every word. The students seemed appeased that their first day netted each of them an average of 95 between the two grades (indeed, that was an A). The students who wanted their A were content, and the students who struggled academically were ecstatic with the grade. You could tell that a few of them did not have their heart in the STRONG program, but they played along because they received a better grade than usual. I was conquering the uncertainty in the backs of the students' minds that this program could make them more successful in life. After all, it had already improved most of their grades, in only one day.

I walked down the hall at the end of the first day and another teacher stopped me in the hall. "Hey," he said. "I saw one of your students with the bright orange wrist band on." The teacher told me how he asked them what it was about, and they informed him about the STRONG program. "I immediately knew it was one of your crazy experiments," he admitted. He told me that he knew right away we were studying Hitler and WWII. "That's great," he said with a big grin. "Make them think a little bit. That's what they need," he concluded. I felt a little better, knowing that at least some teachers would think what I was doing was a good thing. I was a bit concerned that other teachers (and especially parents) would only see me as a cruel teacher who preyed on unsuspecting young minds. I guess in a way I was, but the primary intent was to let the kids understand that there is something within them, within us all, that wants us to go along with the group, be told we are special, and become something greater than everyone else. I walked back to my room with a bit more confidence heading into the second day of the STRONG program. Little did I know that on the second day, a mutiny would threaten to destroy our little classroom utopia.

The assignment for the second day (again, all kids were on time and ready to learn) was for the students to memorize the words that the acronym STRONG represented. That was a pretty easy task, and all students made a 100 on the quiz. As I began to do our mini-lesson on the importance of self-belief, I noticed one student was slouching. I stopped and immediately said, "The class is now down to a ninety for the day," and looked directly at the malefactor. All of the other kid's eyes darted and found the culprit. There was a hurl of harsh words that followed. "Way to go!" "Straighten up!" and "You better act right!" were spat from the students' mouths with a white-hot rage.

Normally, I would have corrected them for being so harsh to a fellow student. Actually, I had only one classroom rule: "Respect everyone at all times, including yourself." That axiom pretty much covered everything, and in years past had always worked like a charm. My students respected me, and I them. They were quiet when people shared out loud with the class, whether it was me or a student. Some very quiet students who never really talked in other classes felt safe enough to share in mine. They knew I would not tolerate kids insulting, berating, abusing, or belittling one another. Here we were, on only the second day, and that class rule had lost its grip on these new STRONG students. I immediately felt the urge to remind the students of our class rule, but instead I kept quiet. This was what I wanted, after all. I tried to create a Hitlerian society where students did not act because they wanted or believed, but because they did not want to be different from the group. In the end, they wanted to help themselves. As much as it chagrinned me, I kept quiet and allowed the baseness to spew for a moment, then continued the lesson.

The effects of my Hitlerian experiment were taking hold faster than I realized. The students were not trying to convince the malefactor to do something wrong; instead, they were trying to use their peer pressure to make sure he did right. There was not technically anything wrong with that; however, the degree of malevolent self-serving that filled their voices was unsettling. I actually began to see my students telling the Jews and other undesirables to "Get on the train," not because they hated the Jews, but because they cared about what Hitler and his Nazi henchmen might do to them. It is what allowed the Night of the Long Knives (a mass assassination that Hitler had some of his leaders commit against others in leadership positions to maintain a feeling of allegiance within his inner circle) to take place within the Nazi party. After just one day in the program, I saw a sinister change in my students; I was not prepared for what happened next.

Minutes later, I caught another student with his legs crossed instead of keeping his feet flat on the floor. I immediately stopped and announced to the class that the group daily grade was now down to eighty. Again, the angry faces, haunting stares, and raging insults were catapulted at the offender. I almost felt sorry for the young man as he realized what he had done, and I wanted to quickly move to correct it, but it was too late. I had seen the culprit, and when

I looked at him and spoke, every one of my students' eyes had followed mine and they knew who the offender was. Even if I said something, what would stop them from remembering who he was and exacting their revenge later? I thought about what would happen to the boy after class; would the other students say harsh words, would they bump him in the hall, would they knock his books out of his hand, would they refuse to sit with him at lunch? The thought of repercussions outside of my class made my stomach begin to roll, and a lump form in the back of my throat. I pressed on, but when I spotted the third infraction in the form of a student not taking notes and just day dreaming, I still didn't suspect the class was about to come unhinged, and the whole society I had worked so hard to create was about to collapse before my eyes.

I had just uttered the words, "The class grade is now down to seventy," when a student in the back jumped up. My eyes quickly darted toward her, and when our gazes locked she screamed, "This is ridiculous! I'm not going to put up with this!" As shocked as I was, ever the meticulous planner, I had prepared for just this situation. You do not just go brainwashing children without your superior's prior approval. I had foreseen this incident happening. This was one of the brighter students in my class, and she was used to making that A. She was the type of student to not just stand by and watch her grade drop to a D (with most of the class time still remaining). Before I attempted this sociological experiment on my class, I had discussed it with the principal. We even considered the possibility that a student or two would get so distraught over this radical change in class policy that they may consider leaving the class. Fortunately for me, I was very near one of the principal's offices. We agreed if any kid rebelled, we would just offer them the chance to stay in the class, or they could go to the principal's office and the principal would hold them there until I could come down and deal with the problem. So, when the girl said she was not going to stand for it, I told her she could stay and go along with it or leave and go talk to the principal about it. I told the class the principal was aware of our new program, and he was very proud and excited for our class to get the prestigious honor. I thought that last bit might deter her, but she was strong-willed; so she grabbed her books and headed for the door. As she walked out I glared at her and spat, "You just stay down there with the principal, and I will be down after class to take care of you!" She did not have the bravery to look me in the eye as she walked past, but kept going out the door. I thought the problem was over. We had our first rebel (Hitler had his, too) and she was harshly handled. She was intelligent and strong-willed, so I was not totally surprised when she was not deterred by my warning. I was surprised by what happened next.

I glared at the class and they all looked terrified. Most of them had never seen a verbal exchange like that between a teacher and a good student. We live in a small town, where teaching is still a respected profession. We have very few problems of this nature in our school, and several quiet students had their mouths open wide and lids straining to keep their eyes in their sockets. I was about to get back to my lesson, when I saw movement to my right. Another student stood and gathered his books, and was heading toward the door. It was a boy who only came to school about two days a week. He had never been a problem in my class, but he'd previously had several run-ins with the administration over discipline that had landed him in detention, in-school suspension, and even out-of-school suspension several times. I did not ask him where he was going since it was obvious, I only warned him. "There is room for you in the principal's office, as well." He said, "That's fine," and out the door he disappeared. I looked at the class and asked, "Does anyone else want to join them and stay with the principal?" Not a person stirred.

I must say I expected a student focused on grades to be unsettled, when they realized they would be penalized for the bad behavior of the other students and saw their grade falling. What I had not anticipated was the student who had nothing to lose. This boy cared nothing about his grades, would most likely drop out when he turned eighteen, and possibly, if he cared enough, go get his GED. He knew the principal on a first-name basis, and loved getting a few days of vacation from school. So he had nothing to lose by bucking the system and getting in trouble. At the least, it would get him a reprieve from class: at most, a reprieve from the entire educational system that irked him so much. The ironic thing is, I had a solution to both kinds of students, and the solution was the same. All I had to do was go down to the principal's office and get both students back on board. When the class was over, and I rushed down to the principal's office; my heart skipped a beat, as the students were gone and the principal was nowhere to be found.

I began to panic. I told my friend, the assistant principal, to hold them there. If they were not there, it must have been because he was not in his office. So, now where were my students wandering? I took a guess that they had gone to the main principal's office. Again, not a big deal, because I had informed the head principal of my class experiment as well. I hurried down to his office, but when I turned the corner to where I could see inside his door, there was no one there, either. There was only one more principal's office to check. I convinced myself they would not go to this last principal. He was not over curriculum or discipline, and was not very visible. He was really over paperwork for teachers like Individualized Education Plans (IEPs), services for students with disabilities (504s), and teacher evaluations. As I quickly walked toward his office, I was pretty sure they would not be there, and I began to worry that they were still missing. As I got closer to the last office, I imagined my students so mad they left school, walked home and told their parents of this foolishness, and were right now speaking to the central office administration or worse, the television news. Finally, I arrived at the last office, and I found out that I was just in time.

Behind the desk was the older principal. He had his elbow on his desk and his head in his hands. His eyes were bugged out and he sat there shaking his head as he faced the students with their backs to me. When I flashed in front of his door, the principal lifted his head from his hands and looked me in the eye. An expression appeared on his face that looked like he had just been saved from certain doom. The students, noticing his gaze, turned to see me and stopped talking. I walked in and shut the door. "I am sorry," I began. "I told every principal in the building but you what I was doing," I continued. "I will take these students off your hands and fix things," I promised. "I was just doing an experiment in my class," I ended. He did not say a word, he only looked up with a perplexed smile, glad to know the horror was over. I motioned for the kids to follow me.

When we left his office, we entered into the lunch room, and I told the students to take a seat on one side of the table. I sat on the other side facing them, and began to explain. "I am so proud of you!" I lauded. I explained how I was doing an experiment to show the class how Hitler brainwashed people into following his ideas. When I had finished they were both smiling and laughing. "We wondered what was going on," said one. "I was so mad at you! I thought you had gone crazy," said the other laughing. Then I told them I needed their help. No one else in the room had bucked the system. They were all being tricked, just like the German people. I needed them to play their part; I needed to continue the experiment to see how long I could fool the rest of the class, and how many students would continue to go along with it. They seemed pleased to be in on the whole thing, and eager to help continue fooling the others. I promised them that they would receive an A for the entire unit because they had recognized the ruse, and had the guts to get up and walk out of the experiment—unlike so many German people. I told them we needed to keep it secret; they were only to tell their fellow students that they had indeed been sent to the office, and Mr. Campbell and the principal had taken care of it. They agreed to only repeat that statement, return to class, and continue to play along like good little students. Little did they know, they were the biggest dupes of all.

You see, there were many in Germany who did not fall for Hitler's plan. They realized what he was doing from the beginning. Some people opposed Hitler, and they were all imprisoned (remember that the first concentration camps were built for dissenters, long before they were built for the Jews or other "undesirables"). That caused many to not speak up, out of fear. Many of Hitler's inner circle, however, knew what was going on. The reason they did not say anything is because they were part of it. They had been convinced by Hitler that their lives would be better if they played along. Hitler made them feel special, because he gave them a promotion, a title, or a uniform. He let them in on a secret that many did not know. They were awed, knowing that they discovered the truth, and enjoyed the benefits of being in a special group. What they had not realized was they had become the worst ones in the entire society. Many did not know the true motives of Hitler. Most of the public did not consider the dastardly end game. So many thought that it was all a bunch of coincidences, and no one could intentionally be that sinister. This core group of people knew the motives behind the truth and decided to become part of the entire scam, knowing all along that their actions would lead even further down the path to destruction. Why should they care? After all, they were getting a pass (or in this case, an A). Who cared what happened to everyone else?

Now that I had the students re-entangled in my web of deceit, I had to make sure the assistant principal knew what was really going on in my room. I walked back into his office, and he was still disheveled. "Sorry those students bothered you." I began to tell him of the entire plot, how I had informed the other principals, and sadly how I had not expected the students would ever go all the way down to his office. He seemed very relieved, as the corners of his mouth began to twitch upwards and the spark returned to his eye. "I bet you were wondering if I had gone mad down there in my room." I said. "Yes," he said. "I just could not believe the story they were telling me. I didn't know what to say, because they were so mad and it was so unlike you. I was just trying to let them speak their piece and get calmed down," he said. I told him there was nothing more to worry about, and he seemed much more at ease when I left.

I walked back to my class with a wicked grin sprawling across my face. I must admit it was fun playing such a huge prank on the class. It was empowering, getting the students to go along with and even believe anything I told them. It was amazing how even the students who were rebelling one moment, could easily be brought back into the fold with the simple promise of an A and telling them they were in a special group. I began to really feel like Hitler felt, I imagine. It was a very profound sense of power, knowing you could control of others' lives with such ease. I walked back to my class, happy that my experiment would continue—but also a little sad. I was sad that more students had not complained. I was upset that nearly every student was still following blindly. I was crushed that they gave up their pledge to the American flag without a fight.

I sat in my room silently for a long time after the last bell had rung. As the laughter and chatter died away in the halls and left me to my thoughts, I began to question if I was cut out to be a dictator. Sure, fooling people is a fun game to play, but when you realize the disturbing truth about fellow humans, the fun soon vanishes. It is not fun being in control of an experiment that shows you how easy it is to get people to do whatever you want. It is painful to know that most people will put a swastika on their arm, a bullet in someone's head, a dissenter in a camp, and a Jew in an oven. Maybe some people would enjoy being the head of such an experiment, but not me. I quickly realized that maybe the person who was being affected the most was me. Maybe this experiment said more about the kind of person I was, instead of the kind of people my students were.

Sadly, I began to consider stopping the STRONG program after only two full days instead of letting it run the entire week as planned. It was a hard decision for me to make. I had put so much effort into it. I had three more mini-lessons to teach that I had spent hours creating. There were so many more valuable lessons to teach my students that would show them an even deeper understanding of themselves. By the time the week was over, they would feel like an actual German made to look inside the ovens at what they had allowed to happen. The real question that began to haunt me was what was I doing to them down deep inside. What would happen to them, when they realized the bright world in front of them was really very dark? How would this experiment, if continued, affect their religious beliefs, relationships with others, and most importantly, their relationship with themselves?

I wrestled with the decision all night. I told my wife about it when I got home. We discussed it while we ate supper and did the dishes. She told me it was my Frankenstein's monster. If anyone was going to kill it, it had to be its creator. She was right. It was a mess that I had made, and I had to make that decision. As I tried to sleep that night, numerous images came to mind. I saw students writing down their strong pledges. I saw kids wearing their bracelets with pride. There was the kid who was so excited about it, sitting on the front row in rapt attention. I saw the two rebels smiling on their way back to class as they agreed to go along with something that five minutes ago, they were so angry about they had stormed out of class. The most haunting image of all was being in the back of the room and watching every student stand, raise his or her right arm, and pledge to a program that they had only known for a day, turning their backs on the flag they had known their whole lives. When I awoke from my restless sleep, I knew something had to be done.

I went into work that morning somewhat melancholy. I knew the experiment had to end, but I was unsure how. It was kind of like a bad romance that had run its course, yet I did not want to be the one to break it off. I thought about the right way to do it that morning before school, but nothing spectacular came to my mind. As the moments until that first class ticked closer, I began to get cold feet. I started to second guess and think about all of the work and how far the students had fallen into my web of deceit. Did it really have to end now, or could it go just one more day? The bell rang before I could decide, and the students filed into the room. There, waiting on them, was the STRONG logo flashing on the Smart Board. Strains of Wagner's "Ride of the Valkyries" (Hitler's favorite) hauntingly echoed from my room. The students walked in, sat straight with feet on the floor, and awaited the day's lesson. Instead of meeting them at the door as usual, I just sat in my seat in the back of the class and watched the opera unfold.

I could not make up my mind if it was a comedy or tragedy. On one hand, I felt like when I told the kids they might all start laughing. As I explained what happened, they might say, "Oh, you really got us, Mr. Campbell." Then we could all have a good laugh, and talk about what we had learned. They might force a strained smile about giving up the pledge so easily. Most likely, they would feel a tad silly for walking around saluting each other in the hall. Maybe at their ten-year class reunion, they would all fondly remember the STRONG program and all sit around telling funny stories about their experiences. I began to consider the possibility that the high drama I saw unfold in my class was no trifling matter. Maybe it was the darkest of tragedies that would shake these young people to their very cores.

Maybe when I told them there would be no laughs at all. Maybe the students would just sit silently and reflect on how they had so easily been duped. Possibly those sensitive female students would cry, thinking they, too would have tended the ovens, guarded the fences, and forced Jews onto the trains. Maybe the boys would feel sad that they were not the big, strong, young men they thought they were growing into, but little sheep just following orders. When they looked into my eyes from then on, what if they only saw a twisted, sadistic old man who got his jollies warping young minds, instead of a man that was trying to help mold them into thinking young people, who could spot a sly trickster from a mile away?

Before I had too long to think about it (and time to finally make up my mind what to do), I was startled back into reality by the ringing of the bell to start the day. Immediately, something happened. All my students snapped to full attention in a standing position, raised their right hands in a bent salute with bright orange bracelets gleaming, and started chanting the STRONG salute. I quickly jumped up and caught up with them, but no one was looking at me. They were all focused on the flashing STRONG logo on the Smart board at the front of the room, but out of the corner of my left eye I caught Old Glory sagging sadly in the back of the room. The flag had been abandoned. The students had turned their backs on her. She only hung there silently and listened while the students who once saluted her every morning now saluted something new, cold, and sinister. The lonely flag was a sad reminder to me of what I had done (and was doing) to those children. That is when the voice in my head said it had to stop.

After the students finished with their pledge and sat down, I walked to the front, stopped in front of them, paused for a second, and decided to use one visual to help me. I pulled up a picture of a cart full of dead bodies from a Nazi death camp. Gathered around the bodies were the citizens of a local town nearest the camp that had allowed this atrocity to happen. The American soldiers forced them to come and see what they had permitted to take place in their own back yards. Most of the people looked away, stared at their hands, or looked at their shoes, unable to make their eyes see the awful reality. I felt this picture would help me show them that my students were actually just like those people. It was a figurative example of what I was trying to do with my experiment. I was the American military, forcing the common people to see what they had allowed to happen so they could believe they were special. As the students looked at the picture, it gave me just a few more moments to find the perfect words; but no matter how much I thought, only one simple sentence came to my head.

I looked around the room with the students in rapt attention, poised myself, then simply stated, "There is no STRONG program." There was no reaction from the students. It was as if I had not even uttered a word. I continued, "I made it all up. This was only an experiment that I did." I paused to look around, and a few of the students started looking at each other nervously. A couple smiled, but there was no real reaction. It was as if they thought I was pranking them, or maybe they did not want the program to end. I went to my desk and pulled out the packet of information I gave them at the beginning of the experiment. "You see these letters I gave you?" I asked. "I made them all up. There is no STRONG program!" I yelled. Nearly all of the students began to look at one another, and a few whispered to one another. There was one student, however, in the very front (the one who had been so excited at the beginning of the experiment) who just sat quietly and looked down sadly. The reality spread like a ripple over the classroom. I saw students begin to question one another, then finally several looked at me. They asked me, "Why?"

I told them it was all to help them understand. I gave them the long version, hoping they would understand my reasoning. I recounted how so many students every year say they cannot understand how the German people fell for Hitler's propaganda, how they say the German people were dumb, and how students always say they would never fall for a ruse like that. I told them I had to trick them, so they would understand how the German people had been tricked. I had to show them how powerful our natural human drive is to be a part of something special, to be told we are destined for better, to be convinced we are going to rise above everyone else. There were a variety of emotions plastered across the faces of the kids. Some were shocked, and sat with eyes wide and mouths ajar; some smiled, as if they knew the joke was on them; some looked upset that they had been lied to; but the ones I noticed the most were the ones who just sat quietly.

There was a family friend in the class. She was one of the nicest, kindest people you could ever imagine. Her dad was the same way; he was the kind of guy that would do anything for you. She sat at the side of the room, not doing anything. She just had a dreadful look on her face, as if she was going to be sick. I quieted the class, and I asked her to share what she was feeling. She put it simply, "I feel like I've been punched in the gut." Then she followed with, "I think I am going to throw up." She revealed she was totally crushed, realizing that she was no different than those Germans. She fell for it because she wanted her GPA to go up and colleges to see her as more worthy of acceptance; she'd thought it would prepare her for the future. She looked at me, then sadly at the Smart Board with the cart full of dead bodies, then down to the floor. I had been successful. One student had gotten my point. I wanted to help young people understand that the Germans were not dumb or foolish. It was human nature to want to be part of the group, to be told you are special, and to follow a leader who knows all the tricks. However, there was still much more to be revealed.

The boy who was not a very good student and had become so engrossed with STRONG spoke next. "I am not going to lie, I am kind of sad it is over. I was more excited for this than anything I have ever done in school," he conceded. I knew he was more excited about the program than anything we had done in my class, but to hear a boy of seventeen say it was the most exciting experience he had ever had in twelve years of schooling astounded me. I was just overwhelmed thinking that nothing, no play, no sporting event, no field trip, no special teacher, etc. had ever come close to the feeling he got being told he was allowed to be part of something special. "I normally don't like school, but I was really excited for this. I guess that means I would have been the first one in line get my Nazi uniform and put someone in a gas chamber." he said as he let his gaze fall to the floor. I could feel his heaviness, as he realized how easily he would have succumbed to the ploys of Hitler. The students were really starting to get it. Just as I started to feel proud of myself, the next hand went up.

"Can we still keep doing this if we want to?" wondered the next voice. I was shocked. Who would want to continue this madness? I had just told them that doing it in the first place revealed that the students in the class were no different than the people who allowed and even helped put millions of people to their gruesome deaths. I guess I just kind of looked at the young man in the back of the room who had asked it with a puzzled expression, because he soon answered my unspoken question. "Some people might not have liked it, but those were the best grades I have ever made in a class" he explained. True, he normally did just enough to pass. To him, sitting up straight and repeating a few words while wearing a bracelet was much easier than studying, completing study guides, keeping up with class work, etc. The sad part, however, was what it implied about his character. He did not really care what it said about his personal ethics; he was just concerned with doing well in the class, no matter what happened to the grade of others. More importantly, he did not care what it implied about what he would have done if transported back in time and place to 1930s and '40s Germany. I realized I was receiving a lesson, too. This served as a sad reminder that under the right circumstances, an event such as the Holocaust could still happen in modern America. What is scarier is that people like this young man would be okay with it, as long as they got something better out of the deal. I hope the rest of the class was listening, as he gave them another layer to the lesson.

Finally, it was time to reveal the lesson of the two rebellious students. "Where are my two rebels?" I asked. Everyone looked at the two students who walked out only yesterday. Those two held themselves in an air of confidence, not connecting what they had done as possibly more sinister than the rest of the class. "Would you guys like to share with the rest of the class what really happened when you went down to the principal's office?" I prodded them. The talkative girl, worried about her A, took the lead and told the entire story in detail. When she was finished, she had a conceited smirk across her face. "Thank you," I said. "*That* is why those two are the worst offenders in the entire class." Her jaw dropped. "What are you talking about, Mr. Campbell?" She protested. "I walked out. I knew about the whole thing. The only reason I even came back is because I wanted my A," she defended. It was time to reveal the sad truth.

"So, you were the only person to know the truth about what was going on and you still agreed to come back?" I asked rhetorically. "You knew none of this was really going to benefit you or anyone else, as far as your GPA, college placement, or future success, but you still agreed to come back? You were more than happy to let everyone else be tricked so you could get the A I promised," I prodded. The smirk was now gone from her face. "Hitler had people like you," I reminded her. "They were called the brown shirts, the SA, the SS, and his inner circle," I informed the class. "They were the ones who knew the truth about what Hitler was doing, yet they went along with it because they got their special uniform, a position of leadership, or a political reward," I spat. "Who do you think got put on trial in Nuremberg for the crimes against humanity committed in WWII: the average German who did not really understand the evil truth behind the propaganda, or the ones in charge who knew the truth?" That was my final salvo. It was all that was needed. Her self-absorbed ship had been sunk, and her spirit was listing as the rest of the students watched the maritime tragedy of her soul.

In the end, there was lots of sharing, debate, and embarrassed or ashamed young people. Our group discussion about the implications of the STRONG program went on for about thirty minutes, then it was time for me to wrap it up. "Don't tell the other students," I implored. "I plan on doing this again, possibly next year or the one after. I am going to need your bracelets back so I can use them again," I said. After all, they were $1 a piece—which added up quickly, for my two classes of students. My eye caught one boy toying with his bracelet, yet he made no attempt to actually remove it from his wrist. Finally he sheepishly raised his head and his hand. "Mr. Campbell, can I keep mine?" "What in the world would you want that cheap, bright orange bracelet for?" I asked. "Well," he replied, "I want it to remind me of the kind of person I am, how easily I was tricked, how excited I was to be part of something special, and how I am no different than the Germans." I was moved. The tone in his voice told me that a cheap bracelet could serve as a powerful reminder, to a young person ready to start their lives in the adult world.

I saw a few heads shake with agreement. The point the young man made was totally valid. Yes, these bracelets would most likely make their way into the cup holders of unkempt teenage vehicles and sock drawers. Wherever they ended up, one day they would be found again. When they were, the teens would pull them out, think about the STRONG program, and remember the powerful lesson they once learned from a slightly insane young school teacher who was willing to risk getting fired to brainwash them into the most powerful history lesson they would ever have. Of those who had removed the bracelets, some returned them to their arms. Some young ladies put them in their purses, while others dropped them into their backpacks; not to be forgotten, but to serve as later reminders of what man is truly capable of doing.

The best lessons are the ones not read, copied, memorized, or drilled into students' heads. The real ones that change lives are the ones they experience. These types of lessons have the students actively chasing the education, instead of the education chasing them. These are the type of lessons that stick with kids for a lifetime. I sometimes ask myself, "What will these students remember about my class at the ten-year high school reunion? What stories will end the phrase, "You remember that time in Mr. Campbell's class when...?" I know it will not be my "amazing" lecturing skills, worksheets, pop quizzes, or study guides. No student will ever say, "Man, do you remember how awesomely phrased question number seven was on that second unit test? What a teacher!" I guarantee no one will ever hear, "Remember that time Mr. Campbell covered three state standards with one lesson? That was incredible!" Students will not remember those things. What they will remember was the time someone made them think, the time they got to experience, when they made a connection with another person, and when the teacher created an environment where they could learn something about themselves on their own. John Taylor Gatto once said, "The greatest type of knowledge is self-knowledge." The teacher who provides the opportunity for this greatest form of knowledge will never be forgotten...no matter how hard the students may wish they could.

The teachers at our school once had to go to an in-service on creative teaching. We had an amazing former teacher who led our instruction that day. He showed us amazing lessons for the most difficult subjects. As we left for the day, I overheard a fellow teacher tell another, "Sure, those lessons were great, but I bet each one took two hours to prepare, for a one-hour class." It was the way it was said that caught my attention the most. The person said it as if implying that putting more time into planning the lesson than giving it was ridiculous. Realistically, that is the way great performances take place. All sports teams spend more time practicing than playing the game, singers spend more time making an album than the listening time of the final product, stage actors spend more time rehearsing lines than the length of the play, and advertising executives spend more time making great commercials than the running time the public sees on TV. For a teacher not be willing (or allowed) to spend more time creating a great lesson than it takes to deliver it is ludicrous, and out of touch with the real world.

Those creative lessons take tons of time to plan, require tremendous creative power, and could get a teacher in serious trouble or even fired, but the payoff is immeasurable. I remember working on that letter I gave the students for hours, to make it look legitimate. I had to develop five new mini-lessons (three of which were never even used). I had to buy the wrist bands, create a pledge, write the fake testimonials from other teachers who had tried the program, and do tons of research. I planned that lesson for weeks; I was a bit disappointed that it ended after three days, and I did not get to continue it for the planned one week. I guess I wanted all of that hard work to be used. Then I realized that it did not matter if it was all used, as long as the goal of the lesson was achieved. An effective teacher must be willing to go to great lengths to create an atmosphere where genuine learning can take place. What I have found is that the more effort that goes into the creation of an amazing and authentic lesson, the less work the teacher does during the lesson. I did not have to bombard the students with worksheets, study guides, tests, quizzes, journal entries, and group activities to chase them with the meaning of the lesson. I just watched for rule infractions, presented the mini-lesson, gave out the bracelets, and then let the real learning happen. When I revealed the truth, the lesson was evident to the students because they taught *themselves* the lesson; I was just the "innocent" bystander.

Sometimes, the version of me that is now five years older, more mature, and wiser looks back on the STRONG brainwashing experiment and a shudder runs through me. I get a little unsettled, thinking about all the things that could have gone wrong. Some kid could have gotten upset and told their parents, who would have gone over the principal's head and called the school board or the director of schools. I cannot even imagine what the director of schools (a proud Vietnam veteran) would have thought if he heard a teacher was not letting his students pledge to the American flag any more. I can imagine one of those parents who is very involved in their child's education getting very upset that his straight-A daughter was receiving a D, just because some other kid did not sit up straight. I think about what would have happened if someone had actually looked it up online and found that no such program really existed, and confronted me with that information in front of the class. There was so much risk involved with this experiment but looking back, I have no regrets.

In the classroom, the old adage, "With big risks come big rewards," still applies. If teachers are not careful, they will become safe. Safe is not trying anything new, unusual, dangerous, or passionate. If we overthink the classroom, we will make ourselves say that they reward is not worth the effort, time, or risk. "What if a kid gets mad? What if a parent comes to the school? What if someone calls the newspaper?" some may fear. It is just that much more important a lesson. When was the last time a student became so emotionally invested in what was going on in the classroom that they let their emotions get the best of them? When was the last time you could look parents in the eye, and tell them that you are doing something in your class that would change the lives of their children and turn them into people who can never be deceived? When was the last time the newspaper came to school and demanded to know what you were teaching, because the community was interested? How great a story would that be, when you told them the truth and let them print that you were doing something creative to change the youth of the community into thinking adults? Instead of seeing only the risks, consider the much greater rewards that go along with them.

Consider what will happen if you choose to not push the envelope of education. How else will young people learn how easily they can be tricked by a smooth-talking person in power? Who else is going to teach them that they cannot belittle other cultures for falling for ruses for which they would have also fallen? What else can show them if they have the power within themselves to stand up and say that something is wrong while everyone else goes along with it? The question is not if these lessons should be taught, but how they should be taught. These lessons must be taught through experience; not preached from the lectern, read from the book, copied from a worksheet, or selected from the multiple choice answers. This is real learning. Real learning is not delivered in nice, neat, sanitized, safe little packages. Real learning is messy, dangerous, and scary, but there is no substitute for it. People never forget it, and once students taste it, they only want more.

"But how will you evaluate if the students are learning?" many will ask. You cannot just give a true/false, multiple choice, fill in the blank test to evaluate this type of learning. Matter of fact, if you ever do use one of those forms of evaluating, you cannot really tell if they learned anything, either. Someone can make 50 percent on a true/false test and not know anything. So, although those prefabricated forms of evaluation appear to be objective instruments of assessment, they really aren't. I prefer to allow them to write an essay about what they learned. Allow them to write an essay with titles like, "What I Learned from STRONG," or "Would I Have Been a Nazi if I Lived in 1930s Germany?" Essays allow you to really see if a student internalized the lesson or made the application. A writing journal could be used; The students could write one at the beginning of the program, after each mini-lesson, immediately after the reveal, and the next day after they have had time to reflect. However, writing assignments are not the only way to access learning.

With lessons that have this big an impact, there are many ways to evaluate the lessons learned. Incorporate math by analyzing the number of people who spoke out against the program, and then research how many people spoke out against Hitler's programs and compare. Use psychology or sociology to find other sects, cults, and total institutions and compare ways they gain control over members. Compare Hitler's style of political power to other totalitarian dictators like Mussolini, Stalin, Pot, Japanese imperialists, and so many others. After the research and comparisons are made, have students create computer-based presentations, display boards, take over one of the bulletin boards in the class, etc. Basically, with lessons this creative, you want the evaluations to be equally as daring. Do not settle for mundane assessments that do not truly allow students to show and express what they have learned, how they have been transformed, and how their lives were challenged by the lesson. In essence, strive to be just as imaginative in your creation of assessments as you were in the creation of the lesson.

The sobering truth, however, of a learning experience of this magnitude is that the real impact cannot be measured quickly. The full impact of the lessons learned will not be able to be adequately evaluated by the end of the week, semester, year, or even four years of high school. The real results of lessons like this are not fully appreciated until ten or more years later. The true results of real lessons will not be measured until the students grow into adults. How they live their lives by the lessons they learned and the things they were taught will be the ultimate result of this type of lessons. Maybe more importantly, it will affect the children theses students will rear and the lessons they, as parents, instill in the next generation. The ultimate evaluation comes when we look around decades from now, and see what kind of community, culture, and civilization has been created by the students that we turn out of our classrooms.

In our fast-paced world of instant gratification, waiting decades for proof that a lesson worked seems to be asking too much. Possibly in a world where everyone has to score their points before their political term is up, their tenure as a judge has passed, the quarterly profit margins have been announced, the play clock has struck zero, or the TV time slot has ended, most people do not seem content to wait and see if what happened makes a real difference. If one considers the governing document that the American founding fathers wrote, the military maxims of Napoleon, or the religious teachings of Jesus Christ, it becomes obvious that the important things of the world are never measured by their impact over days, weeks, or even months. It is the test of time that really determines the impact that something has on the world. Do the standardized test pushers of the educational world like that kind of answer? No, because then student data cannot be tied to end of the year teacher data, end-of-year teacher data cannot be tied to performance bonuses, then performance bonuses cannot be tied to school grade cards. If we really want to change our country (and world) by using our educational system, we have to divorce ourselves from this quarterly profit model of success and realize that real education, as John Taylor Gatto put it, "Should teach you how to live, but more importantly, how to die."

As I think back on that class and the educational journey on which we embarked, I wonder if their lives were changed forever. I contemplate if they will be better parents to their own children when that time comes. I pay attention to the newspapers, look around when I go to the local retail store, and scour the playgrounds when I drive by. I am looking for proof in the real-life assessment that my lesson carried its meaning forward. Maybe it is too soon to tell if the STRONG program's attempt at Hitlerian-style brainwashing really worked. However, I think back to the last day of class that year. As I said my goodbyes to all of those students and watched them walk out of my classroom door, I caught a glimpse of something. It was a bright orange bracelet dangling from the bony wrist of a young boy. It hung there as if to tell me that the lesson had lasted far longer than probably any other I had taught, and there was hope that it would last for decades, permeating future generations. Only time, and the difference it makes in our community, will really tell.

CHAPTER VIII

Make Your Students Die

My first year of teaching, I had a student die. He was only a freshman; I remember when I heard about it, I thought, *Students are not supposed to die.* Nothing any professor in college taught me prepared me for how to deal with this. I could prepare a detailed lesson plan, create a unit plan that covered all modalities of learning, and arrange review questions with every level of Piaget's hierarchy of learning, but I had no idea what to do in a situation like this. I remember sitting at my desk before school, thinking *What am I going to do?* I had no idea what to tell my class, although I felt something needed to be said. After all, a member of our class would never return. You just cannot hide an empty desk, a missing face, and a vacant body. Every time you call the roll where his name was, students will remember that he is missing. The aspect that made this more difficult was that I had his older sister in another one of my classes. In years to come, I would find that this death was not like the other student deaths I would experience, where I went to the funeral and talked to the parents; yet after I left, I had no constant reminder staring at me in class every day. I made up my mind to go to the funeral, no matter how difficult, and try my best not to cry; beyond that, I was at a loss as to how to handle the situation.

As I was walking into the church where the funeral was being held, I saw several of my students in the parking lot. I enjoyed talking to them and trying to encourage them with a smile, a funny word (my go-to tactic with students), and a brief pat on the back. I entered the church and nestled myself into the line trailing from the door to the casket. I looked around to see if there were any other adults I knew, community people, friends, teachers, or coworkers; there was no one. I would have to stand there alone, in a very long line. As I got near the front, I made out the family: mom, no dad, grandparents, what had to be aunts and uncles, and of course his sister, who was in my class. As I got very close to the casket, his sister spotted me. She immediately bypassed several people and came to me. "Thanks for coming, Mr. Campbell." She said. "It's no problem,' I replied, trying my best to stay composed. Then she said something that would break my heart, and give me a lesson that follows me to this very day.

"You know you were his favorite teacher," she whispered, with a smile. With that, I lost all control. I broke my gaze and my eyes flitted around the room, glanced at the floor, and danced across the ceiling. I felt my lip begin to quiver and a tightness entered my chest. I told myself, *Look at her!* It was so hard to look back at her face, which reminded me so much of her brother's. Finally I did, but I was not prepared for what came next. "You know, you are the only teacher who has been here." She said, not really angrily or judgmentally, but more in a matter-of-fact tone. My soul was crushed. I completely lost it. I felt hot tears begin to stream down my face. I could not really talk anymore, and she knew it. I was nearing the casket anyway. Thankfully, it was a closed casket.

I soon met his devastated mother and introduced myself. I tried to tell her how much I enjoyed having her son in class, how full of life he was, how glad I was I got to know him for just a little while, and how much I would miss him. I shook a few more hands, and said a few more words, but I don't really remember who they were to or what I said. I was still in shock from one of the most heart wrenching statements I had ever heard, one that would change my life and drive my teaching for the rest of my career.

As I walked out the opposite aisle of the church, the sister's words haunted me. They played in my head over and over again. I was relieved when I got inside my car. I loosened my tie, took off my coat, turned on some air, and breathed deeply. I laid my head back, staring at the ceiling of my car, and heard those words washing over my mind again and again, pounding against my brain. "You are the only teacher who has been here." It just kept echoing inside my head. *How could this be?* This was the second semester of school. He had four teachers last semester, and four this semester. He had all kinds of teachers from elementary and middle school who knew him and loved him. Surely they knew; it was a small town, and word traveled fast. They had to have seen the paper and heard the talk. Fourteen-year-old boys just do not get crushed by motorized all-terrain vehicles every day, in our town. Maybe it was still early. I looked at my watch. There were still a few minutes before the receiving of friends closed. I looked around the parking lot, yet I saw no new cars pulling in, no teachers I knew walking into the church. It had to be a mistake; surely no kid in a small town from a little high school of only 600 students could die and no teacher come to his funeral. It couldn't be that no one cared. No matter how much I tried to reason with myself, her words stayed with me: "You are the only teacher who has been here."

All of the way home, I just kept thinking on what she said, rolling it over and over again in my mind. I am not really sure how I drove home that day, because when I eventually did arrive at my house, I don't remember anything about how I ended up there. My brain was on autopilot, too busy thinking about the important things in life to worry about driving me home. I still could not believe that no other teacher would come to his funeral. I knew his other teachers, and they were good people. I taught with them, grew up with some of them, and knew that these were not cold, callous people. There had to be an explanation for it, but I could think of no possible reason for only one teacher attending. My mind began to ask an even more haunting question that stays with me to this very day, and has been one of the thoughts that has guided my actions on several occasions. *What if I hadn't gone?*

If I had not gone, there would have been no representative of this boy's school, which he had attended for almost an entire year for seven hours a day, five days a week. Surely, if a person spent that much time in a place, with sup-posedly loving and caring people, he would get to know them on a personal basis. He probably spent more time at school than he did at home (when you take out time for sleeping). I know he listened to me talk more than he listened to his mother talk. Ninety-minute classes give me a lot of opportunity to talk, after all. I know his mother was expecting to see his teachers, his principal, the bus driver, maybe a custodian, even. She only saw me. But what if I had not gone? His mother probably felt that public school was a joke. They say they love your kid; they say they're going to look after your child when they are with him. There is even a law called *in loco parentis* that says the school is supposed to act as the parent when they have them and the parents are not around; yet his parent was at the funeral and the school was not.

I could not help thinking that it all must seem like such a sham to his family. The school says they care, but at the most critical time in his life, the last chance they had to show that love and caring, no one showed up but me. I am not trying to put myself on a pedestal. There is no bragging here. I did not go down there to be the only representative of the school, or to make all of the other teachers look bad. I did it because I was scared. I did it because I did not know what else to do. I think now that maybe I should have gone to the house the day it happened. The least I could have done was called before the funeral. I could have given a donation, taken some food, sent some flowers in our class's name, but I did not do any of that. I just went and stood in a line for a few minutes. I am not trying to elevate myself above everyone else, but I am glad, and yet ashamed, that at least I did the minimum I could have done. Still, I could not help but think that when their mother got her daughter ready to come back to our school the next week, she felt she was sending her off to a bunch of heartless teachers who were only there for a paycheck. I wondered if that girl got physically ill when she looked into the faces of her brother's teachers who did not even come to his funeral, yet had the audacity to say they cared about their students.

Yes, this family and one of my students received a very personal lesson from death, but how many students have? I was nearly 25 years old before this happened. My students needed to know what it was like, as close as we could get to it, without really having to experience the tragedy itself. I knew how much that single event in my first year of teaching had impacted me. I was aware of how it had changed my life forever, and been my guide throughout my teaching career. I did not want my students to have to wait until they were 25 years old to finally have an experience with death that would change their lives and their thought processes. They needed to have that experience as soon as possible. How many stupid mistakes would my students make consciously between the ages of 14 and 25 while saying, "I'm young; I've got plenty of time; it's no big deal; I have all the time in the world to fix this; no one will even remember in ten years." I needed to help them have an experience that would help them see that death is real. A person does not have to be old to experience it; you do not have all of the time in the world; people will remember; it is a big deal; and sometimes you can't fix it (no matter how hard you try).

Yes, the study of life was important, but the study of death was more important. I know because my father saw the sister of that young boy who died my first year teaching, in a local restaurant a few years later. I am not sure how she recognized my dad, but she did, and she immediately came up to him. "You're Mr. Campbell's dad, right?" she asked. When my father confirmed, she said, "You know, he is my favorite teacher. He was my brother's favorite teacher, too. I will never forget him. He was the only one who came to my brother's funeral." When my father told me that, it was just further confirmation that I had to do something. I had to find a way to make my class about life and death. The students needed it, I needed it, the community needed it, and if one family could be saved from the crushing blow that an institution supposedly designed to help kids will not even show up for one child's funeral, then it would all be worth it.

Years later, I saw his sister out in town. She came up to me and talked for a few minutes. She told me she was in school, studying to be a nurse, and everything was going great. She even remembered a few things from class. Not lectures, worksheets, or quizzes (of course), but mostly crazy things I had done, like the time I had almost killed Bitsy. She never mentioned her brother or the funeral, but we both knew. Some things do not need to be said. A few years later, I saw her again at a restaurant in town. She was with her husband this time; when she got up from her table to come and speak with me, she was in her nursing scrubs and pregnant. We had a great talk about how well her life was going, how her family was growing and she and her husband were so excited. Again, there was no mention of her brother, at least overtly, but when she put her hand on my shoulder and said, "You know, Mr. Campbell, you will always be my favorite teacher," I knew what she meant. It was not because I was the best lecturer, created the best worksheets, or made my pop quizzes more of a surprise than anyone else. I think it was because, in some small way, we faced the overwhelming experience of death together.

A couple of years later, there was a girl who was not in my class, but I knew her name and face from just being a teacher in the school. Her mother died, and remembering my earlier lesson, I was determined to go. What if I was the only one, after all? I asked a friend of mine who taught next door (he did not have her in class either), and we agreed we should go. I recounted the previous story on our twenty-minute trip to the funeral home. We made a pact that we would always try to go to any student's (or their family's) funeral, whether we had them in our class or not. As we arrived, there were a few cars in the parking lot already. At least that was a good sign. As we entered, there were several people standing around, but as we made it to the room that allowed us to see the casket, I was shocked by what I saw.

There was the fifteen-year-old girl from our school, dealing with the death of her mother (without the presence of a father), and she was standing all alone. I was in shock. I had never seen just one person standing by a casket before. Usually there are too many people around that casket, but not here, not on this night. As we entered the room with the casket, there was one other person there for moral support; sitting off to her side was her fifteen-year-old boyfriend. I was shocked. If you know anything about teen-age love, let us just say it can be fly-by-night and fleeting. I appreciate the young man standing by his girlfriend, but they had only been dating for a couple of weeks (and would not be dating a few weeks later). She really had no one with any real, strong connections there to support her. As my friend and I approached the casket, something even weirder happened.

I have never been at a funeral when I was the only one at the casket, but that is what happened. The girl who was standing by herself did not see us, and walked out the side door. There my friend and I were, left to visit the body of a person I did not know, trying to support a person I barely knew. We both stood there awkwardly for a few minutes, stared at this strange face, and walked back out of the building, only finding a few teacher friends of mine to speak to on the way. I later found out that she had a couple of aunts who were at the funeral. However, they kept stepping outside to smoke; that is actually where she went, when we approached to check on where they were. You may ask if I am glad I went, considering the person I went to support did not even know we came. Yes, I am glad, because the point was not to be seen. The point was to make sure there was at least one adult from our school there to show that someone cared. As I mentioned, there were several other teachers already there when we arrived, and I was glad to see it. There is no doubt that this girl can say, "More people from my school came to my mother's funeral than my own family."

A few years later, I had the misfortune of having two students whose fathers passed away in the same week. That had never happened to me as a teacher before, and to have it occur twice in the same week was quite rare. The first one was rather painful for me, because I inadvertently broke the vow I'd made when the student died during my first year of teaching. I must admit, sometimes I can be detached for a teacher. My family does not take the local paper, and my class is so far out on the fringes of the campus I often miss much of the daily hustle and bustle of the school. I had a very good student miss a day in my class. That is no big deal, but then he missed a second day. That was unusual, for a good student to miss two days of school in a row. Luckily for me, he had several close friends in that class whom I could ask about him. I asked if he was indeed absent that day, which they confirmed. Then I asked if he was sick, and they all said, "No." I just figured he was maybe out of town with his family, and if anything was amiss surely his friends would have told me. The next day, at lunch, my fellow teachers were talking about his dad passing away, and going to the funeral. I was shocked. How could no one have mentioned that? How could his best friends not have said anything, especially when I gave them the chance?

I was totally in shock, and also saddened. Yes, I was heartbroken by his loss, but I was also crushed because I had violated my maxim of always going to the funeral for a student or the family of a student. I had not violated my code intentionally, but it felt the same to me on the inside. I immediately wondered how his mother felt. He only had four teachers that semester, and I had not bothered to even come to his father's funeral. I had to rectify the situation as best I could. During my planning period I called the home, and his mother answered. I told her who I was, explained the situation, and begged her forgiveness. I even told her about my experience as a first year teacher and how I had come to develop my credo. She was a very kind lady, and so gracious to accept my apology. She explained her husband was sick with cancer for years, and they had expected it for a while. She told me that it had been hard on her son the past few weeks, to which I was amazed because he had presented a calm façade at school. She only asked me to do her one favor.

"Keep an eye on my son at school, will you?" she implored. "You know these teenage boys," she said. "They are so good at not letting their parents inside to know how they are really feeling." She was spot-on in her analysis of teens. "I just worry about how he's going to deal with it, and that he won't let me know how he's doing," she confided. The other end of the phone got quiet, then I heard her sobbing. It really hit me hard, and I too began to cry quietly at my desk. The cry I should have had at the funeral had not been allowed to escape. I gave her a few moments to compose herself, and I gathered myself as well. I asked if he and his friends were close (I was doubtful, since none of them told me about his father's passing), and she assured me he had good friends to talk with and comfort him. It's always good to have friends to talk with when you are going through a tough time, but it's good to have an older person with a few more years and a bit more experience to confide in as well. I was determined to hold up my end of the bargain; it was my repayment, for not coming to the funeral and breaking my oath.

The young man missed several more days, during which time I scolded his friends a bit for not letting me know what the young man was going through when I gave them the opportunity. "Sorry," they offered. "You asked if he was sick," they countered, and protested, "we thought you knew." I think I got the message across that they were to tell me if anything tragic happened to a classmate in the future. The next week he returned to class, where he naturally had missed some assignments. I told him that when he was ready we would work on them slowly, because I knew he had other classes to take care of as well. Frankly, I felt a bit foolish even working with him to make up his missed work. How silly my class work seemed, in comparison to what he was going through. One morning, he showed up to my class before school to work on some missing grades. This time allowed me to make good on my promise to his mother and vindicate myself, at least a bit, in my own eyes.

I heard the knock on my door at about 7:15 that morning, a full thirty minutes before school started. When I opened the door, there was the young man I was expecting, looking as he always had. He was still the tall, thin, quiet boy hiding behind his glasses and forcing a small smile when he talked. I let him in, and he took his normal seat in the class, about ten feet away from my desk. I gathered up all of the papers he needed, and told him what material we had covered in his absence. Then I prepared myself to make good on the promise I made his to mother. I told him I was sorry for missing his father's funeral. "My mother told me that you called and why you missed. It's okay," he reassured me. Then I told him I also had no idea his father had been sick for so long, and I was sorry I had not done anything to help the family during his illness. Again, in his quiet way he told me it was fine. He had not told many people about it, so he did not expect me to know. Then, I told him if he ever needed anyone to talk to, someone who would not judge, someone who could keep a secret, someone to yell at...whatever it was, he could come see me. He looked sheepishly at me and then the floor, then said, "Thanks." Then I asked him the one question that caused the first real change I had seen in his expression the entire year.

It was a simple question: "How are you doing?" That's it, just those four words. Judging by the way he responded, I think he had been waiting for someone to ask him that for a long time. He looked down, closed his eyes, and began to sob in a quiet way; if you couldn't see his body trembling, his shoulders shaking, and his hand come up to cover his mouth, you probably wouldn't have even known he was crying. No sound was made. My mind immediately flashed back to a educational psychology professor I had in college, who told me that nothing was as emotionally powerful as touch. I left my chair, quickly crossed over to his seat, pulled up a desk as close to his as I could, and just put my arm around him. There was a flood of tears from his eyes that washed away years of hospital visits; seeing his dad deteriorate every day when he went home; the painful talks his dad gave him about becoming the man of the house; the times he saw the weariness in his mother's eyes; the times he had screamed into his pillow, praying to God his dad's cancer would go away; and the times he'd told everyone he was okay, when what he really wanted was to cry while someone put their arm around him. Then I learned something that my college professor had not told me about the power of touch.

Touch is powerful not just to the person receiving (in this case, the hug), but also to the person giving it. As soon as he put his head down into both hands, I too felt the tears begin to flow down my own cheeks. I didn't say much for a while. I'm not sure if he even knew I was crying, until I spoke. I tried to say some words that didn't sound preachy, but let him know it's okay to cry, get mad, get sad—to grieve. I also told him that it was normal to not truly understand a moment like the passing of a family member for days, weeks, or even years, when the full gravity of it sank in and the visits, preachers, meals, and condolences stopped. Mostly, however, we just sat quietly, and cried together. In a few moments, after we were finished crying, we wiped our tears, shook hands, and agreed that if either of us ever needed it, we were to meet again before school, lock the door, and just have another good cry. We both smiled, and he went on to class that day. We never did have another pre-school crying fest; I can only hope it was because he did not need it.

The next year, because of my location in the school, I did not see the young man very much. He earned a scholarship though, in golf, and went away to a college in a neighboring state. It was doubtful that our paths would cross very much in the next few years, if ever. When I went back to school the next fall, I learned something interesting. His mother was now working at the central office of our school district. When the end of August rolled around, and I knew that her son would have left for college, I called the central office and asked for her. She seemed a little shocked to be hearing from me again, but quickly remembered who I was. I asked her how she and her son were doing, if he had gotten off to college, and if she missed him. We had a short talk, and it seemed that all was going well for them both, but then I had to let her know that I had not forgotten my promise. I told her that if he ever needed me, I was still in the same place, still getting to school early, and my door was still open to him if he ever needed anyone to talk to, someone who would not judge, someone who could keep a secret, someone to yell at, whatever it was he needed. Even if it was just to meet again before school, lock the door, and have another good cry, he could come see me. It was the least I could do, for violating my oath.

I know what you're thinking. *I thought this was a book about lessons so outrageous that you could get fired? What's so crazy about helping kids in tough times?* There is nothing crazy about helping kids, but it is the impact these life and death events had on me that made me determined to work them into class. This lesson landed me in trouble with some people. I decided that these moments of life and death implications were when real life lessons were learned. They were educational experiences that would never be forgotten by my students or myself. These were times that students would look back on in twenty years and say, "I will never forget the day..." I had to try and recreate these experiences of life and death in my classroom as often as possible, and that disturbed quite a few people.

I have always loved teaching World War I. I am not sure why I love it so much; it is such a sad and depressing war. Just men staring at mud, being physically beaten down by the mundane madness for years, until their spirits and youth were crushed. I love the poetry, too. The violent, dark, and depressing lines of Owen, Sassoon, and the other Lost Poets are my favorite. Poems of rats, shell shock, gas attacks, and the slaughter of millions have for some reason always fascinated me. When I teach, I do not just focus on what state standards and standardized tests tell me are important. I also teach what I love and feel is important to me. For some reason, I believe that if I loved a subject, some of that love will rub off on my students—and it does. So, even though there is very little about WWI in our textbooks, I teach it longer than any other unit in our course of study, and the students love it.

I decided years ago that since WWI was fought by people not much older than my students, I would try to place them in a situation as close to that of the soldiers of WWI as possible. For that unit, we do not sit in desks or chairs; we sit in our trenches with ramparts made by upturned desks shielding us from the enemy. There is a no man's land between each side that only I can breach, in my god-like narrator status. We have a theme song that plays every day when they enter and leave the battlefield, titled "Life, Birth, Blood, Doom." (If you have never heard it, it is a literal assault on the senses, just like WWI.) We write letters home to our parents, boyfriends, fiancés, brothers, sisters, and politicians. We snipe at each other with paper wads; we make propaganda posters; and we fly our handmade airplanes over the trenches. At the end of the unit, we review by answering questions that allow one side to bomb the other, "killing" their soldiers. However, that isn't what the students remember most.

The first day of the unit, the students make their own paper gas masks. The first year I tried it, I just gave them a gas mask that I drew on a sheet of white paper. What I noticed a few days later was that some students had cut theirs out voluntarily. The next year, I decided to give the kids scissors and colored pencils. The students spent a lot of time customizing them to include eyes that see through the glass panes, graffiti, camouflage, etc. Some kids even began putting string and yarn on theirs, making straps to hold them around their necks so they would always be ready. Some even cut out eye holes and used elastic to hold them to their faces, so they would always be prepared. And what was the grand reward for all of their trouble? They received five bonus points on their unit test if they survived. It was not very much reward for all that work over a two week period, but the real reward was they survived WWI.

I would call out, "Gas attacks," and the students had five seconds to get their masks in front of their faces or they would "die" in our game. I call the attacks during class time at first, and manage to kill a few unprepared soldiers. The students who die early on tend to lose theirs, cannot get the masks out of their bag in time, etc. After a couple of days, I start to call the gas attacks all over the school. At lunch when they are carrying their trays, during class change, in the bathroom, and anywhere else they think they can escape the horrors of war. Before long, we transition to the hand sign for gas attack (extended arms, tapping the shoulders with both hands). This requires them to not only be listening at all times, but also to be watching. No matter where I move in the room, the kids' heads are on a swivel, watching my every twitch.

By this time, over the half of the class is dead. Perhaps they could not get their backpacks off their shoulder, into the floor, and masks out and onto their faces in five seconds. They did not bring their mask with them to lunch. They left their mask at home. They did not see the sign. In other words, they were not attentive soldiers. However, there are still a few good soldiers out there, and the last few days the game becomes so real that some have said they feel like they are getting PTSD. Once I was at the mall doing some Christmas shopping with my family, when we stopped in the food court. Across the way, I saw one of my students from that class. She was with her dad and brother having a meal. I silently stalked across the food court, skulking behind columns, lurking behind crowds of giggling teenage girls and hiding behind flower pots, until I was right behind her father. I stepped right behind him while she was talking to him, and so as not to cause a panic in the mall, signaled gas attack. I saw her lift her gaze from her father's eyes, stopping mid-sentence to stare at me; all of the blood drained from her face. Her father, noticing the speechless, jaw-dropped expression turned to see me. With a wicked grin on his face, he then looked back at his daughter. I thought I would have some explaining to do, but to my surprise he smiled, knowing full well what had happened. That's when I realized his daughter had told him all about it. He understood everything—the mask, the attacks, the hand gestures, every detail—because his daughter had told him. You see, when you make your class a matter of life and death, teenagers do strange things they'd never do otherwise—like talk to their parents about their school day.

Once during that unit, our school had our annual intramural volleyball tournament. When the winner of the homeroom classes was determined, they played the teachers in a game in front of the school. So, there I was on the front line, knees bent and swaying, ready to receive the serve, when under the net my icy stare meets that of one of my students. He says casually, "Mr. Campbell," and points down to his sock. He reaches down into his sock, pulls out a folded piece of paper, unfolds it and holds it to his face. It is indeed his gas mask. "Go ahead and call it, Mr. Campbell. I am ready," he sneered in confidence. I was elated. Even when he was having fun, he still came prepared with his gas mask. He was a good soldier worthy of surviving.

Once a girl came into the class one morning, and she was frantic. "Mr. Campbell can I have another gas mask?" she begged. "I am sorry" I replied "we don't have any more in the commissary. What happened to yours?" "Well, I took mine to work last night (she worked in a local restaurant), because I thought you might come in to eat. I even had it in my pocket, so I could grab it in an instant. I was making a pizza by the window, when I see this bald head (evidently my most distinguishing feature), and I thought it was you. So I whipped out my mask to get it on before you came in the door and killed me, and that's when I lost it," she said. "Lost it where?" I asked. "In the pizza sauce. It landed right in the tomato sauce, and I pulled it out to be ready, but then saw that the bald head was not yours. I took it to the sink and tried to clean it off, but it fell apart," she said, almost in tears. She began to rummage through her notebook and then pulled out this red crumpled piece of paper that I could not even tell was ever a gas mask. It was disintegrating, falling apart. There was no way she could cover her face with it. "So, can I please have another one?" she pleaded. "I'm sorry," I said, "but the store room is all out. We were supposed to get a new shipment in today, but the road was cut off by the heavy bombardment last night and the lorries have not come up with supplies yet." She trudged to her desk with the wadded-up, tomato-stained piece of paper and flopped down, waiting for the inevitable.

The students get so involved in this game of life and death that they begin to feel the emotional strain of survival. I remember we read several poems and discussed what was called "shell shock" in WWI. The strain on soldiers to survive death in a war-torn environment has always taken its toll. In the Civil War, it was called "soldiers' heart;" in WWII, sometimes they said, "He stood too close to the cannons;" and today they use post traumatic stress disorder, or simply PTSD. No matter what you want to call it, people are put under tremendous mental stress when they have to worry about death coming from all angles. It seems the uncertainty of not knowing when, where, and how your death will come, but expecting it any second, frazzles the psyche of those individuals. After a couple of weeks of constantly looking over their shoulder in class for me, watching for me at work, doing school work while darting their eyes around to look for the gas sign, being sniped at and bombed by classmates during review games, and being "killed" at the mall, the kids actually began to feel the strain as well.

I never really thought that a game could do that; one day a student of mine helped me realize it. He came into the room, and I was just standing beside the door. As soon as he rounded the corner from the hallway into the room and saw me standing there, he jerked his arm up to his face as he already held his mask prepared. *A good soldier,* I thought. There was something in the way his head was snapping around looking for me, the frantic way his hands moved, and the bulging in his eyes that made me take special notice, but then he told me something that confirmed my suspicions. "I feel like I've got shell shock," he said. "I'm so nervous. I take this gas mask everywhere, in every class, just waiting. I can't stop looking for you to walk by my other classes," he confided. I smiled a little inside. I am not trying to really scar the kids (although sometimes they may have their doubts), I just want them to get a little taste of what it is like to feel unknown but certain doom searching for them. They were starting to get it, but I was really surprised by what I heard next.

"The other day," the student continued, "when I was at home, I thought my dad was acting just a bit weird. He was just looking at me, with his face a bit too happy, like he was up to something," he explained. "I became convinced that you had called my dad and told him to call a gas attack on me at home," he said, to my total amazement. "The whole time I was in the shower, eating supper, and even sleeping, I thought he was going to run in and call an attack." The boy was becoming paranoid. The good news for him was that he only had one more day to survive, and then it was all over. I was amazed by how deeply these students were adapting to their pretend roles as soldiers. They were actually experiencing the same emotions as real soldiers, albeit on a much smaller and less deadly scale. *For what?* I thought. *Five measly points on a test?* Then it came to me that it was much more than just the meager grade bump that drove them. I dare say if there was no grade attached at all, they would still feel and react the same way. There is just something innate about the challenge of living, the will to survive. It makes all of us, students included, want to continue to be part of the group. Once a student of mine, who had woodworking class later in the day, asked if he could make a wooden plaque with all of the survivors' names on it to hang in the classroom. I thought it was an excellent idea. A student was so motivated by an activity in my class that he wanted to use his natural proclivities in another class, to create something to show his pride in having participated in mine. I was honored.

Never underestimate the desire to live, however, because it can get you fired. Once I had this girl in my class who was a total type-A, a go-getter: 100 percent grade motivated. She didn't just have to get the A, she needed the 100. I must say she was not the most intelligent student I ever had, but her drive to have perfect grades was overpowering. She would do anything to achieve it. She once made a 99 on my test (no easy feat), and asked what she could do to improve her performance in my class. Her oldest sibling was a doctor, the next was a college professor working on his doctorate, and she was not backing down from the educational gauntlet they had thrown down. At times, this drive of hers became a bit unnerving for me. I saw that she was more focused on grades than learning, which bothered me, but I could not foresee the problem this would turn into with the gas masks.

This young lady was sitting in the lunch room selling yearbooks at a table with a friend one day during our WWI unit. I walked by on my way to eat lunch, and I immediately planned my attack. Lunchrooms, the gym, and the hallways are great places to catch kids without their gas masks. I snuck up behind her and called the gas attack. She jerked around, yet remained seated, open mouthed—with nothing to do but await her impending doom. As I counted down the five seconds on my fingers and got to zero, she jumped from her chair and screamed "No fair! I'm working for the yearbook. You never said you could kill me in the lunchroom. I'm not even in your class. I'm still alive!" I saw the veins bulging from her neck, the red in her face, the clenched fists, and I knew this girl really wanted her five points on the next test. I just walked away...smiling. The next day she actually came into class with her mask in front of her face like she was still part of the game, but when I listed the surviving soldiers on the board, she was not one of them. She just dropped her mask and glared at me for ninety minutes. I could feel the flaming stare burning holes in me the entire period.

She came in the next day pouting. She would not speak to me, did not want to answer questions in class, stormed out of the door as soon as class was over, etc. I even saw her boyfriend in the hallway; he looked scared. I knew him from another class of mine, and he said that she had been emotionally torn up all week because of it. "She has been talking about nothing but that crazy gas mask and how you cheated for days!" he confided. Sensing potential trouble, I developed a plan. The midterm was coming up, and I try to call all of the parents at that time just to let them know how their children are doing, and talk to them a bit about how the class is going. I figured this would be a good time to talk to mom, and make sure she understood my side of the story (not that teenage girls ever get worked up and tell anything but the truth, whole truth, and nothing but the truth). I sure am glad I called!

When I talked to the mother, she was very kind. She even started with, "Oh yes, Mr. Campbell, she talks about your class all the time, especially lately." The girl in my class had shared with her mother what was going on, and believe it or not, it was pretty accurate. Her mother told me that she had been crying the past couple of days since she "died," and she had been talking with her about it. However, her mother totally understood what I was trying to do, and was 100 percent behind me and the lesson I was trying to teach. The mom even told me her daughter was there in the room with her and listening to our conversation, so she understood that her mother and I were on the same page. It was a bit of a relief, because sometimes type-A kids and their type-A parents can be a bit touchy about grades, especially with my antics, but it was good to see that there would be no potential drama with the parents and the school.

Something else her mother said was that her daughter did not like history. She said it was boring, and had even waited an extra year to take it, compared to most of her classmates, because she just dreaded the monotony and boredom so much. However, here she was talking to her mother about a subject she had never enjoyed, crying about dying in a game she had never liked, and upset she did not get to live on in the WWI experiment, which she had never wanted to know about before. By the end of the class she had gotten over it (amazing what time can do for a teenage girl's frame of mind), and I even learned something else amazing from her boyfriend.

It was nearing the end of the school year, and he came rushing up to me in the hallway one day between classes. "You're never going to believe this, Mr. Campbell!" he said. He began to tell me how he called his girlfriend the night before, and when he asked her what she was doing, she told him something that he could just not believe. I thought it was going to be making a voodoo doll of me and sticking it full of pins, but amazingly it was not. Instead, she was watching a television show on the History Channel with her father. The boyfriend knew how much she always disliked history, and he just had to ask her what was happening. "I thought you hated history?" he asked. "Well, I used to, before I had Mr. Campbell's class," was her response. Then he told me the best part was yet to come. "You'll never believe what show she was watching!" he said, eyes widening and even standing up on his toes in excitement. "A World War One show!" he blurted, with hands upraised. "Can you believe it?" he asked. Actually I could not believe it at first; then it started to sink in.

If you make your class a matter of life and death, kids will want to live. It does not matter if it is a class they usually like, something they dreaded taking, or even a topic they deplore; the drive to live will make them get involved. That was the key for this assignment. It was engagement and involvement. It made them feel like what happened was relevant to them, personally. It was real learning, not fake; their actions had an impact on the outcome. No one was really going to die; five points on a test was only going to make a decimal point's worth of difference on their final average. Yes, it really was just a stupid piece of paper drawn to look like a gas mask—but that wasn't the point. The point was that it was life and death, just like it was in WWI for real people. They feared dying, just like those men had so long ago. They wanted to live to see another day, just like their great-great-grandfathers had. When they realized that their lives were cut short, it mattered. I think I never really considered how impactful this lesson would become to kids, but I had a few more experiences to go before I finally grasped the power of this teaching technique.

One thing that really surprised me is the lasting impact it had on the mindset of my students. I often see the students from my U.S. history classes the next year, when they are seniors. I know they have a lot of important stuff on their minds in their senior year, like college, jobs, sports, the opposite sex, hair, clothes, video games, the opposite sex, the ACT, the SAT, graduation, and the opposite sex. What really amazes me is that many of my former students cannot shake the gas mask experiment. Several times over the last few years, I have been walking down the hall and as I round a corner, I see one of my former students. They always have a mildly shocked expression on their faces. I chalked it up to them saying something about a student or teacher that they didn't want me to hear, talking about something personal they didn't want a teacher to know about, or maybe they really just did not enjoy me very much as a teacher. One year, though, an honest student finally let me know why so many of my former students get shocked looks on their faces when I surprise them in the hall.

This girl was very honest; she wasn't your typical A student. She was the kind of student I really enjoyed, the type to let you know where you stood with her. If you were boring, she let you know. If the class was great that day, she let you know. I always appreciate students like that, because they really hold up the mirror and let a teacher see how he or she is doing. I saw her in the hall a few times the year after she had my class and survived the WWI gas attacks. Each time I saw her in the hall, her head would snap around, she would get this shocked look on her face for a fleeting moment, and her arm would spasmodically jerk toward her backpack. Finally, one day she just stopped me in the hall and said, "Mr. Campbell, every time I see you I still think you are going to call a gas attack and kill me. It makes me so nervous. I can't help it. I still reach for my gas mask in my backpack, even though I know it isn't there, and I know it's over. I think I've got PTSD!" I have conducted very few lessons that last until the next day, much less the next year, but the gas attack is one of them. I really do think it's because they feel it is a life-and-death situation, at least metaphorically. If they get a little PTSD and have a few humorous flashbacks, then they really can start to understand (notice I said start to, not fully understand) an infinitesimally small bit of what it was like to be a soldier and face uncertain death every day. I cannot really try to kill my students and actually harm them, but this little lesson allows them in some small way to experience what it is like. That one girl's hallway confession made me feel that I was staying true to one of my teaching maxims: "Nothing is real until it is experienced."

Several times in class the following years, I have former U.S. history students for other classes, such as sociology or a class on special topics in history. Sometimes I get students in all three classes that I teach. Several times, I have been in one of those other classes when I look at one of my former U.S. history students, and there they are with their gas masks on, just staring at me as if to say, "I am still ready." There have been kids who tell me they laminated theirs and they are going to keep it forever, for what I am not sure, but I will confess this; I have no students who keep their worksheets, tests, lecture notes, or study guides laminated as a treasure from my class forever. There are still former students who, when they see others in the hall with their gas masks, come to my room and ask how many have survived. They want to know if any class has beaten the number of students who survived in their class (the record is seven, from a class of 28), how long they have left, and if the wood plaque is still up. I have never had a former student stop by my room to ask if any current class has surpassed the number of kids who passed a test that their class did, how many days I have left in my Cold War unit, or if I still have a plaque on the wall for who made an advanced score on their standardized test. Something special happens when your class becomes a matter of life and death.

I know many of the other teachers get a kick out of seeing my students try to survive WWI in my class. I have a friend who teaches way down the hall from me, near the lunch room. He gets just about all the traffic from the school, funneled right by his door. He always notices when it is WWI time in my room, because he sees so many young soldiers toting their gas masks with them everywhere. One day, he came to my room with a huge smile on his face. "I've been having so much fun with your students this week," he confessed. "Really? How's that?" I asked. He went on to tell me how as the students come by, he saw how nervous they were; so he decided to start playing a little trick on them. He would let them walk up close to him as he was standing by his door. Then he would look over their shoulders, raise his hand, and say, "Hey, Mr. Campbell. How are you?" He said it was so much fun to see kids scatter to the sides of the hall, throwing down their packs to dig for their masks, covering their faces, then turning around to proudly face—an empty hallway. Not only do I get to teach my students about the fear of uncertain death that comes with WWI, but other teachers start doing my job for me. I have yet to have another teacher help my students review in the hallway, give an impromptu mini-lecture as students walk by, or create and hand out worksheets to my students about my class as they walk by. There is something special about this type of assignment that not only gets students excited and involved, it even draws other teachers into the adventure and makes them want to get involved.

I took the lessons learned from the death of a student or one of their loved ones, figured out how to make those real lessons of life and death meaningful to our discussion of WWI, and reaped the educational rewards for it. Later I began to apply those lessons to other topics. We started doing duck-and-cover drills from the Cold War era during our study of the 1950s and 1960s. We watched the Civil Service videos about duck and cover from the era. Then, any time I called, "Duck and cover," the kids had five seconds to get into the fetal position with necks covered and up against a wall. Oh, the fun we had in the lunch room with that one. I realize that the possibilities are only limited to my imagination, as people all throughout history have been faced with life-and-death situations. It could be an Indian raid drill from the frontier days, an outlaw raid drill from the days of the Old West, a wagon train simulation from the pioneer days, or even a bomb drill from World War II in Japan to teach them the fear of the powerful bombs created to fight Japan, and the folly of even trying to hide from them. If you are creative, there are many ways to apply this premise to many classes in many places to create an environment of learning, and not just a lesson.

This tactic can easily be applied to other subjects. If a teacher is studying diseases in Biology, a scenario could easily be set up to see how the contagion spreads, and who lives and who dies. Maybe a teacher could even work a now-popular zombie apocalypse theme into the scenario. Nursing classes could conduct a survey of death in their classes and take field trips to cemeteries, mortuaries, morgues, and funeral homes. They could also bring in hospice nurses, ER doctors, and a person whose elderly parent had recently passed. Basically, the teacher could create an entire unit dedicated to studying death.

How impactful would that be for students who plan to dedicate their lives to helping people who are sick, and facing life and death circumstances every day? English classes could interview the elderly to see what they have learned about life and how they feel about the prospects of death, and work that information into an essay. The class could even collect the essays into a small book. Math students could use a relevant community story (like a young child whom everyone knows that contracts cancer, a high school students who died in a car wreck, or maybe a local soldier who dies young in the military service of our country) that involves death and then analyze data and statistics about the topic, while also talking with the people who knew them or the family to gain a human perspective. There is no limit to the power of this technique except the creativity of those willing to use it.

Making your class a matter of life and death is one of the most important ways a teacher can transform a class, from something students cannot wait to leave into something they will never forget. Sure, if done right there will be people who get upset. Students will not want to die in the game. Other teachers will think all that goes on in the class is goofing off, when gas attacks start getting called in the hall and kids are scurrying for shelter. Some will say that the kids are being scarred emotionally, and their snowflake-like innocence (including those who rack up body counts in the thousands during one video game, see many homicides on TV before they are adults, and experience the deaths of their own friends and family members) will be destroyed forever by this dreadful teaching tactic. Others may even say that it is a morbid infatuation with death that is unhealthy for kids. Do not let the naysayers dissuade you from trying this tactic. You will soon see that it has become the talk of the school, the memory of that class that the students cannot shake, and a life-changing experience when kids realize that people throughout history faced matters of life and death—and to a point, so did they.

CHAPTER IX

MAKE YOUR STUDENTS CRY

I felt sorry for the girl. She was crying so hard I felt like I should look away, so as not to cause her more embarrassment. I thought the tears would stop after a few minutes, but they did not. I searched around until I found a Kleenex and handed it to her, hoping it would help her compose herself, but that also failed. Her tears awakened a strange feeling inside my teacher's soul. On one hand, I was happy that she had been so moved; yet my heart was broken for this sobbing mess, slouched and heaving in front of me. When I planned my class during the previous school year and summer, I wanted a powerful reaction, but I was not prepared for this; a seventeen-year-old young lady, sobbing uncontrollably over a 100-year-old history book.

Remember the young lady who kept her class copy of *All Quiet on the Western Front* to finish, even when it was not required of her? I saw her about a month later in the hallway after school. I asked her about the book, and she said she was still reading it, and about halfway through. She said she loved it, and would finish it and bring the book back to me. There was no foreshadowing of the powerful emotional exchange we would have when she did return the novel. About a month later, after my first period class, I was speaking with a student or two. She walked up to my door with the book in her hand and I knew she was there to return her novel. Not one to just take the book, I hurried the others on and asked her what she thought of the book. I wanted to see if she felt the book was worth her extra time and effort. I wanted to see what she learned.

"So, what did you think?" I asked nonchalantly. Huge tears came to her eyes as she demanded, "Why did the book have to end like that?" I was totally caught off guard. I never had a student cry about anything we read in class, much less an entire novel read on her own time. "What do you mean?" I asked. "They all died!" she blurted. "I thought at least one of them would make it, but they didn't, not even the narrator. They all just died." I told her that she'd missed a lot of discussion in class about the book, but that was the point the author was trying to make. He lived through the war, but was totally transformed by it. It was, at heart, an anti-war piece. He wanted the reader to get to know (and even love) the characters in the book, then experience the loss just like millions of families around the world did because of World War I. My answer did not suffice. "But not one lived? There couldn't be just one who made it through?" she begged me to change my answer. It was obvious there was something more on her mind.

"Do you have a family member who is in the service, or a veteran?" I asked. I felt that was why she was making the emotional connection so deeply. I was surprised when she answered, "No." What was it about the people in the book that grabbed her and made her feel so strongly for them? Her answer floored me. "I was thinking that there are soldiers right now in Afghanistan, fighting for our country. They are sleeping with their heads in the mud, freezing at night, going hungry, losing loved ones, and dying," she said. "The sad part is, I go all day, even weeks and months, without even thinking about them," she admitted. Then the tears really began to flow. She quickly ran out of dry spots on her hand to wipe the tears, so that is when I dug out a tissue for her. The small piece of paper had no chance against the raging torrent of emotion; soon it lay soaked and mangled, much like her own soul. Her eyes were red, her face and neck were blotchy, and she took a seat in front of my desk.

We talked for a few minutes about anything she wanted to discuss. I asked her about different scenes in the book, what was her favorite chapter, what certain passages meant to her. I was trying to get her mind off of her crying; I felt embarrassed for her. Nothing worked. She just kept crying. As fate would have it, the fire alarm went off right in the middle of our conversation (one of our many state mandated drills). As we walked out of the class, I was a bit relieved that she would have a few minutes to gather herself before she had to move on to her next class. I could just imagine her walking in with bleary eyes and a red face, and all of her friends demanding she tell them what was wrong.

They would never believe she was crying because of an old history book that Mr. Campbell made them read. As we walked out, I explained that she had a few minutes to gather herself before she had to return to her class, but I had to get busy doing my paperwork necessitated by the fire drill.

I was so overwhelmed I asked our dean of students if she knew the girl. She said she did, so I shared with her what had just happened. "That is amazing, considering what her home life is like," she said. I was a little shocked, so I stood there quietly while she finished her paperwork, not even looking up. I am not sure if she even knew the effect what she'd just shared had on me. I do not know exactly what she meant about the student's home life, as I did not know the girl on a deep level; she was only in my room for a few days before she transferred. My mind began to race, however, as I thought about the implication of what she just told me. I saw warning signs of a home that did not care much about education and did not have much money. In high school appearances are extremely important to many students, but this girl often wore her hair twisted up in a knot on top of her head, sweat pants, and socks with flip flops (even in the winter). I guess it could be said she was not part of the in crowd. She was not the typical A student, and I never saw her mom or dad at a parent-teacher conference or school activity (no matter if it was academic or sports related). I was now even more overwhelmed by what just happened. A student without much extrinsic motivation from her parents about education (or most likely any other thing for that matter) was so moved by a book she read on her own time that she stood in front of me, an emotional mess, because of how it made her feel.

As we walked in silently beside one another after the fire drill was complete, I wanted to thank the student for what she did for me. After we were back inside the school and ready to part ways, I stopped, turned to her, and extended my hand. She took mine in her own, but in her eyes I could tell she was not really sure why. "I just want to thank you," I said. "What for?" she asked, her still-bleary eyes staring back into mine. "Why, for making me feel like a real teacher, of course," was my reply. Then I proceeded to tell her how I struggled with what book to read that year, how I even considered not using it because it was below their grade level, and the new standards said I was only to use texts that were at their grade level or a little higher. I told her how I was not supposed to use fiction because the new standards said informational texts are what would help them in their jobs. According to the experts, I was supposed to focus on speeches by politicians, laws, and government manuals. As I concluded, I looked her deep in the eyes, still shaking her hand, and said, "Thank you for showing me that I made the right decision." She managed a smile, the red blotches were still around her eyes and neck. Then she turned and walked on to class, and I walked into my classroom, sat behind my desk, and had a good cry of my own.

I wondered what we were doing to our students when we let standards created by people who had never spent one day in a classroom override decades of personal wisdom of the teacher. It is heartbreaking that we allow people who are in charge of trying to create workers for our economy tell us which books are appropriate for young people to read, when history had shown us that certain books had inspired people to read them for hundreds and sometimes even thousands of years. I shuddered when I realized that millions of young ladies like the one who just walked away would never get the chance to be moved by a great piece of fiction, because fictional writings (and therefore creativity and imagination) were not welcome in our texts (or our classrooms) anymore. As I dried my own eyes with a tissue from the same box that had failed to stop the young lady's tears moments earlier, I declared that I would never stop using the materials that I knew worked, because they had been tested by me (and many teachers like me) over the years. What is more, they had been tested by young minds for ages, and found to be life changing.

One of the main problems with young people today is that our society has evolved to disconnect them from the real world around them. Just think about it. We have kids' meals, cartoon channels, kids' movies, children's literature, etc. It is possible for a child to supposedly become an adult, yet spend very little time with an adult or doing adult things. Many parents are so busy working to provide consumer goods that they leave their children early almost every day, and often with strangers in day care, where they are surrounded by dozens of other children just like themselves. When children begin school, they find themselves surrounded by other people who are their exact same age. They learn to play games on the TVs in their own rooms, while their parents watch the television and dream of more consumer goods to buy in other rooms. The other members of their families might take their dinners in their own rooms, so as not to miss a second of TV, internet, social media, or games, thereby losing the small time they have to actually talk to one another and share what they have learned. In sports, they are again separated into groups with age as the determining factor. They have children's church on Sunday, where they have dumbed-down, sanitized, safe lessons, and never get to be around many adults.

Their grandparents are ostracized by society, because they do not know how to program the latest electronic gadget or who the latest pop culture icon is. A few years later, when the grandparents can no longer work to acquire consumer goods, they are totally removed to a home, where the families will rarely visit and decades of real-world wisdom will be lost to the world (and the child) forever.

If there is an opportunity for me to use a work of literature that helps transfer some wisdom from those who acquired it in the real world, I am going to use it. I do not care if it is fiction or if some computer program tells me it is the wrong grade level. After all, are not grade levels just contrivances created by the same absentee experts who create educational standards? It is time to reconnect students with the wisdom of the herd that they are missing in their safe, sanitized, and dare I say it, boring, lives. It is time we stopped treating children like children, and started treating them as they have been treated for thousands of years; as productive members of society, worthy of living with the adults and learning from one another to create a powerful culture.

I remember when a man raised in the Great Depression told me that the last penny his father ever spent on him came when he was nine years old. "My dad was going to town, and I gave him a dollar to buy me a fifty-seven-cent pair of overalls. He put fourteen cents with my dollar and brought me back two pair. My dad never spent another penny on me as long as I lived," he said. He was not bitter, and there was no sadness in his voice. It was just matter of fact; he was nine years old and ready to grow up. Later, he told me that he remembered the first time he got "paid like a man." He was eleven years old, and he and his brothers were working for a neighboring widow. They were helping her with farm labor, and at the end of the day the boys lined up at the door waiting for their ten-cent payment for the day of hard labor. This man was in the back of the line, because he was the youngest. As the lady doled out the wages, he received a dime just like all of his brothers. "Excuse me, Ma'am," he uttered. "I think you have made a mistake. I don't get the same pay as my brother, because I am just a boy. I usually get half pay, so I only get a nickel," he finished. She bent down so she could look him straight in the eye and replied, "I watched you boys work all day, and I didn't see any difference between the way you worked and your brothers worked. Why don't you just keep that dime?" The old lady reached down and placed her hands over his dirty palm, folded his fingers over his shiny new dime, and that was it. He worked like a man, and could buy his own things; therefore, he became a man.

How many young people are ready to work with the big boys, change lives, read like a scholar, solve problems, raise money for charities, work in homeless shelters, discuss things with retired people...basically, grow up and start living? Many times all we do is try to relegate them to some form of perpetual childhood; we refuse to allow them to mature. If we ever want to produce a generation knowing how to work, raise families, be part of the community, serve their country, and take care of one another, we are going to be forced to let them grow up—even if that means letting them order from the adult menu, watch the news, tackle powerful tests, wrestle with adult problems, get scared, and even fail.

For the last several years, I have taught social studies: American history, mostly. I know that there are a million jokes about history teachers showing movies. All too often, that stereotype is true. Even we social studies teachers make jokes about it. Once at my school, the social studies department thought a fellow teacher was showing too many movies. He took a sick day once and returned to have his room decorated like a movie theater, complete with a mobile popcorn cart in his room. He was not amused. So, it is with great caution that I ever show a movie. There are years where I have shown one movie in its entirety, but never more. Mostly, now I rely on video clips to portray certain aspects I wish to discuss. There was one year, however, that I had some time in class, and had just watched a movie that amazed me. It won an Academy Award, and another very experienced teacher told me the kids' eyes were glued to the screen when he showed it in class. After seeing what happened in one girl's life, I knew it was the right decision, stereotypes or not.

If you have never seen the movie, *Life is Beautiful*, you have missed a treat. It won the Academy Award for Best Foreign Language Film, Best Original Dramatic Score, and Best Actor for Roberto Benigni during the 71st Academy Awards ceremony. I wondered about the aspect of it being a film that has subtitles when I considered it for class. After I watched it, I was convinced the kids would love it, regardless. However, I did ask a personal friend of mine, who had shown it in class, his opinion. "At first, the kids are excited to watch any movie," he told me. "But after they realize it's subtitled because it's in Italian, they begin to complain and groan. After ten minutes," he assured me, "no one will care. It's that good," he said. Now that I had an experienced teacher's confirmation, I decided to try it and show a complete movie, foreign language and subtitles included, and hope for the best.

I remember watching the movie the first time, and it was powerful. Maybe it was because my wife and I had just experienced the birth of our first child, but the story of a father's love for his son was overpowering. The film is about an Italian Jewish family during WWII. The dad is not big or strong; his only attributes are his wit and sense of humor. He uses his skills to win the hand of his wife; then years later, they make his son have a very adventurous childhood. When the Nazis move to force the Jewish residents into concentration camps, the father uses the opportunity to turn the worst days for his child into his best days, as he weaves a magical tale of a birthday surprise he will never forget.

My teacher friend was right. After just a few minutes of watching the movie, the students forgot about the foreign language and subtitles and were avidly watching the film. The students really enjoyed the movie, and the spectacular ending had a huge impact on the class. When I flipped the lights on at the end of the show, there was one girl in tears. She was crying and wiping her face with both hands. The class had a discussion session about the movie, and as she regained her composure, I asked her to share her thoughts. She related her own beautiful story, about her grandparents and how they had met during WWII. Her grandfather was an American soldier who met the love of his life while stationed in Europe. As her grandmother was trying to make it through the fighting and to American lines, her train was strafed by German fighter planes. She eventually did find her love, and the young lady's grandfather was able to secure her travel to America, where they were married. This young student in my class loved the movie, like many of the other students in class, but for her it was because of something different. This piece had spoken to her.

Sometimes movies get a bad rap for not being as "artistic" as books, poems, and other written works. I suppose because it is a relatively newer medium, it just does not have the nostalgia that other forms of art do. The truth, however, is that a great video presentation can be just as powerful as a piece of writing. The secret to selecting the right movie is the same as selecting the proper writing; find something that makes a connection with the students. Just as *All Quiet on the Western Front* brought a connection to the mind of the student when she realized there were still soldiers currently suffering through many of the same conditions as those in the novel, *Life is Beautiful* reminded this young lady that her own family endured something very similar to those of the characters on the screen. She came to understand that on the horrific canvas of war, love sometimes paints a picture so lovely that it brings tears to one's eyes.

A few days later, the crying student's mother (who just happens to be a teacher at the school) came to me between classes. She related to me the discussion she and her daughter had after school about the film. The family got the movie and watched it together, all being impacted in the same way and ending with everyone having an impassioned cry. That weekend, the grandparents came over and they watched the movie again, and once more they all huddled together as the tears flowed. The teacher told me it was as if some strange Italian man had written the story of their family without ever knowing them. That is what great works of art do: they make us see ourselves. While reading the wonderful book *Out of Our Minds* by Sir Ken Robinson, I found that the description of theater was the connection between performer and audience. I realized that it was much the same for any artwork. Real art is the connection between the piece and the person viewing it. In this case, the piece of art made a powerful impact on a family that they will never forget.

There are many instances when some visual art really had an emotional impact on students in my class, but the shock of my life came from the most unsuspected source. I remember going to a workshop on teaching history where a fellow teacher said he used the music video "One" by Metallica. It is the first video released by the band, replete with hair swinging, heads banging, faces grimacing, voices growling, and guitars wailing (enough to make some older folks cry, already). However, as I watched the video, I realized despite what many may say about heavy metal music, the video was very powerful. The song is about a soldier from World War I who was hit by a landmine, which caused the loss of his arms, legs, and face. The wounds trapped him in a hospital room, never to be able to move or communicate. Metallica actually wanted to use clips from the World War I anti-war movie *Johnny Got His Gun*, which has a very similar premise; however, the film company that owned it would not approve it. Metallica ended up buying the rights to the film and creating a beautiful video, almost eight minutes in length, that feels more like a miniature movie than a music video. I spent hours crafting my lesson to make sure they kids did not miss the message of the film because of the contemporary feel of the visual piece. When the lesson was over, one girl showed me that the message hit its mark.

As we prepared to watch the video (complete with a handout of the lyrics to the song, the words from the movie clips used, and questions to consider at the end), I asked how many had already seen it. Only a couple of students raised their hands. I then inquired how many had ever heard any Metallica song in its entirety. All of my students raised their hand but one. I looked around to find that it was a nice straight-A student who sat on the front row, who was the only one without her hand raised. Anyone could tell this young lady was from an upper-middle class family; classical music was far more likely to be heard in her home than heavy metal. I decided to probe more and asked her with which types of music she was more familiar with, what she heard most often. Sure enough, she informed me she took classical piano lessons and listened to mostly classical music, with some jazz piano mixed in for good measure. I was interested to see what the class thought of the video, but especially curious to see how she reacted. Nothing could prepare either of us for what we were about to witness.

When the song begins, it is rather slow and somber, but gradually builds to an epic guitar riffing, hair swinging, head banging tour de force. Interwoven with the gradually rising musical crescendo is this horrible story of a broken young man. He is trapped in this hospital bed, unable to move anything but his head. Every day, this nurse sees his agony and wishes she could do something to help. Inside, the soldier wants nothing more than to die; however, with the inability to communicate, he knows he will never make his wishes known. One day, he has a dream about his father, who tells him to use Morse code to let the world know his wishes. The soldier does all he can do, which is twitch his head, to relay the message. At first no one can tell what he is doing, but eventually the nurse notices and brings in the military officials to investigate. They discover that he is saying "Kill me," over and over again, but the military officials will not hear of it. No brave soldier who gave his body for the service of their country will be put down like a wounded animal. The poor nurse, however, who has to care for the man every day and is the closest thing he has to a friend, cannot stand it any longer. She decides to kill the young man and stop his suffering. One night she sneaks into his room and removes his ventilator tube, pushing his chest down with her bare hands as she turns her head away in tears, unable to look at what she is doing. After an agonizing few moments, as the nurse feels the breath slipping from the soldier's lungs, a military officer happens to be coming down the hallway; he sees what she's doing through the door. He rushes in and pushes the nurse away to preserve the soldier's life. The music video ends with the lonely, wounded soldier lying alone in a dark hospital room, begging to be killed, twitching SOS, SOS, SOS...over and over again. All the while, the music comes to a powerful conclusion. It is a very compelling video indeed, but nothing prepared me for what I saw from the young pianist in the front row.

The formerly happy-go-lucky classical pianist was sitting frozen, in rapt horror. As the song began (when the music was still quiet and melodic) I looked at her, and she'd seemed very interested in the song. As the song really began to rev up and the guitars began to wail, she'd looked a little surprised. When the song was coming to an end and the guitars were screaming, the hair was flying, and the heads were banging, she looked absolutely terrified; like a child who had seen his first horror film. If you can imagine a kid who has just found out there is no Santa Claus, only Krampus, that was the expression she had on her face. It was as if she had come to the reality that there was a much bigger musical world out there than the one she was exposed to, and it was not always pretty. Sometimes, as in this song, it could be violent and scary; now she had to confront that frontal assault on her senses. As the video came to an abrupt end, with a visual fade out showing the man with no legs, arms, or face quietly held prisoner in his hospital room, while back at home his family raised a toast to peace, I saw a twinkle in her eye. As we sat in darkness in the room with only the light of the overhead projector, a tear caught the light as it escaped her eye and made its way down her cheek.

As the class sat quietly, I turned on the lights so we could have a discussion and answer the questions about the video. As the students finished their writing, I prepared to lead the discussion. The last question they had to answer was "If you were the nurse, would you kill the soldier in the bed?" I felt it was a powerful way to end the study. I came to her in the discussion and asked her what she would do. Her answer was "I would want to, but I don't know if I have it in me to kill a helpless man in a bed like that." We had a wonderful discussion about the Hippocratic Oath, mercy killings, what is life, who has the right to end life, etc. When the bell rang and the young pianist made her way toward the door, I asked her what she thought of her first Metallica video. She said, "It was awful." She went on to tell me that it was so powerful; the guitars sounded like guns, and the video of the man interspersed throughout made it very emotional. I asked her if a trained classical pianist reared on Chopin ever wanted to hear another Metallica song. She looked at the floor, then cocked her head back, allowing her formerly tear-filled eyes to look up and to the right for a moment. Then a wicked little grin crossed her face, and she said, "I think so."

It does not really matter if what you use in your class is written or visual. There are works of art that can have a very powerful effect on you students. Some teachers may say that written pieces are a higher form of art, or that heavy metal music videos cannot be considered artwork, but I disagree. Art takes many forms in our culture, and what teachers should be looking for is those works that elicit the response we are trying to evoke in our students. Whether the response we are looking to generate requires the use of a poem, diary entry, song, music video, or a guest speaker, that choice is the role of the teacher. The teacher is to use the wisdom they have accumulated to decide what works best to achieve the desired results. Only the classroom teacher knows the students well enough to make the right choice, and if the proper selection is made, the impact can be extremely powerful. No canned lesson plan, state standard, formalized assessment, school superintendent, state level educational bureaucrat, or million-dollar philanthropic association can tell a teacher how to make these choices. This type of decision can only be made through personal wisdom, trial and error, and knowledge of the students.

Once when my sociology class was doing a fundraiser for a local principal who was fighting Lou Gehrig's disease (ALS), I saw another tear that changed my teaching career. My students decided to create shirts as a fundraiser to help this man, who has a wife and three kids. The amazing thing was that after they had created the shirts, designed advertisements for them, created social media promotion sites, taken preorders, and placed the order for the shirts, there were still questions unanswered. As I sat in a chair in the room one day leading a discussion about what we needed to do for the next phase of the project, one innocent young lady raised her hand and asked a question that was integral to the project, yet somehow had been left unanswered. It was a simple inquiry: "What is the money for?" The question was one of the most pertinent to the entire project, yet somehow in my own ignorance, I failed to understand that not every student knew what Lou Gehrig's disease was. I saw several heads around the room nodding in agreement. Obviously, the majority of the class did not know the answer.

One must understand the type of person this principal was. He was one of those guys who was just always around in our community. The story about his fight with Lou Gehrig's disease (which had just become public knowledge about four months before) had been featured in our local paper and on our local TV news programs. I was sure that all of my students were aware of the situation, but obviously I was wrong. More amazing to me than the fact that most of my students were not fully aware of his situation, was the idea that they had been working so hard to raise money for a man they really did not know anything about. I realized I had failed in one of my most important jobs as a teacher: to make objectives clear and concise at the beginning of the assignment.

I sat down in my chair, looking them all in the eye, one by one. I began to talk to them about the kind of man the principal was, how I'd known him for much of my life, and what the disease does to a person's body. I began to explain to my students how the nerves no longer carry their electrical messages to the muscles, the muscles begin to wither, and eventually the muscles die, leaving the body unable to move. As I told them of how eventually my friend would be left without even the ability to speak or lift his head, I felt something welling up inside of me that threatened to become so big I could not control it. I went on to tell them how eventually the muscles of the diaphragm become so weak they can no longer expand the rib cage; with that, I could no longer contain my emotions. Just the thought of a childhood friend dying this terrible death in front of his wife and three kids was too much, and I began to cry. I cried while I told them about how he would not be able to work those last couple of years of his life, and how he would be ineligible to keep his work insurance because of that. I sobbed while I told them that his wife, who once saw him as her protector, and his children, who once thought of him as the strongest daddy in the world, would watch him turn into a weak, frail shell of his former self, no longer able to even speak to them. They would have to watch him die a very slow and agonizing death. Unable to really look up with my bleary eyes, I went on to tell them that in the last years of a person's life with this disease, the healthcare costs rocket to over $200,000. And I concluded with telling them all of the money earned would help offset the healthcare costs that would inevitably happen in the coming years, taking the burden off of his family. When I finished, I gathered myself and looked around at my class. To my surprise, many of them were crying with me.

At first I was stunned, because all of these students had done so much work on the project without even knowing who this man was or what the money raised was going to do. I am not sure if they were so excited about the project because they were doing something different other than worksheets and quizzes, they were able to help someone and make a real connection to a person (whether they really knew this person or why he needed their help or not), or maybe because I had been so passionate about it. I cannot be certain. What I can say is that after the tear-filled talk we had about who he was and why he needed the help, the students became more involved and intense than any other time during the project. I asked how many students knew the principal personally, and only three raised their hands. I was stunned. I had just figured everyone saw him around at ballgames, more attended his school in their elementary years, their parents knew him, they had read about him in the newspaper, or had seen him on the news. When I realized my folly, I was determined it was time to make it right.

After school that day, I called the principal and asked him if he could come down to my class to see the fundraiser they created, and just let the kids get to know him better so they would have more investment (not that they needed much more) in the project. I wanted them to personally know who they were helping, and what kind of person he really was. He was able to work it out so he could slip away from his school for a few moments to come and speak to our class. He gave about a ten-minute testimony to my children that had them crying again. Here was a man whom they had never met, and they cried with me when I spoke about him, and now they were crying again as they listened intently to his life story. He concluded his talk by saying, "I am glad I have this disease, because if I did not, I would never have gotten the chance to meet all of you, and you are some very special young people." Not only could I tell the students had been touched during his talk, but what happened after he left was amazing.

The students worked with so much tenacity that I was shocked. The way they worked to sell the shirts, advertise them, organize them, etc. was amazing. It took me a while to realize I'd missed a very important step in the process, in any process; helping the members understand the clear goals of the task. I think it helped me better understand what the goals were, as well. Not only was the goal to get my students to use their skills of advertising manipulation (which we had been studying in class), but I realized part of it was to help them understand the importance of making connections. Finally, when I told them my perspective, and more importantly, arranged the meeting between them and the person they were trying to help, the project became real. So real that the students did what I only saw happen a handful of times in my class; they were overwhelmed with emotions and cried. When a teacher realizes how to make a project or lesson this real to student, do not be surprised when the most amazing things happen. The difficulty of making things about rigor, relevance, and relationships becomes a moot point when you get students so emotionally invested in something that they cry.

When I spoke with the principal later that day, he said, "I don't understand it. Kids aren't supposed to like their principals. I am supposed to be old and stuffy. I am 'the man,' and young people aren't supposed to like the man." Fortunately, I had helped the students make a connection with someone that touched them so deeply that a teenager cried about a complete stranger: an old stuffy principal, no less. Imagine the surprise of my class, when that same principal showed up a few days later with a bus and ordered all of my students to board it. They all complied after a few moments of indecision, trying to figure out if it was a joke or for real. He limped aboard the bus and announced that he was taking the entire class to his favorite restaurant for lunch. "I love this place, and eat here at least once per week," he announced. "Some of their food is kind of different, but all I ask is you try one spoonful of everything. This will probably be the last time I ever get to eat with most of you, and I hope that in the future, if you ever eat it again, you will remember our meal together." His voice echoed through the bus. I had so much fun that day just watching him go from table to table and interact with the kids encouraging them to try new things. Many of the students liked the new foods, and some did not, but they all had an experience that day—and it was not just culinary.

If you work with teenagers, helping them make connections to people outside of their age group is something that does not happen often. I am sure this lesson can be applied to many other subjects and situations, by any teacher willing to invest a little creativity into their lesson planning. Find ways to make them care so much about science they create a connection with someone that is life-changing. What if they took a cold case from the police department and used their knowledge of science and forensics to solve the case? Can you imagine when the mother of the victim showed up and thanked the students for giving her the peace of mind of knowing what happened to her child? It would be life altering. In language arts classes, could the children find people with amazing stories and write a short biography about them? Can you imagine what a person would think, who had many trials throughout life and possibly feels like they are not appreciated, unwrapping a box with their life story inside? How would a handicapped person (and the student) feel if the woodworking class showed up and built them a ramp for their house? What would happen if a business class created a fundraiser that supplied a seizure dog for a young child in the community who could not afford one? There are a million ways to help kids get involved with people in the community and create such powerful emotional bonds that crying occurs.

Once, I had a student who thought he and I had become emotionally close. I must admit, after having him in three different classes over the years, and coaching him in football and powerlifting, I grew to know and like the young man. However, my personal ethics as a teacher reminded me that I should never treat students as friends, or even refer to them as such. They were my students and I their teacher; the line needed to remain to ensure that I did not handle situations incorrectly. When I assigned or graded classwork, it needed to be as a teacher and not a friend. When I enforced school rules and policies, it needed to be fair and unbiased, done like a teacher and not a friend. I think most students understand that. I was put in a very delicate situation once when this young man asked me a personal question during class.

I was teaching an advanced placement biology class one year, and this young man signed up. I must admit he was not an overly studious young man, and I felt he took the class mainly because he liked me as a teacher. At first, I thought taking a class for that reason was a bad one, until my principal told me that it is hard to learn from a teacher if a student does not enjoy their teaching style or personality. After I thought about it, I allowed him to stay in the class although the work was often challenging for him and he often received C grades. I was in class lecturing one day when some students asked me a couple of questions, and we meandered a bit during the answer. I was getting ready to move back to the topic when the young man raised his hand. He asked me point blank, "Do you consider me a friend?" I must admit I was a bit surprised. I have never had a student ask me a question like that, and I was really not expecting it to be asked during class. For a moment, I considered asking him to stay at the end of class and he and I would speak privately, but then I thought it was good for me to discuss such a policy in front of the students.

I curtly answered with a definitive, "No." He was shocked. He did not really say or do anything that most students could notice, but I saw his jaw grow a touch slack and his eyes open a bit as his head leaned back a little. I proceeded to explain how it would not be proper for a teacher to consider his students friends for a variety of reasons, like equal enforcement of rules, fair grading, etc. I went on to say that once my students graduated from high school, I had no problems possibly seeing them as friends and even peers (indeed, it was a tad strange the first time a former student became a coworker, but I adapted easily). After we discussed my reasoning for a few moments, we quickly returned back to the lecture topic. I felt good that I was able to explain my reasoning behind why I carry myself the way I do with my students, and I even noticed several students nodding in agreement. I thought all was well, and done with, but I would soon find the contrary.

Because I coached this young man in a couple of different sports, he was also familiar with my wife and two small children. My family often came to our competitions and fundraisers, and knew most of the athletes on my teams. The next time we had an event and my wife came, unbeknownst to me, this young man spoke to my wife about the discussion in class. Later that evening after the kids were in bed, my wife recounted the events to me. "He just came right up to me, like he had something very important to say to me" she started. "He told me that he asked you in class if you were his friend," she recounted. "He even told me that he had prepared himself for the answer and felt he could take it, no matter what you answered." She continued, "But when you answered 'No', he told me he fought back tears on the inside." I must admit, I was shocked by the conversation. The young man had appeared to take the answer well; besides, I did not really think that most guys would be emotionally scarred because a teacher said they could not think of a student as a friend until after they graduated. I never really said anything to the young man about that conversation he had with my wife, but surely he knew we discussed it. One day, if we stayed acquainted and even became friends after he left high school, I was determined to tell him so.

After high school, however, this young man joined the military. I even went and had dinner with his family at a local restaurant before he left for his first tour in Iraq (he eventually served two). After he left the military, he moved back to our town. I spoke to him a couple of times when he called me to let me know he made it through his deployments and was now out of the military. My kids and I have a tradition that on Veterans' day, we always go and have dinner with a veteran. I thought it was a good idea to let my sons grow up getting to know actual veterans on that day, rather than just saying it was a day we thought about veterans when most people really do not. My sons would get to see that people they know from their everyday walks of life are veterans. They would grow up knowing that these people, although they appear like everyone else now, sacrificed their lives for us in years past, and we are not to forget their sacrifice. I decided that year we would take this recently returned former student out for dinner.

We agreed to meet at the same restaurant where we ate before he left for his first deployment and have lunch. I did not tell him that it would be a special Veterans Day meal for him. However, when we showed up with handmade cards for him, he got the message. My boys, four and six at the time, took construction paper and doubled it over to make him a card, and drew on it. I wrote him a special Veterans Day card as well. He loved looking at my boys' pictures of him and reading their messages, and then he got to my card. I was honest and told him I appreciated his service and his sacrifice for giving up some of the best years of his young life to go and serve our country, but the real treat came in the P.S. of the card. I included some words I thought he would enjoy finally hearing. A simple final thought at the bottom of the card, *Happy Veterans Day, from your friend, Alex Campbell*. This time there was no Mr. or veil between teacher and student, just a heart-felt thank you between two adult men. He looked up from his card with a smile on his face and those tears that he had suppressed several years before welled up in his eyes. I could not help but think that instead of being peers, we had switched places. In my eyes, at least, he held a place of greater esteem, for although I was a teacher and worked hard to help young people, I never put myself in harm's way in a foreign land for my country. Now, it was I who felt unworthy to be considered on the same level, and it was my tears that were suppressed inside.

When crying does occur, prepare yourself for the critics. There will be those who say, "Yes, that was nice, but how does that prepare them for their standardized tests, their career, or real life?" People will say you are traumatizing the children with themes that are far above their limited understanding. Some teachers view crying in their room as a bad thing, but I have come to view it as a positive. I quote legendary coach Jimmy Valvano, "If you laugh, you think, and you cry, that's a full day. That's a heck of a day. You do that seven days a week, you're going to have something special." I've made it a motto in my class. If kids can do either and think, they have experienced a real half day, and if they do both, then they have experienced what most young people never experience in school. If they can take that one step further, and experience both of those for another person and not just themselves, then they have done something that hardly any young person will do throughout our culture. You can teach all day, but if there is never a real connection made, then the efforts are fruitless. Remember that the point of teaching in a way that students may cry is not to get them to cry, but to get them to care. Creating a climate where a teenager cares about others is the point. In a culture where so many people consider teens self-absorbed, the ability to get them to care for others, and even care enough to cry, is a powerful tool in any teacher's arsenal.

As a matter of fact, getting students involved on a level where they feel like crying is the only way to prepare them for real life. How else will our students learn to be loving parents, and create loving homes for their children? How will these future business leaders of our country create the type of workplace environment where people will *want* to work and be productive? Where will future politicians come from who want to pass laws because they need to do what is right for the common citizens, instead of what is right for a huge political action committee, a powerful corporation, or a political party? Where will our future social workers come from who approach each case like it is someone's precious child, not just another file of paperwork waiting to be done so the workday can be finished? If we as a society, and that includes teachers, do not realize it is our responsibility to train up our children to care for others, then we are doomed to the same old self-absorbed, me-first, selfish generation about which we currently complain.

I honestly feel that teens are not by nature self-absorbed and narcissistic; that takes years of hard work on the part of the adults and the culture of the society. Think about how much effort goes into making young people care only about themselves and people of their age. How else can we expect our children to grow up, except as spoiled brats who believe the world must revolve around them, their social class, their age group, and their desires? The only real way to combat these feelings in our youth is to actually teach them about others, which will also teach them about themselves. When they cry during a movie that reminds them of their grandparents, it teaches them how to understand and become emotionally invested in their grandparents instead of seeing them as relics from a bygone era that have outlived their usefulness. When they learn to cry for a principal at a local school, they realize he has a life outside of work and is not just defined by his vocation; he has a family, fears, and hopes just as they do. When a young lady cries because she realizes that she has forgotten the soldiers of her own country who sacrifice for her every day, she has learned a very valuable lesson about sacrifice, patriotism, and how to live the opposite of a self-absorbed life. When a young lady experiences a powerful music video that leaves her reeling and considering the impact that war has on everyone (both the nurses and the soldiers), then young people began to really become properly enculturated. It is the only way to fix what Sir Ken Robinson describes as the "continuous present" that young people are doomed to continue because they have been cut off from the past and their futures by age segregation.

So, for all of the quantitative data people out there, I know you are thinking, *But how do we measure the learning that has taken place in a classroom where children are taught to care?* Do we just bottle up the tears and whoever has the most tears in their vial at the end of the semester gets an A? I'm not saying that we should make the caring the only thing that we grade, or even the primary thing in which students are categorized. It is but one of the many aspects that run through the climate of the classroom. If a teacher goes in and says, "Okay, today we need to have a good cry that lasts for three minutes after this story," then that teacher will be sorely mistaken. You cannot plan it; you can only create the environment for it. A teacher will never be able to predict when it will happen, but when it does, it will become a very special moment that both teacher and student will never forget. It will be a day that you look back on and think that you might not know exactly how much was learned or what was internalized, but you know that something special took place in the hearts of your students. At the end of a day, week, school year, or career, for what else can a teacher really hope?

CHAPTER X

LET YOUR STUDENTS REFUSE TO DO ASSIGNMENTS

I t was a beautiful day, and the sun was so nice that my workout partner and I decided to do some of our lifting exercises outside after school. As we sweated through our workout, I noticed this young man getting out of his vehicle in the parking lot that faced us. It is not unusual to see people coming and going not too long after school dismissed, but this guy seemed to be looking at me. As he continued to walk, he did not head toward the door or the main entrance of the school, but toward us. He walked right up to me and stuck out his hand. He introduced himself as the fiancé of one of my students. Despite the fact that I had never met him, I quickly realized exactly who he was and why he made it a point to come and see me. After introducing himself, he squeezed my hand very firmly, pulled me a bit closer, looked intently into my eyes, and said a very impassioned "Thank you." His eyes seemed to pierce my soul. I could feel a tremble in his voice as he spoke, and although I never met the young man again, I would never forget the lesson I learned from him.

It all started a couple of days before when my American history class was covering World War I. After we go through the causes of the conflict, we spend a couple of days discussing the brutality of trench warfare. I have my students flip over their desks and create a trench system in my class. I show them pictures of trench foot, trench mouth, trench rats, lice, etc. while they sit in their trenches. Then I try to get them to experience the living conditions by making them wear wet socks, throwing rubber rats into their trench, and making them wear hillbilly teeth. We have a lice-picking competition, off of woolen sweaters. Later we read excerpts from soldiers' diaries about the trench conditions, before the students complete their capstone assignment of composing their own letters home from the front lines. My students often do an amazing job with the letters, and really let their creativity flow. I enjoy walking among the trenches and reading the letters as the students work. As I meandered through the front lines, enjoying the writings of my students, I came to a young lady who had done absolutely nothing.

I will be quite honest that in my younger days as a teacher if I gave an assignment with fifteen minutes of class time for a student to work on it, and I came around to find that a student had wasted the time, I would have been upset. I most likely would have (and often did) dress that student down for not obeying my wishes and wasting time. I am not sure why, but instead of getting upset that day, I decided to just calmly ask her why she had not written anything. As I towered over this tiny young lady, I asked her why she had not written anything, she simply responded "I can't." She did not even look up, but I detected something very odd and mournful in her voice. This student was an excellent worker. She always did what was asked of her, and many times even more. She was never disrespectful, and made excellent grades in my class. I am not sure why, but I decided to say nothing at the moment and wait until after the class was over. I continued around the class reading other letters for the next five minutes or so, and when the bell rang, I spun and asked the young lady if she would stay and speak with me for a moment.

As she gathered up her things, I returned to my desk and plopped down, curious about why such an excellent student had not worked on her assignment, and also planning a little about how to deal with the offense. She walked up to my desk, and for the first time, I got a really good look at her face. She was under a tremendous amount of emotional strain; I could see it in her nervousness (her hands were trembling), and her eyes were nearly filled with tears. I looked through her tears at her bloodshot eyes and asked her very simply why she had not written the letter, when I had given her time in class to do so. Nothing prepared me for the shocking reply she gave me. "I am not going to write your letter," she said flatly. I must admit that I am a fun-loving teacher who likes to do exciting things in my class, create activities that the students (and I) enjoy, and leave my students with an experience they will never forget. However, I am also a teacher who keeps order and discipline, and likes things to be done the first time I ask. I felt some rage building up inside of me about a student basically telling me they did not do my activity, and curtly saying they were not about to do it in the future, either. I started to rip into that girl and give her a good lecture about who the teacher was in the class, how much effort I put into the assignment, how I expected things to be done when I assigned them, and how she needed to care about her grade and what she learned—but there was something about the emotion in this girl. I swallowed all of that rage and anger I felt creeping up out of my teacher's soul, and decided to ask a very simple follow-up question. In my teaching career, I have never been more thankful that I asked a question than at that very moment.

It was a very simple question, but a very poignant one. "Why?" That was it. I am not sure why I was able to ask it, when what I really wanted to do was explode with some teacher sarcasm about who the boss was, and how she needed to understand that I knew more than her and I was in charge. She looked down for a moment as if gathering herself, then raised her head to look at me, her eyes now unable to hold her tears. "It's my fiancé," she said. "He's in the military, and he leaves for Afghanistan in a few days," she croaked. "I tried to write the letter, I really did, Mr. Campbell, but every time I put my pencil to the paper all I could do was think of him," she gushed in a torrent of emotion. I just sat there, the former rage gone and replaced with compassion. "Every time I tried to write, I just thought of how he would be experiencing many of the same things in just a few weeks, and I could not bring myself to write it," she concluded. I was shocked.

Many times, as adults we think we experience so much more than the children we teach. Teachers often acquire the mistaken opinion that because we are the adults in the room, we are the only ones with adult problems. It often takes a slap from reality to make me understand that many of my students have seen and dealt with more adult situations than I have in life. I have never seen one or either of my parents die, my daddy go to jail, or my father get drunk and tear the house apart. I've never had to go live with relatives because my mom and dad are not fit parents, discovered my dad's body in my house in a pool of blood after a suicide attempt, and never come home to my clothes in a trash bag on the porch and a note saying to go live with my aunt. These are all things that my students or my friends experienced as mere children trying to grow up and get an education. It is quite clear to me that many students are learning, experiencing, and being challenged more at home than they are at school. I realized that this was just another example of how my simple little make-believe project in school could not come close to the lesson she was getting outside of school.

I had to think about how I was going to deal with this issue right in front of me. Could I really just allow a student to refuse to do her assignment? Should I punish her for not doing what I ask? What if the others students heard that she got away with refusing to do her work? The first question I asked myself was why I even gave the assignment in the first place. I reasoned that I gave the assignment so the students could feel what it was like to live in those awful conditions that the average soldier lived through during WWI. I also wanted to evoke the emotions that families, friends, and lovers felt when they were ripped apart. Sure, I wanted them to use proper grammar and include words we had learned that described the battlefront, but the main object was to get them to feel. I had the answer that this traumatized young lady standing in front of me with her head down was waiting to hear.

"Do you know why I gave this assignment" I asked her. She shook her head while barely raising it enough to peer at me from under her eyelids. "I gave this assignment so the students would feel what it was like to be at war or to have a loved one go to war," I continued. "Do you understand that?" I asked. She nodded the affirmative. I proceeded to tell her that she had shown me that she did understand what it was like to feel those emotions, when a loved one leaves for war. Her head finally began to raise a bit and I could see a shocked expression spread across her face. "I can tell that you felt something today," I explained, "and I guess the writing was really for me to read to see if the students could understand what it felt like. Let's leave the writing to people who cannot show me that they feel something. I know you felt something; it's written all over your face." A relieved smile stretched across her face. "Really?" she asked "You aren't mad?" "Of course not. Actually, I am going to give you a hundred on your feeling today," I informed her. "A hundred?" she asked, amazed. "Yes, a hundred. You deserve it. After all, what other student cared so much about a soldier going off to war that they cried?" I reminded her. "Thank you for understanding, Mr. Campbell," she said. She quickly turned and made for the door, wiping her eyes as she went.

I sat and thought as she disappeared. It felt weird to allow a student to refuse to do work, and even weirder to reward them with a 100 for doing so. I learned a very valuable lesson that day, though; the most important thing a teacher should ask themselves when designing class activities is "What is the purpose of the activity?" If my purpose is for students to practice writing, then they need to write. If I assign a short speech and the purpose is for them to work on their oral communication skills, then they need to speak in front of the class. Whether they need to write down their speech or not is inconsequential. From that day forward, I always ask myself, when I am planning my class ahead of time, what the purpose of the assignment is. My purpose that day was not to torture a young lady's soul in class any more than it was already being tortured outside of class. I was not there to make her think horrible thoughts about her fiancé's future. I did not want to see her have an emotional breakdown in class, in front of the other students. I only wanted her to feel, and she was able to demonstrate that to me more effectively without writing the letter than if she had.

So there I was, face to face with her fiancé. He came to school to find the teacher who allowed his young love to not do her assignment, because she was too worried about him. As we grasped hands and he looked at me, I could see that he was appreciative in a way that I had never seen before. No mom or dad ever came and thanked me like this at a parent-teacher conference. No student ever shook my hand like this when I assigned a worksheet. No graduate ever looked into my eyes like this when they received their diploma. And surely, no boyfriend ever drove down to the school to thank me for giving a standardized test.

As he walked away, I felt a sense of smallness in the world. Here I was, a "big-time" high school teacher with my college degree, professional teaching license, and my shiny school identification badge; yet I was trying to equip teenagers with the skills they need to handle situations like the leaving, sacrifice, and possible deaths of their loved ones. That day, I realized that although I considered myself the expert on war in my classroom, I had a real expert sitting there silently refusing to do her work, for fear of breaking down in front of her friends. The real lesson of the effects of war on loved ones was being given at home, while I prattled on and on about the front, shell shock, and the communication trenches. This time, it was I who became the student while a young girl and her fiancé became the teachers. It was one of the greatest lessons I ever learned.

Some people may find it hard to allow students to refuse to do assignments. What if a student lies to me to get out of work and tries to use the ruse again? What if the girl is honest, but her friends hear about it and they use it with less genuine intentions? What if a parent finds out their child received a ninety on an assignment they did, while another student received a 100 on the same project that they did not even complete? I guess those are all things that can happen, but a teacher just has to be able to risk it sometimes. When and which students to risk it on requires lots of wisdom on the part of the teacher, and knowing the students. My mentor teacher in college told me that the most important thing a teacher could ever do is know their students. She was right. If a teacher does not put in the time to get to know his students, then making these decisions becomes very difficult.

There is nothing that can replace the real-world decision making of an experienced teacher. Unfortunately, the ability to make these decisions is one of the things that are being phased out of the modern, industrialized classroom. The pressure is increasingly put on more experienced teachers through bloated bureaucracy, mounting paperwork load, required increases in before and after school duties, and exploding test administration, preparation, and grading. Most teachers have given up fun, critical thinking assignments altogether in favor of test preparation. More and more experienced teachers are hanging it up rather than put up with the new intellectual hoop jumping, which leaves our students at a distinct disadvantage. I am not saying that younger, less experienced teachers cannot be effective. It is only that these new realities of the modern classroom put even more of an emphasis on the importance of finding great young teachers, with the intangibles that really can transform a classroom. Is it worth the risk to allow students to refuse to do work? Absolutely. This was not the only time a student told me they would not do the work I assigned.

When I was a young teacher (still ignorant enough to believe in homework), one day I assigned a little work to be done at home. There was this very sweet, quiet girl in my class. She always did whatever was asked of her to the best of her ability, although that ability was, educationally speaking, quite low. I did not know too much about her, as she had just moved to our school a couple of months before. I ascertained that she was not my greatest student when rated on her academic merits, but she was a very kind young lady who was excellent to have in class. One day I gave them a small homework assignment, and after class this quiet young lady was waiting to speak with me. "I am not going to be able to do your homework tonight," she said. I was more than a little taken back by her bluntness. There is just something about a student refusing to do what I asked that got under my skin in those younger days. In this case, there was just something very grating about the matter of fact way she laid it out for me. "Oh, really, why is that?" I asked with a very questioning tone maybe even laced with a hint of condescension. "Well, I have to go to the hospital," was her quick, short answer. "Are you going to have a procedure or something? Because if you are going to be out for a few days, you need to go to the office and apply for a homebound teacher so you will not get behind in your studies," I gladly informed her. "No, it isn't me," she said. "It's my dad," she continued. "He is dying."

I could feel the blood drain from my face. All of the self-righteous indignation left me immediately. I stood there in total shock, and beckoned for her to tell me more. She recounted how her father was much older than her mother, but her mother had died of cancer a few months ago. Right after her mother's passing, her father began to have serious heart problems. It was just her and her younger brother struggling along, while her father was in and out of the hospital. She had a much older sister who lived hours away, but her sister had decided to move back and take care of my student and her younger brother while also looking after her dad. Her older sister was going to pick her and her brother up after school and drive them an hour to the hospital so they could spend the entire night with their father, possibly for the last time.

That quiet little student administered a quick lesson to me in the importance of what happens after school, and the lack of importance in homework. As I progressed through my teaching career, it was experiences like this one (and others) that convinced me of the importance of what was happening after school in so many students' lives. I know that not every student had a dying father or a fiancé leaving for a war zone, but nearly every student of mine had something more important than homework to do. Whether it was sports, clubs, a job, family time, religiously affiliated groups and meetings, hobbies, unstructured play, or a million other possibilities; there was always something real that my fake homework interrupted. How arrogant was I to think that there was never anything more important than my homework to most (if not all) students? As it turns out, if I was really honest, there were probably few if any times that my homework was ever more important than what was going on in a young person's life outside of school.

As I became a parent of two very energetic little boys, I soon found out that it did not have to be a serious illness to make family time more important than school work. So many families are incredibly busy, and time at night or on the weekends becomes a very precious commodity. Events like the two mentioned above, and countless others that I experienced, convinced me that it was okay for students not to do homework. My final inspiration to put the nail in the coffin of homework was when I was studying World War II. The American government created a board to oversee production and labor. Their main goal was to keep workers happy and production high. They did this through a series of measures: paying employees well, allowing them to join unions, and not requiring overtime. What the government and companies soon found out was that people liked to be well compensated for a hard day's work, without being forced to do more. Results even showed that more production at a lower price could be achieved by working employees hard but restricting it to an eight hour work day, instead of paying them more money for overtime while requiring them to work longer hours. Eventually, after much research, I decided that I would no longer give any homework to any class (except my advanced place-ment classes). I made a pact with my students that if we worked hard form the time the class started until it ended, I would assign no homework. I also made a pact with my own family that I would bring no work home with me from school. I started going to school earlier and working harder when I was there, so I would not interrupt the precious time at night and on weekends that my family deserved of me.

Often it can be hard for educators to admit that there are more important things going on in the lives of our students than our subjects. Sometimes, we teachers overinflate the importance of solving matrices, memorizing the steps to balancing an equation, or memorizing the four main causes of World War I. We need to realize that education is important, but so are family, friends, hobbies, recreational activities, religious affiliation, and community involve-ment. The truth is that those things will last much longer than the facts, data, memorization, short cuts, and test-taking strategies masquerading as education that we most often try to cram into the minds of our youth. Twenty years from now, my students will be hard pressed to remember any academic lessons I tried to teach them, but they will still have their families, friends, and hobbies. It is time that teachers stop being so pompous and consider our students when making educational decisions. It may be something as simple as really trying to understand our students by asking the innocuous question "Why?" instead of just assuming that there could be nothing more important going on than our subject. Educators, use your wisdom, know your students, and allow yourself to be challenged. You may find out that it is okay to let students refuse to do their work. It might turn out to be the best lesson your students will ever receive from you.